THE PATH TO PARADISE

THE PATH TO PARADISE

The Inner World of Suicide Bombers and Their Dispatchers

Anat Berko

Translated by Elizabeth Yuval
Foreword by Moshe Addad

PRAEGER SECURITY INTERNATIONAL
Westport, Connecticut • London

Library of Congress Cataloging-in-Publication Data

Berko, Anat.
The path to paradise : the inner world of suicide bombers and their dispatchers / Anat Berko ;
foreword by Moshe Addad ; translated by Elizabeth Yuval.
    p. cm.
  Includes bibliographical references and index.
  ISBN 978–0–275–99446–4 (alk. paper)
  1. Suicide bombings—Palestine.   2. Suicide bombers—Psychology.   3. Palestinian
  Arabs—Interviews.   4. Women suicide bombers.   5. Arab-Israeli conflict—1993-
  I. Title.
  HV6433.P25B47   2007
  956.9405′4–dc22   2007000050

British Library Cataloguing in Publication Data is available.

Library of Congress Catalog Card Number: 2007000050
ISBN-13: 978–0–275–99446–4
ISBN-10: 0–275–99446–5

First published in 2007

Praeger Security International, 88 Post Road West, Westport, CT 06881
An imprint of Greenwood Publishing Group, Inc.
www.praeger.com

Printed in the United States of America

The paper used in this book complies with the
Permanent Paper Standard issued by the National
Information Standards Organization (Z39.48–1984).

10 9 8 7 6 5 4 3 2 1

This book is dedicated to Reuven, my husband,
and Tzlil, Yechiam, and Keshet, my children.
My thanks to my mother for her endless support,
and to my late father, who was a beacon to me.

CONTENTS

Foreword by Moshe Addad   ix

Acknowledgments   xi

Introduction   xiii

1. Dispatcher of Palestinian Suicide Bombers: "Find Me
   Sad Guys"   1

2. The Role of the Dispatcher: "Everybody Has His Job: I
   Dispatch the Suicide Bomber and He Explodes"   14

3. Organization: "The Dispatchers Don't Send Their Own Sons
   to Blow Themselves Up"   25

4. Dispatchers Are Held in High Esteem: "I'm Considered
   Someone Who Does Something Good"   36

5. Dispatcher Macho: "My Father Taught It What It Means to
   Be a Man and Didn't Allow US to Be Cowards"   44

6. Sheikh Ahmad Yassin, Hamas Founder: "The Shaheed
   Doesn't Die, He Lives with Allah"   50

7. Women in Prison: "She Poured Boiling Margarine
   on My Face"   69

8. As Machiavelli Said, "The End Justifies the Means"   80

9. The Book of Mug Shots: "Huda Can't Talk to You Now,
   She's Having Her Face Done"   90

10. The Value of Women: "I'll Never Do Anyone Any Good,
    Anyway"   96

11. The Terrorist's Dream: "I've Wanted to Be a Shaheeda Ever
    Since I Was a Little Girl"   113

12. Double Standard: "Sure, I'd Attack a Kindergarten! I Am Able
    to Look at Your Children—and Explode!"   125

13. Is the "Other" a Human Being? "Do Israeli Mothers Feel Pain
    Like We Do?"   137

14. A Teenage Shaheed: "My Classmate Enlisted Me as a
    Shaheed. He Was Paid and Gave Me 100 Shekels"   147

15. Paradise: "All That Is Forbidden in This World Is Allowed
    in Paradise"   159

The Last Word   171

Notes   177

Glossary   179

Selected Bibliography   181

Index   185

FOREWORD

Since 1993 Israel has been subject to a perverse and deadly form of terrorist attack whose slogan is "I seek death if Jews die with me." Murdering Jews and trying to destroy the State of Israel has passed from wishful thinking to practice. The deliberate murders make no distinction between children, the aged, women, cripples, men, left-wingers, and right-wingers, it is total slaughter as the means of justifying the ends: the destruction of the Jewish people in their own country, and wherever they may be found.

The blind hatred of Jews has dispelled the fear of personal extinction. The reward of the-future-after-the-suicide, a hedonistic afterlife in a utopian Muslim paradise, is a potent motivating factor. In addition, the Qur'an promises that whoever dies a martyr's death for the sake of Allah, the *shaheed*, does not actually die, but rather lives in the presence of the Lord of the universe, with an emphasis on "Allah spoke the truth." Not only that, but according to the Qur'an, the shaheed's family will also be rewarded. The suicide bomber will receive material benefits, he will be able to see the light shining from the face of Allah, bathe in the rivers of paradise, and live forever.

The suicide bomber has rights not given to others. The uniqueness of the suicide-bombing candidate fortifies him for the mission he plans to undertake. To commit suicide as a martyr for the sake of Allah, to be a *shaheed* or *shaheeda*, is an honor granted by Allah, and as such cannot be refused. The brainwashing and intensive indoctrination carried out in the mosques, educational system, and media burrow into the souls of the faithful and are gradually internalized in potential suicide candidates, so that when called upon they surface, accompanied by a sensation of self-exaltation.

It is not suicide committed out of despair, but rather an act of hope accompanied by an elevation in status. Some of the suicide bombers experience a connection with the omnipotent Allah. They sacrifice their bodies for the sake of a hedonistic eternity, for the benefits their families will receive in both this world and the next and to protect the light of Allah.

According to Surah Al-Nisaa,[1] Verse 74, "Let them fight for the sake of Allah, those who sell the life of this world for the life hereafter, and whoever fights for the sake of Allah and slain or is victorious, we will reward him greatly."

Islam, which comes from the Arab verb meaning "to turn oneself over" demands that the individual devote himself to the will of Allah and whoever accepts Islam as his religion is called a "Muslim," that is, a slave to the demands of the Islam as they are transmitted through the Qur'an Surahs.

As early as January 624 AD, the faithful were called to the "holy war" against the tribe of the Quraish in the Arabian Peninsula. Three hundred of the faithful enthusiastically came to join battle, firm in the belief that whoever fell would live eternally in the next world, where all good things awaited. In fact, it was a great victory, a perfect jihad.

For some suicide bombers, the act of self-sacrifice for the sake of Allah means the purification of their past lives in the gutters. They enlist because of the plainly stated promise that such purification is certain, and they swear allegiance and sacrifice themselves to the accompaniment of exploding buses and the deaths of scores of completely innocent people.

The author spent long years talking to the dispatchers of suicide bombers, to male and female suicide bombers who were arrested on their way to carry out attacks, and hours speaking to Hamas leader and founder Ahmad Yassin. In addition, the author also spent great amounts of time in what seemed almost like natural meetings, despite the unique circumstances, with Muslim mothers and women whose sons and husbands had become *shaheeds*, and with Muslim clerics and others. The purpose of this book is to clarify, insofar as is possible, the complex situation in which Palestinian suicide bombing terrorism takes place and the mind of the suicide bomber.

Professor Moshe Addad
Head of the Department of Criminology
Bar Ilan Univesity, Ramat Gan, Israel

ACKNOWLEDGMENTS

My thanks to the many members of the Israeli security forces, especially to the prison services, who gave unstintingly of their time, to The Institute for Counter-Terrorism (ICT), The Interdisciplinary Center Herzliya (IDC), and to my mentors Profs. Moshe Addad and Yuval Wolf of Bar Ilan University and Prof. Ariel Merari of Tel Aviv University, all of whom made this book possible. Thanks also to Elizabeth Yuval for her translation and to Rami Tal, who edited the Hebrew version of this book for Yediot Aharonot Publishers (2004).

INTRODUCTION

"Anyone ever hit you with a plank? That's the Israeli occupation," said the suicide bomber spitefully. "If I think that once I had a house, a wife, a child—it's like I'm asleep and dreaming. '*Halas*' (Enough). Now I live in prison."

We sat across from one another in the offices of a maximum-security prison, separated by a table with a faded Formica top. Behind me a railing, brought from somewhere or other, was leaning against the wall. Rifat stared at one of the wooden posts. I could read his mind and he didn't try to hide what he was thinking. I could feel waves of hatred washing over me, his eyes flashing it in my direction. "If you let me go, I'll come to Jerusalem. You don't want me to get out of prison . . ." he said aggressively. I had asked that tea be brought to us, sweet and minty, the way it is usually prepared in the Arab Middle East, but he refused to drink it. "Today there is a fast, we fast twice a week;" it was a decision reached by the Hamas members in that prison.

Unshaven and with a thick beard, he was wearing a long white *galabiya* and his head was covered by a large white skullcap, crocheted and coming down to his forehead. There was a kind of star in the middle, like a Star of David. At the time I never imagined that in January 2006 the fundamentalist Hamas movement would take over the Palestinian régime in fairly democratic elections, displacing Fatah to become the ruling party. There is no way of ignoring its victory. There are those who say it was elected because the Palestinians were fed up with the corruption of the Fatah régime. That was undoubtedly one of the reasons, but it was also because of its avowed intention to destroy the State of Israel and establish a radical Islamist state on the ruins, from the Jordan to the Mediterranean. Major General

Moshe Ya'alon, the former chief of staff, explained it by saying that "there is a struggle against the West and its culture, and Israel is a stepping stone, to be conquered and destroyed as the Muslims march toward a worldwide Caliphate. Khaled Mashal [head of the Hamas political bureau], Ahmadine-jad [the president of Iran] and bin Laden all say the same thing..."

The guard who brought Rifat to the meeting warned me to be careful. "He's a suicide bomber, he got on a bus in Jerusalem with a bomb on his back. He pressed the detonator hoping to kill as many Jews as possible, but it didn't explode."

I didn't lower my eyes, despite the waves of hostility, suspicion, and hatred he sent in my direction. It was like being in a cage with a tiger: you have to keep looking the beast in the eye, and most important, not show fear. In the interviews I had had with other suicide bombers I didn't feel the same boiling violence. I had spoken to all the prisoners without handcuffs, although the guards disapproved. One of the security officers had told me that "someone serving 50 consecutive life sentences has nothing to lose, so killing another Jew means nothing to him..."

It was a fairly surrealistic situation: here I was, a Jewish mother, Ph.D candidate, and at the time, a career officer in the Israel Defense Forces, sitting across the table from a serial killer. Between 1993 and 1996 there was a wave of suicide bombings, the bombs blew up in buses, open-air markets, restaurants, coffee shops, everywhere. After 1996 many people in Israel thought—and hoped—that it was over, but unfortunately, they were wrong.

I researched the topic for my doctorate in the Department of Criminology of Bar Ilan University, focusing on the moral nature of those who organized and dispatched the suicide bombers. Then I began dealing with various other aspects of suicide bombing terrorism, particularly the female suicide bombers who, for whatever reason, remained alive.

Throughout the entire obstacle course I was helped and supported by my husband, Reuven, who is a specialist in Middle Eastern affairs, and thoroughly familiar with both the Arabic language and the Islamic religion. There were times when I came back from visiting a prison barely able to breathe. On the one hand, an academically-oriented doctoral candidate was trying to discover the scientific truth about suicide bombing terrorism, acts committed by the men and women with whom I had held conversations which were, generally speaking, empathetic and calm. On the other, a human being wanted to make heard the cry of victims whose voices had been silenced by terrorists. And there are other cries which are never heard: every victim of Palestinian terrorism leaves behind friends and family whose lives are changed beyond recognition. There are thousands of people who wake up in the morning, every morning, and only in the fraction of a second between sleep and the surfacing of memory do they have peace. They are children without mothers, without siblings, fathers without sons to say Kaddish over their graves, wives without husbands, schoolmates and comrades in arms left alone, every possible permutation of horror, with no relief.

While researching the subject I discovered that many Israelis thought suicide bombing terrorism had only begun with the second intifada (September 2000), repressing the horrendous attacks of preceding decade. It would seem that such "forgetfulness," or the activating of defense mechanisms of repression and perhaps even collective denial have helped Israelis continue living fairly normal lives under the constant threat of uncompromising, mass-murder suicide bombing terrorism. It is the sort of terrorism that makes no distinction in its choice of victims, civilians and military. Boys, girls, men, women, all are targets for suicide bombing murderers, and it seems to be the terrorist organizations' preferred type of attack.

One of the female suicide bombers who was captured said, "Why should you have something and we should have nothing? Why should your children be happy and ours sad?" The question, oversimplified and perhaps even childish is directed at every Israeli, and, actually, at every citizen of a Western country, as the terrorist attacks in New York, Madrid, and London have demonstrated.

Like the skyjacking of airplanes by Palestinians in the 1970s, the epidemic of suicide bombing terrorism has begun to spread throughout the Western world and beyond. Its scope has increased and it has reached the Arab world itself, and today even women and children serve as living bombs.

For a number of years I held conversations with those who had dispatched suicide bombers and with suicide bombers whose missions had failed, and with many others who helped me clarify and understand suicide bombing terrorism by letting me see matters directly through their eyes. In most cases, and for a variety of reasons, the names mentioned in this book are fictitious. However, everything is based on conversations with real people. Anyone who is familiar with the details of the incidents will know the identities of the individuals involved.

CHAPTER 1

Dispatcher of Palestinian Suicide Bombers: "Find Me Sad Guys"

It is often assumed that suicide bombers freely and voluntarily chose to commit suicide. How valid is that assumption?

In most instances, the suicide bombers who blow themselves up do volunteer, like the young woman from a village near Jenin (a city in northern West Bank) who told me that she had looked for the local Fatah operative to offer herself as a suicide bomber. "In any case my life wasn't worth anything and my father wouldn't let me marry the boy I wanted to, so I found a Fatah operative in Jenin and volunteered, to get back at my father . . ."

Mahmoud, a suicide bomber dispatcher with a long history, responsible for the deaths of many Israelis, is serving several consecutive terms of life imprisonment. "I didn't tell him [the suicide bomber] to kill himself. He wanted to and I helped him . . . I asked them to find me guys who were desperate and sad."

Where do you look for a potential suicide bomber, male or female? Often someone suspected of collaborating with Israel will volunteer to carry out a suicide bombing attack to clear his (or her) name. Sheikh Ahmad Yassin told me that "if a Muslim loses the true path it is important for him to find it again, because otherwise his wife will be labeled 'wife of a traitor,' and his son, 'son of a traitor.'" One such example is Ayat al-Akhras, who blew herself up in a supermarket in the Kiriyat Yovel neighborhood of Jerusalem on March 29, 2003, to clear the name of her father, who was suspected of collaborating with Israel.

Sometimes, the motive is suspicion of "imperfect" moral behavior, according to the norms of Palestinian Muslim society. In such a case, even the mother of two very young children will be sent to blow herself up, as happened to Reem al-Riyashi, who carried out a suicide bombing attack at the Erez crossing in the Gaza Strip on January 14, 2004. Did a young mother really decide of her own free will to commit suicide and murder?

"I have an implant in my leg," she wailed when the metal detector beeped, and the soldier at the crossing believed her. It is hard to remain impassive when assailed by a crying woman. It cost him his life. Al-Riyashi crossed through and blew herself up, along with the soldier and other security personnel. Without a doubt she wanted to kill Jews, and she might also have been motivated by nationalist and religious factors. But what about her children, her responsibility, care, and love for them? Maybe it was her last chance to escape before her husband abused her physically, because apparently he was tired of her, or perhaps because there was another man in her life, or just a rumor about it. For her it was an honorable way out and prevented not only her from being humiliated, but her family as well.

I remembered something I had heard in that context, "Not a *shaheeda*, a *sharmouta*" (i.e., not a woman who died as a martyr for the sake of Allah, but just a whore), and I heard it from Murad, an Arab journalist who accompanied me several times when I interviewed individuals outside Israeli prisons. He added, "It was better for her to die than to be murdered, and she even took a couple of [Israeli] soldiers with her, so all her sins were forgotten. And there is something I want you to know: if someone decides to be a *shaheed*, every bad thing he ever did is canceled, even if it's a question of a woman who slept around. It's like what a Muslim on a *hajj* feels like. So, a lot of men commit sins and say to themselves, "I'll go on a *hajj* and everything will be erased, so I can do anything, I'm going to run wild!"

Sometimes, the suicide bombers are "volunteered" and accept offers to participate in suicide bombing attacks after their emotions have become inflamed and their baser impulses take over, as sometimes happens at the mass funeral of a wanted terrorist killed by the Israeli army. Sometimes they are recruited for training in the "struggle against the Zionist enemy" with no intention at all of becoming suicide bombers. Only later do the recruits discover themselves forced to commit *istishhad* (the death of a martyr for the sake of Allah). In one sense, the suicide bombers are victims of Palestinian society. Nazima was in prison for security violations. She was 22, had finished the tenth grade, was nice-looking, and lived in a refugee camp. She was caught while on her way to carry out an attack at one of the West Bank settlements. Hand grenades had been taped to her body. It was unclear whether those who dispatched her planned for them to explode when she was shot trying to penetrate the settlement, or whether she was supposed to throw them. In any case, her dispatchers obviously planned to turn her into a *shaheeda*, although she herself had no intention of dying.

"My family, those are my only friends," Nazima told me. "You can't trust anyone, not even your relatives. There are children they talked into it by exploiting their youth. I knew three children who were sent to carry out attacks, they were 13, 14 and 17. They died before they even entered the settlement, killed by tank fire. Hamas adopted them and made them members after they died."

Nazima was wearing tight, faded jeans, a tight, colorful blouse and her long black hair was tied back in a ponytail. She had a lot of blue-black eye makeup on; it brought out the black in her eyes. She looked like every other Israeli woman her age, her Western clothing making her stand out from the other prisoners in the wing, who were all wearing traditional Muslim dress. She was the seventh child in a family of ten children, a daughter of her father's first wife. "My father is 70, he was a police officer and the Palestinian Authority retired him. My mother is 55 and takes care of the house all the time. My father's second wife is 40, and the two families live separately." According to Nazima, her father's family came from a village near Ashdod and her mother was born in a village near Beersheba. Her mother told her about how the Jews shelled them and how they fled from their villages, although judging by her age it is hard to believe she could remember anything, and it is more probable that she heard stories from other people. During the interviews I heard many stories about the experiences of refugees. In 1947, after the Israelis accepted, the Arabs rejected the UN partition plan and the armies of all the Arab states attacked the Jewish state that had been established in Eretz-Israel. In the wake of Israel's War of Independence, the Arab population which fled during the fighting, concentrated in refugee camps established in places like the Gaza Strip (which was Egyptian), the West Bank (which was Jordanian), Lebanon, and Syria. Only Jordan absorbed the Arab refugees as citizens, and the term "Palestinians," meaning Arabs living in Israel and the territories, only came into use around 1967. Though there is some truth in the stories, they are often elaborated with imaginary experiences. The younger generation is brought up hearing them and imbued with the trauma of being a refugee, perhaps the longest stretch of refugeedom in history.

Nazima talked about daily life in the refugee camp, about good relations with neighbors, and mutual aid. "It was a good life in the camp, and even though it was a camp, people liked each other and took care of each other."

It wasn't difficult to get her talking. The need to talk, to tell her story, was very strong. "There are girls who come and offer themselves. I never offered myself. I didn't want to die in an attack. About three months before the attack I started training. I didn't know it would be like that, I didn't think I would die and I didn't want to die. They [the recruiters and the dispatchers] planned for me to commit suicide, but I didn't ask for it. They offered me an explosive belt and other things but I didn't agree. At first they didn't force me, but things turned out the way they did. I was a spoiled child and I didn't plan to die."

It is very possible Nazima was pressured into carrying out an attack, perhaps because of "immoral behavior," but it was hard for her to admit it. However, the hints were broad. "I come from a well-respected family, and because of what I did I'm sure they get even more respect. They didn't know I went with *shabbab* [the guys], if they knew they would have prevented me. Girls have taken part in attacks since the intifada started ... if it's a girl, they look at her as though she did something heroic. People look at a girl [who carried out an attack] with more respect than a man."

Nazima spoke emotionally about the special way people treated her because she was a terrorist-operative. I asked, "Did preparations for the attack give you, as a woman, more freedom of movement?"

She said, "We aren't living in the West. When I left the house for military training I would tell my father that I was going to visit a girlfriend. My father doesn't stop me from visiting my friends. No one asked too many questions. That was how I could go to training sessions for three months. I would get into a car that came for me in the refugee camp ... There was always another girl in the car so that I wouldn't be alone with a man ... Sometimes they covered my eyes until we reached the training ground of Shuhadaa Al-Aqsa [Al-Aqsa Martyrs] ... I was never alone, there were other girls in training as well ... and the boys would ask what made me want to work with them, they wanted to know if there was something going on at home or if I had been forced to marry against my will ... They didn't want anyone with a social stigma, just an ordinary person."

There have also been reports that female suicide bombers are sexually exploited by the members of the organization or cell, and that sometimes their savings are taken before the attack "because in any case, she is going to blow herself up."

In Arab society, where boys and girls are kept separate from the cradle, any romantic or even social association between the sexes is considered taboo and may lead to the woman's being physically harmed. That is not the case, however, in situations of antioccupation military activity. There is a sense of being alive, of adventure and excitement that goes far beyond military missions. In addition to the women recruited for terrorist attacks, there are others who help with recruitment and dispatching, all of which help to generate a "permissible" association between the sexes. However, the men's claim that they are looking for "an ordinary woman" is unconvincing. Not one of the ten Palestinian women who carried out suicide bombing attacks acted in a way that could be classified as normative according to the criteria of Palestinian society. It is likely that Nazima was looking for friends, and not just women friends. She wanted the physical excitement of being involved in a military-like adventure, of forbidden meetings, and of sneaking out of her boring house. She said that at the time she even started keeping a diary to record the thrilling training sessions.

"The men treated us with a great deal of respect, as though we were their sisters. I knew two of them beforehand. One of them was a salesman and the other was a relative of one of my girlfriends." In fact, people from the same small area are often recruited, including friends who are the first line of communication between the dispatcher and potential suicide bombers. In Nazima's case, the connection was made by a close friend.

"I had known her for four years. We met at the mosque. She was 21, engaged to be married and studying at the university. She used to be in the car when I got in, so I wouldn't be alone with men. They would let her off at the university and take me for training.

"My friend didn't choose that path, the path of death. She had been in training but stopped. That was how she knew the people. She helped them recruit girls for attacks. I think maybe she had a secret role, to bring girls there. Maybe she pretended to be my friend to exploit me, my best friend dragged me into this, and I am angry with her.

"I wanted to learn how to use a weapon but I didn't want to die. I had a friend who introduced me to the boys, and when I asked for weapons training they offered me an explosive belt and things like that . . . I said I had only come to learn how to use weapons, I wasn't willing to die. The boys told me to sign a document saying that I had chosen to engage in training, so that no one would say they had forced me . . . I don't know if they also make boys sign such a piece of paper . . ."

Apparently, having the woman sign is a way of preventing a blood feud with her family. They might not only kill her, but might harm the man who influenced her to engage in activities where she would not be watched and supervised by her father or older brother. Often such supervision becomes terrorism directed against the women and children in the family.

Nazima: "They [the recruiters and trainers] contacted my friend and she told me it was urgent I get there . . . to some house. They came for me with a car and they used to change the pickup point all the time so that no one would be suspicious."

Nazima was clearly excited and her voice was unsteady. She continued talking, staring at some point on the white wall behind me. "I went into an unfamiliar house. There was an older man there, and other, younger men in the same room . . . and then he told me that the following Monday I was going to carry out a suicide bombing attack, *istishhad.* He said, 'Get ready, prepare yourself . . .' I was very surprised when he told me I would be a *shaheeda.* I wasn't planning to die like that. At first I thought he was kidding, but no, he wasn't kidding. He said, 'You prepared yourself, you trained, you know who we are, who the operatives in the organization are, and you have to do it.'"

Her face became sad and she continued, "I told him that I only came for the training, not to carry out a suicide bombing attack . . . and then we argued. I told him I wasn't strictly observant when it came to religion, I didn't wear traditional clothing or cover my hair, didn't pray at all the prescribed times and actually sometimes I prayed and sometimes I didn't . . . I also said that

I watched television and listened to songs, things devout Muslims usually don't do, and that I hadn't planned on becoming a *shaheeda*, otherwise I would have been more scrupulous in my religious behavior."

But the dispatcher wouldn't give in. "I found myself screaming at him ... I thought it was a joke, but my friend told me it was the real thing. I asked him if I could start all over from the beginning, to forget that there had ever been a connection between us, I would forget them and they would forget me. They refused, naturally, and said, 'You know everything about us and we aren't sure of what will happen once you leave this room, maybe you'll tell someone about us, maybe you will make the mistake of talking about us ...' I swore by the Qur'an that I wouldn't tell anyone anything. They said, 'We are an organization, not just people, and that [oath] means nothing to us.' They were afraid of me and for themselves, that I would tell who they where and where the training camp was."

In the end, Nazima yielded to the pressure. "I began counting the days until I was going to die, because they forced me. I hate the idea of dying, I like living, I was very spoiled. I was afraid to tell my father, to ask him for help, because then he would know I had had military training with boys, and without permission ... When they told me I was going to carry out 'an action' I cried a lot, I almost fainted, everything went black before my eyes. I didn't have the courage to tell my father because they warned me not to tell anyone. A few times I almost told him, but in the end I couldn't. Now that I'm in prison, I think that if I had told him, maybe he could have done something, because he is a fairly important person and he knows a lot of people, but I didn't have the courage then."

It became apparent that Nazima was less afraid of telling her father about the planned "military action" in which she would become a *shaheeda* than she was about his reaction to the fact that she had been meeting boys without his knowledge or permission. In Arab society, any relationship between a man and woman is forbidden unless it has been arranged by the father for the purpose of marriage. Even such a relationship is subject to an extremely strict behavior code, and an engaged couple is only permitted to meet if chaperoned by a family member.

Nazima: "My parents sensed there was something different about me, that I had changed. Beforehand I had always smiled. They asked me what happened to me all of a sudden because I was yelling and nervous all the time. Why? Those five days, from Monday until Friday, felt like a thousand years. I begged the 'older man' who was in charge of military affairs to release me. He said '*halas ya-binti*' ["That's enough, my daughter!"]. I kept telling him that I wasn't religious, I didn't pray, and he said, 'When you die you will be closer to Allah. Allah will forgive you and allow you to enter paradise even though you didn't pray.'"

And Nazima incidentally noted that "the older man" didn't look like a particularly devout Muslim.

"So that was it. He wouldn't let me off the hook and I didn't wear an explosive belt, I had hand grenades instead ... I thought I was going to die, not go to prison." Nazima became furious with the "older man" every time she thought about what had happened to her: "In prison I die a couple of times every day. I feel it would be easier to die than to stay in prison ... I planned one thing and something else happened instead. All I wanted was military training ..."

She was also angry with the friend who helped recruit her. "She was the one who told me it was urgent that I meet them. After they told me about the attack, she came to my house to ask what they wanted. We had a fight and I yelled and threw her out of the house."

"If you could talk to her now, what would you say?"

Nazima answered angrily, "I can't begin to tell you what I would say to her, considering that I'm in prison. Nothing she could tell me or say to me would be enough to make me stop being angry." Her black eyes were full of tears. Obviously, she thought her friend had used and sacrificed her.

I asked, "Are there parents who want their children to commit suicide?" She shook her head and said, "I don't think there is a single parent who would agree to that. Anyone who says anything else is lying. Maybe there are parents with a dead friend or relative who would agree to revenge. I don't believe parents know their children are going to blow themselves up. Only the dispatchers know."

The dispatcher is a very significant figure in the well-oiled machine that produces suicide bombing attacks. Often he is involved in recruitment as well. When Mahmoud the dispatcher asked for "sad guys," he meant those who were social nonentities and had no status but who might get recognition by dying, those with low self-esteem who are usually not involved in social affairs. He meant men and women who have trouble finding themselves, sometimes influenced by anger and bitterness at their marginality, and who are willing to try anything to feel they have worth and to win the approval of society or their families. One of the suicide bombers whose mission had failed told me that "Making my mother happy is the most important thing in the world" although of course he did not mean that his death would make her happy.

Many of them have no father figure or a father they can't identify with. In some cases, the relationship is ambivalent, for example if the father took another wife after the suicide bomber's mother.

The mother is the most significant figure for both the dispatchers and the suicide bombers. Any conversation about their mothers causes a great rush of emotion and usually makes them cry. That happens despite the fact that Arab society oppresses women and expects them to obey and remain submissive to the men in the family (the father, husband, brothers, etc.), and to preserve "the family honor," which morally speaking is the woman's responsibility.

Often the immediate family knows nothing of a son or daughter's desire to be a *shaheed*. In general, parents strongly oppose their children's committing suicide, even if it would mean having them recognized as *shaheeds*. A suicide bomber who was caught quoted her father as saying "The dispatchers trade in the blood of the *shaheeds*."

If a typical profile could be drawn of the suicide bombers of 1993–1996, those who carried out their attacks after the Oslo Accord between Israel and the Palestinian in 1993, it is hard to do the same for the suicide bombers of the second intifada, the Al-Aqsa intifada, which began in September 2000 and as of January 2007 has not ended. However, there has sometimes been a so-called "lull in the fighting" since Abu Mazen took over the chairmanship of the Palestinian Authority.

There is also general anarchy, particularly in the Gaza Strip, and the armed Palestinian terrorist organizations do as they please, one example of which was the murder of Musa Arafat, a relative of Yasser Arafat, in September 2005, when armed men broke into his house in the middle of the night, riddled his body with bullets, and threw it into the street. As of this writing, Hamas, which is dedicated to the destruction of Israel and to the establishment of a radical Islamic state on the ruins, won a sweeping victory in the Palestinian Legislative Council elections in January 2006 and the future is uncertain. We now witness violent Fatah-Hamas and exchanges of gunfire in the streets. Suicide bombing attacks are still carried out in Israel's cities. Hezbollah (a Lebanese Shi'ite terrorist organization), supported by Syria and Iran, has become more involved, and there are reports of Al-Qaeda cells having been established in the Palestinian Authority. It should be noted that when terrorism operates from within a population that does not legitimize it, terrorism is reined in. Sometimes the local population collaborates by not voicing opposition, either out of fear or out of belief in the rightness of the path taken, as was made clear during the second Lebanon war in the summer of 2006, which broke out following the abduction by two Israeli soldiers by Hezbollah. Hezbollah fired rockets from within and in close proximity to residential dwellings in Lebanese towns and villages, targeting Israeli cities, believing that the IDF would not return fire at areas inhabited by civilians.

However, it can be stated that in most cases suicide bombers are not the young, uneducated, single individuals they were in the past, nor is the extremist religious element as strong as might be supposed. Neither the dispatchers nor the suicide bombers are religious fanatics. For some, the process of becoming more religious takes place in an Israeli prison, where they receive religious instruction from other prisoners. But in most cases, religion is an integral part of the preparing the suicide bomber for the attack.

Suicide bombing attacks are the Palestinians' strategic weapons. They have no conventional means at their disposal to confront Israel. Murad, the journalist who accompanied me on many occasions, said, "By now, there are not only religious *shaheeds*, there are secular ones as well ... A suicide bombing attack has an enormous psychological effect, it sows terrible fear ... People talk about the balance of terror with Israel, scaring [the Israelis] with suicide bombers who disrupt their normal daily lives ... You can't go into a coffee house in Israel today without first being checked by a security guard ..."

The father of Hiba Daraghmeh, who blew herself up at the shopping mall in Afula (southeast of Haifa) on May 19, 2003, described how his daughter began studying religion intensively in the weeks before the attack. Hanadi Jaradat, before blowing herself up in the Maxim Restaurant in Haifa on October 4, 2003, devoted a great deal of time to memorizing Qur'an verses in the company of several women who belonged to the Palestinian Islamic Jihad.

Religion (as translated into the *fatwas* of respected sheikhs such as Yusuf Qardawi and Muhammad Tantawi) and nationalism combine to produce a fertile medium for terrorism to grow on. In addition, there is often the desire to revenge the deaths of relatives, hatred for Jews, and a loathing of the Western world. The dispatcher is admired as a militant, masculine figure and is a role model for many young men. Another incentive is the financial reward promised to the *shaheed*'s family, paid after the attack has been carried out, and not least is the promise of direct passage to paradise, releasing them from the world of evil and suffering, which most of the suicide bombers believe to be a genuine matter of fact.

However, many of the suicide bombers do not have financial difficulties, their standard of living is average in comparison with the rest of Palestinian society (where the standard of living is fairly low to begin with, and which has seriously deteriorated in the more than six years of the current intifada). The terrorists led by Muhammad Atta who carried out the attacks on the Twin Towers and the Pentagon in the United States on September 11, 2001, were not members of the proletariat, but were educated, well off, and enjoyed freedom and economic plenty in the West.

In addition, not only do they generally not have economic problems, but most of the suicide bombers also do not have an emotional disturbance that prevents them from differentiating between reality and imagination, despite the fact that some of them were identified as having disturbed borderline personalities, often splitting the world into absolute black and white, sometimes having suicidal thoughts, and even having tried to harm themselves in the past. They often become captives of their own fantasies and dream about their families and society regarding them as "*shaheed* heroes" and about murdering Israeli civilians. They fantasize about looking like the *shaheeds* in the posters hung in the streets, which feature them striking heroic, macho poses. They imagine, sometimes down to the last detail, the "hero cult" that will spring up around them after the attack and even make up the dialogues praising their acts. Especially important are the respect and honor their families will receive. The wishful thinking of being a local and national hero is a catalyst for *istishhad*. Parents, as previously mentioned, do not usually encourage their children to become *shaheeds*, but they find it hard to prevent them from identifying with the dispatchers and the *shaheeds* and from regarding them as role models.

The Palestinian family has lost much of its patriarchal power and is suffering from a process of disintegration. The mother of a terrorist I met said that "the parents are the last to know." When the children of Muslim families living in Western countries grow up, they experience a conflict between life at home and in the immigrant community, and Western culture. Cultural conflicts and the process of the deterioration of the patriarchal family occur in Muslim society when it is not hermetically sealed off from processes of globalization, and when it is exposed to the Western media, which undermine conventions and the structure of society, religion, and family. Often potential *shaheeds* view the religious individual, the ideologue, and especially the suicide bomber dispatcher as a source of the authority which, in the past was indisputably in the hands of the paterfamilias.

Potential suicide bombers describe the "sensation of being uplifted," a kind of elation, when they reach the decision of *istishhad*, that is, to become *shaheeds*, and become emotionally detached, behaving mechanically on the way to the target. However, if something breaks through the trance-like state, there is a chance he (or she) will repent and change his mind. That is balanced by fear of the dispatcher, whose expectations he does not want to disappoint.

Shafika reached the place targeted for the attack, a crowded city in the center of Israel, wearing an explosive belt. Then she saw a mother with a baby. "The baby reminded me of my nephew," she said, "and the way he looked made me think he didn't deserve to die." She contacted her dispatcher and asked him to get her out. In the meantime there was a suicide bombing attack at a different site, and her rescue was delayed. The dispatcher, said Shafika, was very angry with her. "He said that a lot of people had an interest in the attack, and screwing it up was out of the question."

The baby she said she pitied was an exception. In most cases, the intended victims of a suicide bombing attack are not perceived by the suicide bomber or dispatcher as victims, and therefore human emotions toward them are irrelevant.

The potential suicide bomber and his dispatcher dehumanize their victims. Only in rare cases, such as that of Shafika, are emotions from the suicide bomber's normative world transferred to the victims of terrorism. Often dispatchers, terrorists, and suicide bombers told me that until they were put in prison and met Jews, they did not regard them as human beings at all. That is the result of Palestinian society's having demonized the Jews in every possible way, including by calling them "killers of the prophets, bloodsuckers, descendents of monkeys and pigs, enemies of Allah," expressions which appear in books, articles, speeches, sermons, textbooks, children's magazines, etc. All Jews are demonized, as is everything related to Western culture, making it possible to recruit more living bombs. It is meeting with prisoners, male and female, that often makes gestures of closeness and humanity possible.

While the suicide bomber undergoes psychological preparation for the attack, practical plans and preparations are made: intelligence is gathered, the explosive device, belt or vest is prepared, the method is decided on, and a human network of liaisons, support individuals, and escorts is prepared to transport the suicide bomber to the site of the attack.

Before he is dispatched, the suicide bomber is usually filmed for the media. Carrying a copy of the Qur'an and a Kalashnikov assault rifle, and wearing a headband (usually green, which is thought to have been Muhammad's favorite color) inscribed "there is no God but Allah and Muhammad is his prophet," he reads his prepared statement. The text he recites has been carefully dictated and is in effect a kind of verbal contract that will not allow the suicide bomber to change his mind. Making the "will" public after the suicide bombing attack is an act of propaganda that nourishes the *shaheed* cult in Palestinian society. The tapes also serve to increase the motivation of future recruits.

More than two thirds of Palestinian suicide bombing attacks have been carried out by lone terrorists driven to the site by car, one of whose passengers is a guide familiar with the area of the attack. But there have been instances in which dispatchers used two suicide bombers in a joint attack, hoping both to increase the number of casualties and to create a dynamic of commitment which will not allow either one to change his mind. The pattern of attacks carried out by Al-Qaeda is different, preferring a large number of suicide bombers for simultaneous attacks. On September 11, 2001, for example, nineteen suicide bombers coordinated their activities. The same was true for the attacks on July 7, 2005, on the buses and underground trains in London, in which a number of suicide bombers coordinated attacks in different arenas. The group activity of cells of suicide bombers is similar to that of the criminal subculture, and perhaps even a "thrill" subculture, a group that acts on its own, committed to itself. Such a group will not permit a suicide bomber to change his mind or repent, and the lone suicide bomber must obey group demands regarding the mission. Without doubt, terrorist attacks carried out by large groups of suicide bombers have enormous psychological effect. They are retained in the public consciousness and remembered as milestones on the global jihad terrorist map. In addition, through the communications media they fuel the minds of those who have been recruited to bin Laden's ideology. They pave the way for the recruitment of endless columns of suicide bombers who regard the groups as role models. Western society, for which human life is the supreme value, finds it difficult to define and understand the suicide bomber's behavior. One of the fathers of modern sociology, Emil Durkheim,[1] said that man had become the god of other men, and therefore every attempt to harm human life was a kind of blasphemy, suicide's being such an attempt.

Suicide is usually characterized by an unbearable emotional pain that the individual feels only death can end. In the case of voluntary suicide bombers, the pain will end, in his or her fantasy, in the passage to an afterlife in paradise, so that pain will be replaced by supreme bliss in the concrete sense, physical bliss, which is perceived as a reward of paradise. For Palestinians and Arabs in general, the power of collective society and the individual's need to satisfy it are immense, while the person has no value or significance.

Durkheim[2] also says that for society to be able to compel some of its members to commit suicide, it must be a society in which individual personality has very little value. For someone to be so marginal he must be almost completely submerged within the group. One of the female prisoners in prison for security violations told me that "none of us has her own life."

Thus it can be seen that suicide depends not only on the individual circumstances of the bomber, but on social circumstances and dictated norms which enable society to accept the act. The collective social force encourages the individual to commit suicide, while in Western society it would be expected to deter him from doing so.

The messages characteristically broadcast to Palestinian society were made evident in a poem read on a Palestinian television program called *Message of the People*. It was read with much pathos by a young woman wearing a green head covering.

> Goodbye my mother, my father, my brothers,
> Beloved among men,
> Do not mourn for me if you see me return,
> Borne upon [men's] shoulders,
> Do not cry for me if I die as a *shaheed*.
> For my joy at the moment of my meeting
> With Allah is the most beautiful of promises.
> I carried out the *shuhadah* and I am happy
> Kiss me for the last time,
> Look at the happy expression on my face
> Wrap me in a *kafiyeh*,
> And cover my face,
> And cover my face with the flag of the homeland,
> And if someone asks of me say that I went far away
> I will never return,

I will never return,
I am going to eternal paradise.
Do not cry, oh my mother,
Do not cry, oh my mother,
For I live in [your] hearts.
I have traveled all the roads
And I will scatter my soul everywhere.
The stories of my deeds
Will be told from generation to generation.
My beloved, give voice to your joy!
Mother, give voice to your joy!
If I arrive carried on [men's] shoulders,
Then I will marry
Those of the beautiful eyes [epithet of the *houris*, the 72
    black-eyed virgins of paradise].

"Warrior of the Emperor! You are absolutely forbidden to return alive from the battle. Your mission demands your death. Your body will die on the battlefield, but your soul will live. It chose the death of your body as a way of achieving victory." Such was the Emperor of Japan's battle order. Propelled by that spirit, the kamikaze ["divine wind"] pilots crashed their planes on the decks of the American aircraft carriers during the Second World War. A similar message is sent to the suicide bomber. The dispatchers are like the cannon that shoots the mortar shell. Without them there would be no suicide bombing attacks. Who makes the decision, what are the dynamics between dispatcher and potential suicide bomber, male or female? Who is behind the suicide bombing attacks? Ordinary people or psychopaths motivated by insane hatred?

CHAPTER 2

The Role of the Dispatcher: "Everybody Has His Job: I Dispatch the Suicide Bomber and He Explodes"

"Someone who dispatches suicide bombers? Around here there is no argument, around here, people are happy about it." That was what Saleh told me at our first meeting. He was a Palestinian dispatcher who had sent two suicide bombers to carry out a double mass-murder attack inside Israel. The first explosion killed many soldiers who were waiting at a pickup point for rides to their bases. The second killed and maimed those who rushed to take care of the wounded. I interviewed him during the summer of 2000, a few months before the second intifada broke out.

Saleh looked me straight in the face, waiting to see if I would lower my eyes in embarrassment or fear. He said, "On our side I see only victims. It's not a question of nationalism. No one thinks we're going to get our land back with a suicide bombing attack. They say, if a mother cries here, then a mother has to cry there too. I admire a man who attacks soldiers, but not one who attacks women, children, ordinary civilians. I'm the most respected person here."

When he came into the interview room I stood up and held out my hand for him to shake, as if to say, "This is a meeting between two people, you can speak freely."

Saleh was tall. I could see him looking over my head and then his eyes moved down, looking me over, trying to size me up. It was the inquisitive look of a strange man, crude and direct. The hand that loosely shook mine was sweaty and unpleasant. Did he feel insecure? Was he uncomfortable shaking hands with a woman? But there was something arrogant and defiant about him, direct and uninhibited.

Nevertheless, at first it seemed difficult for him to hold a normal conversation. He made a point of talking about local politics, including the issue

Ashkenazi Jews (Jews of European origin) versus Sephardic Jews (Jews from Middle Eastern and North African countries) in Israeli society. I told him I had no intention of debating with him, but that rather I wanted to discuss his personal and family life. His Hebrew was fluent, and he told me he could read and write it as well. He had a large vocabulary and expressed himself clearly and unhesitatingly. There was something manipulative in his attitude. He tried to turn the discussion into an exchange of opinions about the murderous Palestinian violence directed at Israeli civilians, and sometimes it seemed that he was trying to get me to support it. How absurd, I thought to myself. Sometimes he would pause, and then look me right in the eye again, quite impolitely. It was very annoying, as though he were investigating me. He thought I would lower my eyes, or at least show signs of being uncomfortable. In fact, I did feel uncomfortable, but I knew that if he sensed it, he would try to control the discussion, which was unacceptable. I looked directly at him, metaphorically straightened my spine and continued, ignoring his provocations. I knew that if this were happening in the street, I would cross to the other side to get away from him.

After we had been speaking for about two hours I said, "Our children are the same age. My parents came from Iraq, and I grew up speaking Hebrew but acquired a passive knowledge of Arabic."

He raised his eyes to the ceiling. Previously he had spoken almost nonstop, but now he seemed to be having trouble finding the right words. "The conflict is between nations, not between people," he said finally, almost in a whisper, his head hanging. "I have Jewish friends and I always felt good when I was with them. Even now they can't believe I was arrested. Not all of them are in favor of peace. What about Jerusalem? They release thieves from prison but they don't let security prisoners out. Here, most of the inmates are PLO [i.e., Fatah]. They are admired . . ."

He spoke of the suicide bombers and of himself as a dispatcher: "Among us, someone who dispatches suicide bombers has status. Society respects him and helps his family." Saleh seemed very self-centered. He had a great deal of anger bottled up and ready to explode. He told me about his life before he was arrested. His father was a plumber who worked for the Rehovot municipality and his family had a clothing factory in Gaza. Financially they had no worries. Saleh finished high school and studied economics at Al-Azhar University in Cairo, but his father objected. "He wanted me close by," he said, "and children did what their fathers told them. But that was then, and my children don't," he said in a tone of anger and bitterness.

Exposure to Israel's Western society in the wake of the Six Day War in 1967, in which the Arab countries joined forces to destroy the State of Israel, created a crisis in Palestinian society and undermined its patriarchal family structure. The father was no longer omnipotent and sometimes his children, who worked in Israel, supported the family. Young Palestinians often felt themselves caught in a conflict between their closed, traditional society and open Western society. Many of them became deeply jealous of the Israelis, sometimes of their Western way of life. The lives of Arab families revolve around the extended family and the community, and the children are less exposed to the outside world and have less direct contact and interaction with it, most of their information coming from the media. In the West, at least according to some educational philosophies, the children are the center of family life and in certain cases decide its agenda

Hamas [the Islamic Resistance Movement], the Palestinian offshoot of the Egyptian Muslim Brotherhood, provided an answer for the conflict created. It established a social, educational, and religious network (da'wah), which embraced the local residents and created an economic and spiritual need for its services, especially in education and welfare, with the stated intention of promoting its fundamentalist Islamic ideology.

The process did not take place in a vacuum, and at the same time there were opposite processes. In 2000, former Israeli Prime Minister Benjamin Netanyahu, who at the time held no political office, told me there were many changes for the good taking place which were dependent neither on us nor on the Arabs. "Arab society," he said, "has always been closed and subject to very clear religious and cultural control. Today it is exposed to a certain amount of modernization and more channels of information are opening up. Whereas Israel is fairly ready, for the Arab régimes it poses a definite threat.

"In Iran today thousands of satellite dishes receive American sitcoms. Young Iranians see how the stars of the shows dress and they hear the music. That creates pressure on the political and religious establishments, which try to stop the flow of information, but it is doubtful whether they can succeed."

My own children are not particularly obedient, and certainly do not fear their parents as we feared ours. When we were around my late father, who came to Israel from Iraq as a young man in 1949, we were very careful of what we said. "Ayib," he would say in Arabic, for talking like that. He would usually say it when my sisters and I called each other names. "Girls don't talk like that," he would say. My mother, who came from Iraq as a child, had no objection to what we said. It should be noted that Arab children are under the thumbs of their parents, whose influence is completely different from that of parents in Western families.

Saleh tried to describe a situation similar to my own, and said that children were no longer completely dominated by the fathers but expressed their own desires. They even dared to defy their parents.

"When they put me in prison I was 27. Now I'm 30. I liked my job. I got married in 1990, ten years ago, and I have three children. The oldest is a boy, he's eight, my daughter is six and the youngest is also a boy, three and a half. I went to prison when he was just three months old. I didn't see my family at all for five months. My father died"—and here he used the Hebrew word *niftar*, usually used only by Jews to refer to the death of a Jewish person, since it does not mean "died" but rather "released" from performing the religious duties commanded by the Bible—"and they wouldn't let me call my mother. It was just revenge. She was 80 and very ill. All together we're ten children. Five boys, five girls. I'm the youngest.

"At first it was very hard. Now my family has gotten used to the situation, they know what they have to do, they're waiting for me to get out. I've been sentenced. I was sentenced a month ago for an attack. Now my children ask questions that I can't answer. I write letters. My family helps my wife. At least that's something I don't have to worry about. My brothers take care of my wife before they take care of their own families, bring her what she needs. They take care of my children's school, food, clothing. . . .

"Someone who dispatches suicide bombers? Around here there is no argument, around here, people are happy about it. If women and children are killed maybe it's different, it's individual. Of course we believe in peace, there are children named 'Abdul Salaam' ["slave of peace"]. Peace where everyone has their rights. [When] I was outside, you could feel that something had changed [after the Oslo Accord], things were going in the right direction, whoever didn't believe wasn't alive.

"For us, money isn't important. The most important thing is that I return to my family. They told me I'll get 22 terms of life imprisonment, not one. But I was sentenced on the basis of reasonable doubt. I was accused of aiding and abetting suicide bombers. The whole story is based on a bag they found at my house full of explosives. One of the workers left it there . . . it's a real problem. He was killed, the Palestinian Authority killed him, maybe they asked the Israel Security Agency, because right after the Oslo Accord was signed you had the feeling that there was cooperation on matters of security, to fight terrorism and promote the peace process. That collapsed because of the suicide bombing attacks carried out by Palestinians against the State of Israel . . ."

Saleh believed that at that time Palestinian Authority and the Israel Security Agency combined forces to prevent terrorist attacks. He was referring to the wave of suicide bombing attacks which engulfed Israel during the 1990s. In fact there was such cooperation, although not of the sort Saleh suspected. During the current intifada (September 2000 to the present) there has been no such cooperation, and the Palestinian Authority has either collaborated with the terrorists or turned a blind eye to their activities.

Nevertheless, Saleh stated in no uncertain terms that life under the Palestinian Authority was preferable to life under the Israel occupation. "Ever since the Authority has been in the Gaza Strip there has been an emotional change. You can move around in Gaza, you can go out at night, no one will bother you. During the [first] intifada [1987–1993] after seven or eight at night everyone was at home—no one was allowed outside."

Like others I interviewed, Saleh was very interested in the ethnic issues in Israel. On one hand, he was impressed that Jews had come from different places with different cultures and managed to create an entity like the State of Israel. On the other, he tried to make light of it, to undermine the foundations of Israeli society. Saleh said, "[In Israel] there is discrimination. You think there is democracy? No racism in Israel? Why isn't the Prime Minister a Sephardic Jew?"

I understood that he was intelligent and trying, on the most personal level, to make me, as an Israeli Jew of Iraqi extraction and therefore a Sephardic Jew, feel inferior and deprived because the Prime Minister wasn't Sephardic. "You relate to all Arabs as though they were criminals. All Israeli Arabs are citizens, but not everyone is treated the same. There is racism. I am talking about democracy. They talk about reconciliation to get a few Arab votes. The Jews have water, electricity, a sewer system, the Arabs don't." Questioning Israeli society, its human fabric, and moral structure, was a recurring theme in many of the conversations I held with suicide bomber dispatchers.

Unlike Saleh, who spoke Hebrew, Mahmoud, also a suicide bomber dispatcher, refused to speak anything but Arabic. He sat across the table from me, an uncertain, suspicious look on his face. He was short and thin with dark brown eyes, thin brown hair, and a little moustache. His brown clothes were unsoiled and it was clear that even in prison he cared about his appearance and was careful to keep clean.

"The world I live in, as a Palestinian, is full of dilemmas. Should I live with my mother and the rest of the family in the refugee camp or should I leave everything. They took my land, should someone rise up and do what I did? That was a dilemma for me, it was the last choice I made regarding my life. Either I would live in prison or with my parents ... Even a Jewish mother loves her son, but sometimes she wants to keep him safe, sometimes she sends him off to war because there's no choice ... The dilemma of whether to live, marry or whether every Jewish mother wants to send her son off, but not be the one to do it ... In another sense, she has to send him off. It was the same with me, I wanted to live with my family and brothers, but it was my duty to defend my homeland, I felt I owed it to myself. Not things concerning Jews and Palestinians; things about people."

Mahmoud was not afraid to talk to me. He was the ranking dispatcher. His status with the other prisoners was high and he had no fear of being thought a collaborator. At the time, he was serving 46 consecutive life sentences in one of Israel's maximum security prisons. He was found responsible for a series of suicide bombing attacks, which resulted in the deaths of 46 civilians, some of them children. The judges were unanimous: "The murderous behavior of the accused, who tries to lend his deeds an air of ideology, is that of someone whom every human society must rid itself. A person whose goal is to indiscriminately kill and slaughter men, women and children simply because they are Jews removes himself from the humanity created in the image of God and cannot use the defense of his rights as a pretext for his actions. The identity of the victims was of no consequence in the eyes of the accused, and therefore the attacks led [not only to the deaths of Jews but] to the deaths of foreign workers and an Arab."

I told Mahmoud that I was doing research and asked him to tell me about himself and his family. Mahmoud, who initially had insisted on speaking only Arabic to emphasize his nationality, began speaking a mixture of Hebrew and Arabic. "You can speak in whatever language you like. My parents came from Iraq and I understand some Arabic, and what I don't understand, I'll get someone to help me translate," I said half-smiling.

Apparently I said something to thaw the atmosphere. Possibly it was the thought that if I had been born into an Iraqi-Jewish household, maybe I would understand an Arab man better.

He drank some of the tea in the cup in front of him, enjoying the sweetness. He seemed introverted. Most of the time he kept his eyes lowered, embarrassed. Only sometimes did he look directly at me. He spoke in a quiet monotone, at first in Arabic and then in Arabic mixed with Hebrew. "The first time I was arrested for throwing rocks I was in the Ansar prison in the Gaza Strip for 18 days. My interrogation consisted of a beating. I was 17 and I felt it made me stronger. The intifada had the greatest influence on me. I saw the [Israeli] army, how it behaved, my friends who got killed right next to me. We were arrested, beaten—it gave me the strength to go on.

"I'm 29. I was born in Khan Yunis [a refugee camp in the Gaza Strip]. I got married and divorced and fours years ago, I said, enough is enough. I don't have any children. My father is dead, he died 18 years ago. My mother is 60, at home, and my father's second wife has eight children, seven boys and one girl. I was born fourth and have ten more brothers and sisters. My father married his second wife, 'the new one . . .'"

Even if he didn't specifically say so, it is reasonable to assume that Mahmoud feels rejected because he is the son of his father's first wife, who was pushed aside to make room for his second, younger wife. The lack of a father figure—the father's having married a second wife and started anew family, gone to prison or died—is characteristic of suicide bombers and the dispatchers.

"When I was ten, my father died of leukemia. He was a tough man. When we were little, even though we were little, it was important to him that we could do everything. He was a tailor, and I would go with him when I was little to sell things. My father loved us a lot, but his love wouldn't let us be weak, and taught us to be men. A girl spends more time with her mother, and the boy learns more from his father. I remember my father used to give me a lot of responsibility and had me go and sell material myself. I would sell it and do the accounts and even pay salaries. Our house was modest but nothing was lacking.

"I went to school, graduated and even studied at Al-Jama'ah Al-Islamiyah University in Gaza, but I never got my degree. I studied the fundamentals of Islamic law and the principles of religion. I'm not very religious, that is, my family is religious, but not very religious. My studies were erratic because I kept getting arrested. I signed up for three years but I didn't study consistently because I got arrested all the time.

"All my brothers are married and study. I have one brother in prison in Israel and one who was deported. When they deported Hamas he went to Syria.

"We're not allowed to have visitors in prison. Only my mother comes to visit. At first my brothers weren't allowed to come. But there was a hunger strike and now a brother or a sister can visit every other week for 45 minutes."

Talking about his family made Mahmoud very emotional and he sank into a gloomy reverie about other, better days. "Our home was good, there were no problems between brothers and sisters, the family was good and united. My brothers and I were alike, there was no difference, we lived the same way but they weren't all smart. If they had all had the same intelligence, all of them would be in prison. My parents left their land. In 1948 they lived in Hamah, a small village near Ramla. I heard the Jews did all kinds of things to hurt them and that's why they left. They left the village and went to live in a refugee camp."

Mahmoud said he knew Jews. When he was 15 or 16, he worked in supermarkets in Petah Tikva, and Herzliya during the summer vacation.

"I didn't like the work. At first I had to work to continue studying, to support myself and be responsible. But on the other hand, I worked on my land [i.e., land he felt belonged to him, not the State of Israel], and that bothered me.

In 1996, Mahmoud was responsible for the murder of Hayah, a soldier serving in the southern command, at the same time I was an officer in the women's corps of the southern command in the army. She stood at an intersection waiting for a ride in a military vehicle which would take her to her base. There she would return her equipment and say goodbye to her comrades in arms. Just 19 years old, a few days later she was to be married.

A suicide bomber dispatched by Muhammad put an end to all her dreams. He arrived at the intersection looking for soldiers in uniform, an earring in his ear and his hair full of gel. Hayah and a male soldier were standing near a public telephone. The suicide bomber approached them and blew himself up. Hayah was killed instantly. Dozens of others were wounded.

I looked at Muhammad and thought about Hayah's grieving family. Her sister was an officer in the same command and under my jurisdiction, so I knew the family before the tragedy. My next meeting with them was during the *Shiva*, the traditional seven-day Jewish mourning period. I arrived at the house after hospital visits to many of the soldiers who had been wounded in the attack.

I kissed her mother, and she hugged me, and I could feel her whole body shake. The house was full of people, many of them soldiers from Hayah's unit and that of her sister. Never in my wildest dreams did I imagine that several years later I would be sitting in the same room with her murderer, calmly having tea with him. Externally, at least, Mahmoud radiated tenderness and delicacy. It was hard to believe that this was the man responsible for suicide bombing attacks which had cost the lives of so many innocent Israelis, left so many wounded scarred forever in body and soul, and destroyed the lives of entire families.

I asked Mahmoud to talk about love. His eyes sparkled, and he acted like an adolescent talking about his first girlfriend. I imagine that my being a woman broke down some of his resistance and the walls he had built around himself at the beginning of our meeting. He looked around as though checking to see if there were someone else listening before he revealed his deepest secrets. It seemed to be more difficult for him to speak about love for a woman than about planning a suicide bombing attack.

He said, "When I was wanted [by the Israeli security forces], when they were chasing me, I didn't want to get married, but my mother said I should, that she wanted me to have a home. So for my mother I went and got married."

The desire to please the mother was a leitmotif in all the conversations I had with dispatchers and failed male and female suicide bombers. Mahmoud said that from the moment his mother broached the topic he felt he had to satisfy her. "To make my mother happy" was the most important thing in the world, even though he knew he was liable to be arrested by the Israeli security forces and that his married life would be over almost before it started, even earlier than he imagined.

"When I got married I was already a wanted man. I was arrested a month after the ceremony. [What happened was that] I left the Gaza Strip and went to the West Bank. I was arrested in Hebron and they brought me to prison. I was married but I couldn't be with my wife all the time. I was embarrassed. Should she come for visits or should I leave her alone? She didn't want to get divorced but I thought about it and it was only logical for me to leave her. It was very hard for her. Enough was enough, there was no relationship, and if you get divorced, each one leaves the other. She remarried. When she did, I was pleased. My wife knew I was wanted by the Israelis before we got married. Maybe I would die, maybe I would go to prison, but she said she wanted me. It was hard for my mother because they were very close. Now they visit each other."

Mahmoud's wife was his cousin and they knew each other from childhood. He said he had a moral dilemma regarding his wife. Many prisoners want a woman in their lives, one living beyond the prison walls, a woman they can fantasize about and take strength from, a woman who will worry about them, write, and visit. In that respect there is a marked difference between male and female prisoners. Male prisoners regard it as a relatively convenient arrangement: the woman outside takes care of the children and keeps the family going. Female prisoners, on the other hand, are afraid that their men will find other women. The few who are mothers know that they cannot rely on men in that respect.

Mahmoud, who knew that sooner or later he would most likely be apprehended and imprisoned, understood that morally and emotionally it would be worth his while to keep his wife. He said that he thought about it a great deal. He loved his wife a lot, he said, and his first reaction was not to give her up. She was very young and Mahmoud knew that they would quickly find her another husband. He did not hide his anger at the thought that his beloved wife would belong to another man. She would share his bed and bear him the children she could not bear Mahmoud. But, he said, it was his great love for her that made him decide to divorce her. "I wanted a different life for her, a family and children," he said. He did not want her to spend her whole life waiting for him to be released from prison, something that would apparently never happen.

"There is no point in talking about her now. It's over and done with." He divorced her and she has already remarried, as he expected her to, but his mother is still in touch with her, for she is not only her ex-mother-in-law, but her aunt.

Speaking about love softened him. He took another sip of tea. Then he said, "Because of my situation now, I don't want to bring up memories about my childhood. I think it was a long time ago, I don't want to remember. My life as a Palestinian . . . I don't want to remember the emotional, moving moments. It's hard for me to explain it . . . The situation the person lives in forces him to forget. So that he doesn't get upset . . ."

The lack of desire to face memories was a feature of many of my conversations with suicide bombers and dispatchers. Apparently Mahmoud and his comrades were afraid talking about their childhood experiences and memories would weaken them, or dull the macho aura they radiate. Any sign of emotion, they seemed to feel, might filter through the cold, murderous façade they had created for themselves, and even more so in prison, in the company of other prisoners. I realized that the arousal of any strong emotion would threaten him.

Nevertheless, he told me about his life with a kind of tranquility. Apparently there was something very soothing about it and it made him want to talk. "Life was very good in the refugee camps. I lived at home. I had a good life, and my neighbors were like family, we were all one big happy family. We ate together, made food for everyone. I had friends there, all the mothers were like a mother to me. At home people fight about stupid things, little things. The world is only sweet when there are problems. It's no good when there are no problems, life isn't worth anything."

The description of communal life was another recurring theme in the discussions I had. Not one of the dispatchers described a difficult financial situation or wretched poverty. Quite the opposite was true. They spoke about a completely normative life, not about families struggling to subsist.

Mahmoud sank down into his chair. I could tell he was thinking about something else. Longing for his home and family were profound. "My mother is strong. She's having a very difficult time, but when she visits me she doesn't show it.

"When I was arrested my parents' house was open all the time for a month or two. Neighbors would come in and ask after me all the time. I had decided that it would be my path even before the intifada broke out ... In Spain Jews and Muslims lived together. Throughout history there was peace between Jews and Arabs, they are cousins. On the other hand, if I live in a house with my wife and my brother comes and throws me out of the house, I will hate him too."

That was a typical claim, raised by many of the terrorists I spoke to when they tried to prove that there was no religious basis for the hatred between Jews and Arabs, and that the struggle was only based on the claim of stolen Arab lands. There is no space in this book for a full discussion of the matter. Suffice it to say that it is very doubtful that throughout history, Jews had personal safety, economic prosperity and religious and cultural freedom under Muslim rule. In the Palestinian Authority, the walls are covered with graffiti expressing the desire for the same sort of slaughter inflicted on the Khaybar Jews: in Saudi Arabia at the dawn of Islam in the early seventh century, the Muslims evicted the three Jewish tribes living there from the homes, killed the men and threw the bodies into a ditch, raped the women and took the children as spoils of war, all with the personal involvement of the prophet Muhammad. Even today, at mass demonstrations and marches the Palestinians can be heard singing "Khaybar, Khaybar, oh Jews, the army of Muhammad will return ... "

Mahmoud continued speaking. "Even before the [first] intifada I decided that this would be my path ... We learned where our lands were and what had happened to them, and we thought that would be the way we would go, and then the intifada began in earnest. The things that happened during the intifada were not the main reasons I chose to do what I did. The main reason was—who I am, where I am, where are my lost lands are, who my father is, where his land is. The things I saw only fired me up. That was the match that lit it all."

His family was not neglected nor did it collapse because of his imprisonment, it became more popular and respected. Respect has financial significance as well. If the Israeli security forces destroy the house of a terrorist, all the neighbors get together to rebuild it. There are amazing descriptions about mutual aid in Palestinian society. There is a rule within Palestinian society that the family of someone who was involved in a terrorist attack against Israel will never be hurt in any way. Not only that, but the members of the extended family, the clan, the neighbors and the organization to which the imprisoned or killed terrorist belonged will do everything in their power to improve its circumstances.

CHAPTER 3

Organization: "The Dispatchers Don't Send Their Own Sons to Blow Themselves Up"

Mu'in, shy, with delicate features, had difficulty opening up when we started talking. He kept clasping and unclasping his long-fingered hands, looking at me without speaking. The conversation took place about two months before the outbreak of the second intifada in September 2000.

He was born in the Jabaliya refugee camp in the Gaza Strip, was married, and had three children, the youngest of whom had been born after his imprisonment. His father had two wives, and he was the oldest child in the family. The father lived with the second wife, but the family had two houses in Jabaliya.

Without a doubt, the children of a first, rejected wife suffer feelings of deprivation and discrimination. The father sometimes sends the long-suffering mother off to live in a shed in the yard, bringing out the younger wife and showing her off.

When a second wife has children, relationships within the family become complicated because everyone wants to attract the father's attention and receive his recognition and love. The financial consideration is also important: the dowry of the younger wife has to be paid, sometimes a drain on already-strained finances. There is also the problem of feelings of deprivation, discrimination, and competition with the new branches grafted onto the original family when the father marries a second time. (One such example is Osama bin Laden, the son of the fourth rejected wife who came from an average Syrian family and was divorced by the father, Muhammad bin Laden. That meant her status was significantly inferior to that of the other wives and she had no support within the family. Osama was scornfully called "the servant's son," and was torn between his desire to live with his mother and the need to be close to his father and the rest of the family.

It was a conflict that had no resolution, and in the end bin Laden was brought up by his father's first wife, who was strict and demanding. Thus bin Laden, like other terrorist dispatchers, suffered paternal deprivation, and had to compete for his father's attention and live as the son of a rejected woman, but also suffered from maternal deprivation because he had been sent away from her. His father died when Osama was 10 years old and his older brother, who in certain respects had been a father figure, also died.[1])

Mu'in began talking about his life. "I was in the Palestinian police force. From there I transferred to Palestinian intelligence. I studied at the Gaza campus of [the Egyptian] Al-Azhar University. My field was literary Arabic. I wanted to continue my studies in Russia. My wife's brother studied engineering in Russia and returned to Gaza. I read about Russia and liked what I read. I know Russian, I learned it in prison. I want to continue my studies there. I want to study medical psychology [sic]. But I didn't succeed and now I'm in prison.

"My father is 67, he has high blood pressure and can't get out of bed. It happened two years ago. My mother is 55. All my brothers [work for] the Palestinian Authority. The Authority gives my family money. Before '48 my father was in the last village on the Gaza side and the Palestinians left it and went to refugee camps. There is a kibbutz where the village used to be. Some of [the people] from the village are still in the Gaza Strip, but they don't have land. My father and mother left the village in '48, my mother was five and my father was 17."

In 1993, when Mu'in was under administrative detention, his brother Yussuf was killed. "He went to the village we left in '48 and carried out a suicide bombing attack in the middle of the kibbutz. No one was hurt. He went to shoot at people, and they shot and killed him. When I got out of prison I found that I had only one brother. I knew him, I would have said that nothing like that would happen to him. How did they convince him? He was so smart!

"In 1993 he went of his own free will. That's hard for the family and children. My mother has only a brother at home who works for Palestinian Preventive Security. I'm fed up with life in Israel. The brother who died was connected with the Palestinian Islamic Jihad. They took responsibility for his attack. I was in prison. I got out five months later and tried to find out how it happened. I thought he had plans for his life. He knew karate... My brother believed he had to commit suicide... Maybe during the intifada he was beaten, he was in prison with a lot of people... If we were at war, I would be happy if Yussuf killed a lot of soldiers, but at war or not, I never would have agreed, ever, that he kill a female soldier. I take responsibility for every word I say. Not a female soldier, not civilians, not minors. If there is a [male] soldier among female soldiers, I don't shoot in his direction. Because if I kill women I don't get money and I don't get promoted. We talk about it in prison, one of the prisoners killed soldiers when there was a war in Lebanon, and all over Europe, killing soldiers is the normal thing."

My feeling was that he said one thing and felt another. It was important for him to tell me he would not harm a female soldier because of her gender, but as in many of the other cases I dealt with, talk was one thing and actions were another. Nevertheless, he tried to make it clear that he himself would never carry out a suicide bombing attack.

"I would never agree to carry out an attack on a bus...I would tell my children...I wouldn't tell them to do what Yussuf did, my brother who carried out a suicide bombing attack. The person who sends people to blow themselves up never send his own son. Did you read the book *From the Hezbollah to Iran*? Nasrallah, his son went out on an attack and died, now maybe they will imitate him."

Not exactly: actually, the son of Hezbollah leader Hassan Nasrallah was killed in an exchange of fire with IDF soldiers in Lebanon, but it happened during a battle, not in a suicide bombing attack. However, I did not want to stop Mu'in, and he continued, "The Palestinian man in the street has a lot of questions, [a lot of people ask] why the sons [of the leaders] don't go [to carry out suicide bombing attacks]. Everyone knows the answer. Leaders are always different from soldiers. That's not a secret. And their sons are different as well. But if something happens, like what happened with Hezbollah, if the son of the leader goes and commits suicide, now maybe the sons of other leaders will go...They would never think of it, they're their sons. People only think about themselves more than about others."

Mu'in was a dispatcher, but his status in the organization was the result of his being the brother of a *shaheed*. When we met again he brought me pictures of his children. He held the pictures out to me as if to say, "What do you think, these are my children, would I send them out to blow themselves up in a suicide bombing attack?" I looked at the pictures and saw the sweet faces of a little boy and girl, holding hands and smiling at the camera. They were dressed in colorful clothing.

Later, he told me that he hoped he would be released and wanted to study psychology in Russia. When he felt he had been talking too long he said, "I think it would be better if we stopped talking today." Obviously, he was afraid the other prisoners would suspect him of being a collaborator, and even though he had dispatched suicide bombers, his footing in the organization was weak, since he had been accepted by virtue of his bother's suicide bombing attack. That was exceptional, since dispatchers usually enjoy high status and respect.

Nevertheless, he kept on talking. "My mother comes to visit. I love her very much. I am her first-born. Her relationship with my wife is very good. She once told me that she loved my wife and sees her like a picture of me inside her. They have a very good life. The relationship with my wife is good, and the relations in my family between my father, mother and [my] brothers is very good. There are no problems there.

"My mother is a very good woman. I say that because of the way she behaves with my wife and the children and my brothers. She doesn't know how to read or write, but she's very smart. The children have gone, and Yussuf . . . the girls are married, they live far away, and my being in prison is hard for her. She hopes I'll come back to her.

"I hope we can get rid of the problem. We will be an independent country separate from the Jewish state. Relations between two countries is bet-ter . . . neighbors. [But] I'm not going to forget the great catastrophe of '48. My mother, if I look at her, has had exactly 50 years of catastrophe . . . Until now she has had a son in prison. Forget about the catastrophes of the past, but a son who is alive and in prison is before her eyes all the time. It is very difficult. She has already made a life for herself. She goes to the cemetery, to my brother, that's one side, she comes to visit me in prison, listens to what I tell her, tells me I've grown, asks about my health . . . She worries all the time.

"The same with my wife, maybe more . . . Maybe sometimes my children, who live with her, maybe she will find a way to change their lives. A woman, her husband in prison, she has children, I know she is busy with them all the time, she does a lot for them . . . What all the children around us lack, she does for them, my wife, she lives for them. The chemistry between us was very good, it still is. She worries about me all the time, waits for me, sits at home, she was studying something but she doesn't have time for that now, the children go to school, to kindergarten. She also helps my father and mother. For the past four and a half years, as long as I've been in prison, she's lived with my parents, only she visits me. Thank Allah I have a wife like that."

The experience of being a refugee was emphasized by most of the dis-patchers. None of them even hinted at a willingness to compromise for the sake of achieving peace. At the outset of our conversation, Mu'in tried to create an analogy between dispatching suicide bombers to blow themselves up in crowded civilian sites and the IDF's military actions.

"The Israeli navy combat units go to places in Lebanon, it's harder than someone who goes to commit suicide. Maybe they jump out of a helicopter onto a land mine, or into an area full of Hezbollah. He knows for sure he might not come back from the attack, and he believes that he is defending the State of Israel and he goes. The difference between him and someone who goes on a suicide bombing attack is that he [the suicide bomber] has no hope, he knows that he will never come back. The Israeli knows he *might* not come back, and that *maybe* he will die, that's the difference.

"Why do I make the comparison? Because all people, maybe they have . . . maybe they are convinced of something . . . If we were at war with Israel, whose side would I be on? The Palestinian side! But I don't want to die,

I don't want to blow myself up, to end my life so that all Palestine might live. That will never happen if everyone thinks he will die...I will be on the Palestinian side. If I kill soldiers as a Palestinian. That's what Yussuf thought, my brother who went to blow himself up. There are people who go and people who blow up. That's the way it is in the world, that's the way it always is, there is the soldier and there is the person in charge, there is the solider and there is the commander."

That worldview is also manifested by Al-Qaeda, whose commanders and those in charge of operations do not carry out suicide bombing attacks, but rather cynically hold the view that "each one does his job...," as Mu'in intimated.

There is no doubt that there is no similarity whatsoever between the suicide bomber dispatchers and the IDF commanders. The call to "Follow me" is still genuine and relevant in the IDF, and commanders, even the highest ranking commanders, lead the troops and expose themselves to the greatest risks.

❖

"My whole life, the most important thing has been my family. I don't bother with myself at all. The agenda of the people around me is more important than I am, that's how I grew up, that's what my mother and fathers and older brothers taught me."

The speaker is Abdallah, a suicide bomber dispatcher, sentenced to a number of consecutive life sentences. He is tall and pleasant, and we spoke for a longer time than usual. He laid out all his complaints about prison and about that fact that his family was not permitted to work in Israel because he had dispatched suicide bombers.

"I was born in the Gaza Strip, in Al-Bureij refugee camp, in 1970. I graduated from high school in 1988. After that I was arrested, in 1990, for things I didn't do—throwing rocks, leading a demonstration and incitement. My father died in 1994. He worked as a laborer in Israel. My mother is a housewife, she's 75 and still lives in Al-Bureij. We are five boys and seven girls. I am number eight and the youngest boy. I'm the only one who went to prison. All my brothers work except for one who is in medical school in Russia. He studied to be a male nurse in Israel but was dissatisfied with the situation in Gaza and left, he had an opportunity to continue his studies and become a doctor. Now he's interning, he finishes this year, and I think he will come back for a visit and weigh his options. He's married.

"I'm single. I studied at the university and getting married would have been hard because then you have to work and support your family. All my other brothers work. They worked in Israel before I was arrested, that ruined things for them financially and emotionally...When I was wanted and the Israeli security forces didn't manage to arrest me...Even now they aren't allowed into Israel. There is work in Gaza, but for someone who is

used to working in Israel all the time—it's better [in Israel]. There are Jews
they know...the relations between them are good, it isn't important, Jews,
Arabs...

"I liked working, not sitting around. I worked in construction in Israel
all the time before I was arrested. During 1988, 1989, I wanted to work
and I looked for work in a lot of places, Tel Aviv, Bat Yam, Jaffa, Netivot,
Ashdod, Beersheba, and I didn't find anything. I was 18. Finally I found
work in a restaurant in Tel Aviv on the waterfront. After that I worked
in Ramat Gan, some of my neighbors were working in construction there.
That's when I knew I had to have a profession, and within a month I learned
to pour concrete, there are people who take two years to learn what I learned
in a month. I had a lot of motivation. A neighbor taught me, I kept asking
him, he told me that in a little while I would be able to pour a column and
stairs, so [I should] think about how to do it. Stairs as well, think about
how to do it. Within a month, with the help of Allah, I learned and I was a
professional. After that I moved on to [building] plans. I would look at plans
all the time. In the beginning I didn't even know which way to hold one..."

His family was the center of his life. "At home the atmosphere was
good, relations were close, we loved each other and couldn't bear to be
apart...Our financial circumstances were good, it was easy. We all worked.
I was at the university and I worked. We brought our salaries home, no difference between us, we gave [our salaries] to our father and mother. Each
one of us, whatever he needed, each one of us used to feel that there was
someone who would support him, that he would never be alone...Even
now I feel that way.

"I worked while I was studying. I supported the family [financially] like
everyone else...They wanted to make me feel they were backing me up. If
you need something, don't worry, you can have it. The girls in the family,
all the girls who were younger than I, all studied at university. The one next
in line after me got her BA in English culture and now she is a teacher, the
next youngest one is studying at the Islamic University. They're all religious
girls, I'm religious. The whole family is religious, but not seriously. If you
compare us with the Jews, we are not ultra-Orthodox. We keep the Islamic
rules and traditions, but we're not extremists. The one who is studying at
the Islamic University is getting her BA in chemistry. The one after her, the
third, is also studying in Gaza, specializing in administration. I was closer
to my sisters, I was their little brother and they spoiled me. I'm OK with
everyone but closer to the girls, I'm fond of them, I feel the most for them.

"At the university, when I was majoring in English, I wanted to change
majors and study politics, political science...My head was spinning. I am
better at political science than at English, but at that time I wanted to
distance myself from political life in Israel. We eat politics, drink politics,
there's politics in the food. I wanted to get away from that.

"When I went into military work [i.e., joined a terrorist organization] I
was on the horns of a dilemma, whether to do the work or not to get into it,

because I might get killed. It was a hard decision to make and I looked at my situation from the family's point of view, because I was a central member of the family. What I was doing was very important, they had great hopes that I would finish my studies. My brothers were married and I lived at home with the unmarried girls, and one of them studied at university, and [it was important] that I help financially and in other ways.

"It was that kind of situation, I had to do one thing or the other, and in the end I made my decision and started military work. My family didn't know anything about it. I was even wanted [by the Israelis] and they didn't know. I didn't want to worry them, to get them started on something like that. Someone who knows about something like that, according to the law he is committing a crime [that is, if a someone knows a member of his family is wanted and shields him, he endangers himself]. It was a really big surprise for them when I was arrested..."

Abdallah also mentioned the importance of relations with neighbors: everyone helped each other, and they especially helped the families of those who were imprisoned in Israel for security offenses. The worse the offense, that is, the more murders the prisoner was responsible for, the higher his family's status was.

"When I was arrested my family began building their house. All the neighbors helped them. It was a small house and they had already laid the foundations...It was very difficult for my mother. For the whole family, my mother, the girls, the boys. They love me a lot, I was away from home all the time, I studied hard, I worked hard, I helped at home, they miss me...When I was arrested they said, 'We lost him...' A lot of times they told me, 'It's a pity you did it...' and 'you had your studies and your work, we hoped you would graduate, work with us, stick it out...' and 'you didn't finish your studies, and now we have lost you...'"

If Abdallah was sorry for anything, it was only for the sorrow he caused his family—he had no pangs of conscience for the deaths he had caused. Nevertheless, for some reason he found it important to make it known that he wouldn't hurt any of the Jews he knew. "At the same time I started doing military work [i.e., when he joined the terrorist organization] I knew Jews, I worked with Jews. There are [Jewish] people I knew, in prison as well. I never thought of hurting them, and if someone else wanted to hurt them, I would try to prevent it. When I was doing military work I was also working in Ashdod, I was a contractor there, and the boss...one day I came to work late. They were pouring a roof. I took his car because I had to go to Gaza, so he sent his sons with me, to Erez, to a place close to my house, he sent them in his car. When they passed through the Erez checkpoint they were shaking with fear. "We're in Gaza. There are terrorists..." At that time I was working for a military organization. If I had wanted to harm them, I could have telephoned one of my friends, not even be involved, kidnapped them. But I wasn't thinking like that at all. If someone had wanted to harm them I would have protected them myself.

"I calmed them down, I said, 'I'm with you, I'm with you in the car.' We arrived in Beit Lahiya and they were really scared, 'We're in the middle of Gaza...' I calmed them down and called my family, bought a couple of things in the grocery store and then we went back to Erez. My brother was working in the [Erez] industrial zone and I slept at his house. On Monday I went back to work. It turned out that [the boys] had told [their father] how Abdallah had done this and that. Most of the time he called me 'Abba,' [Hebrew for "dad"] not 'Abdallah,' and he would say, 'Abdallah is not an Arab' when he wanted to praise me. That's an example of the people I knew. I couldn't hurt them.

"At that time, I wasn't having any problems with myself, whatever entered my thoughts, that I had the right to be free, a lot of things drove me into the army [terrorist organization]. When I was arrested the first time I hadn't done anything. I was detained for nine months that seemed like nine hundred. I hadn't done anything but they beat me and took me out of my home...I tried to strangle a soldier and take his weapon, that was in 1990. It was a difficult time, they would shoot you in the head if you threw a rock, break your arms and legs. Do you remember how the late Rabin said, 'break their arms and legs?'...Anyone who threw a rock got a bullet in the head."

Abdallah blamed Yitzhak Rabin, who was then Minister of Defense, for reacting aggressively to the demonstrations held during the first intifada, but he made a point of calling him "the late Rabin," and there was no bitterness in his voice when he spoke about him. Nevertheless, he felt that his arrest was the first link in a chain of events that led to the serious crimes he eventually committed.

"At [the time of my arrest] I was waiting for Bethlehem University to open. A month and a half after I was arrested it opened. I lost a whole school year. When I was released I wanted to work and study. [But] after I got out of prison they wouldn't give me an identity card, just a card I had to renew every day at the Civilian Administration in Dir Al-Balah. I went there every day. They gave me an identity card after a month and a half. I wanted to get a magnetic card [which enables Palestinians to pass through checkpoints on their way to work in Israel] but they wouldn't give me one because I had been in prison..."

"In Gaza I worked for very low wages. I didn't enjoy working with Arabs. I don't get along well with Arabs. The work is hard and the salary is low. Cheap labor. After we agree on what I'm supposed to do they say, 'Do that as well, Abdallah, and after that you will have more work... You have a contract, you want money' and then he says, 'Now I have no money, I paid for sand and gravel, I have no money...' There were also some Jews who wanted to show what big shots they were, [but] I could be tough too. 'If you're having a hard time right now I'm willing to help you out for a day or two, a week maybe,' but Jews always paid me for my work."

Abdallah smiled broadly while telling me about his work with Jews. It was very strange to hear a dispatcher of suicide bombers say that Arabs broke agreements and did not keep their word.

Abdallah often repeated that the first time he was put in prison he was innocent, and that because of that he could not enroll at a university. The desire for revenge began to gnaw at him. "If someone had suggested that I do something to hurt [the Israelis], like helping someone from Hamas who was wanted by them, I would agree. There was something pushing me to do it. All the time I was looking for my faith, for my honor . . .

"My father was born in Sawafir, my mother in Yavneh, I was born in Gaza, but where should I go to work, where should I go to live? I spoke to a lot of people in Israel and they said, 'There are a lot of Arab countries. Go there.' [But] I was born here. My rights, if my rights are here, why should I go [someplace else]? If you were born in Hungary or [some other] country outside Israel, why don't you go there?"

That was often said during the meetings. My interlocutors suggested the Jews return to the countries they came from. On the other hand, when the idea was proposed that the Palestinians leave for the Arab countries, the response was usually, "It's hard to leave the place I live, where my clan [extended family] lives." I was tempted to ask if they seriously thought the Jews should go back to countries like Iraq, where they were persecuted and from where they were expelled, or to Europe, where they were discriminated against, persecuted, and murdered by the millions in concentration camps, but I could usually resist. The suggestion was recently made again by Iranian president Ahmadinejad, who frequently also suggests wiping Israel off the map, trying to legitimize his ideas through Holocaust denial.

Abdallah spoke bitterly of the way Palestinians were treated at the checkpoints. "When I worked in Israel I had to cross through the checkpoints, [and at] the Erez crossing they used to leave us for two or three hours, they treated me like a dog . . . In Israel even dogs are pampered and kissed. They behaved very badly, soldiers here, there, everywhere. There are Jews who speak and behave . . . He is free to think what he wants, [but what is] important is how you treat me. You should look at people as though they are human beings."

His decision to join a terrorist organization was personal. "When it came to joining a military wing, I didn't consult anyone. I couldn't consult anyone. If I consulted someone at the university [about my studies] I would gain from it, but military work, you can't consult anyone, not your father, your mother, not a good friend. It's something internal, it's up to you and you have to hide it. I thought about it by myself and I made my decision. It was a dilemma. To do military work [terrorism] or to join normal life and keep away from politics. In the end I chose to help military people. If it was the right decision or not, well, this is how it turned out."

Abdallah sounded less convinced that he was right in deciding to join an organization than did other dispatchers. Nevertheless, it seemed that his reservations were the result of personal considerations, of his sadness at having wound up in prison. Like most of the others, he had no regrets for what he had done.

"As for the attacks, I thought a lot about the person who wants to blow himself up or who wants to carry out an attack. No one puts any pressure on him. I didn't understand why they would blow themselves up. There are lots of people who want to blow themselves up. People like that, they have motives, motivation, that make them do things like that . . . I explained some of them. I explained my dilemma about the treatment I got from the Jewish soldiers in Israel, and the same thing happened to other people in Gaza. We are talking about a drop in the bucket. The [Israeli] children were hurt in the attacks, and although I did not take part in them, it was hard for me when a child was hurt.

"I would support a military attack on soldiers, army against army, I don't call that terrorism. Their work was taken from them by force, their rights were taken, so they have to receive their rights. I didn't participate in a military attack, but I wouldn't object to it. I would object to attacking civilians, children. I still love children to this day, it doesn't matter if they are Jewish or Arab. I see a picture of a little child and I keep it. It hurt me that there were others who took part in them, but at the same time, I want to be honest and open . . . Mass-murder attacks . . . People are motivated to carry them out because they themselves were injured, their brothers, members of their families, their sons and daughters, underage, older, there are dead and wounded, someone got his arm broken, someone else lost an eye. If you look at it you see a catastrophe, that was the motive for attacking civilians.

"A lot of times the Izzedine al-Qassam Battalions [the terrorist-operative wing of Hamas] distributed flyers calling for the State of Israel to fight army against army. 'We will not harm civilians, no shooting attacks, no mass-murder attacks, no bombs. We are ready [for such an agreement, of not carrying out attacks against civilians] and even request it.'"

However, as far as can be determined, there is no basis whatsoever in reality for the claim that such material was ever distributed. It if were true, Hamas would not be waging a terrorist war and hiding within the Palestinian civilian population. Moreover, all the suicide bombing attacks were carried out in Israeli cities against bus passengers, people sitting in cafés, in shopping malls, and from the start the intention was to kill civilians. The claim was probably made repeatedly within Hamas as part of its propaganda and psychological warfare campaign directed against Israel.

"There are still dilemmas about that. Even though I am in prison, I can't bear to see the name of a child here and there. I saw an attack against Israel on TV and I couldn't stand to see the name of a child who died or had been hurt. The child who was hurt at Apropo [a suicide bombing attack in a café in Tel Aviv, March 1997. Abdallah was referring to the picture shown on the news several times of an infant whose mother was one of several murdered civilians.] Until now I remember it and it is like a knife in my back . . . There was this guy who carried out the attack at [Café] Apropo, he lived with me, in the same room, he said to me, 'Our brothers, our brothers, we were hurt, before there was Izzedine al-Qassam . . .' [That is, he blamed Israel for killing Palestinians, and the Izzedine al-Qassam Battalions only reacted to provocation.] A Palestinian says, he was under pressure, rape my soul or spirit, why shouldn't I hurt them? What can I say to him?"

He went back to talking about his family. "My mother is very sick. My situation made her collapse. Her illness is much worse. At first she used to come to visit me all the time . . . Now she is in a bad way, she comes every month or two, sometimes she sleeps in the hospital. The situation is hard for the whole family—my brothers, my sisters . . . Even my brother in Russia calls to ask how I am, and so far no one has told him that I have been sentenced to a long term . . ."

The preservation of his family women's honor bothered Abdallah a lot, because he was in prison and there was no one who would watch out for their behavior. He kept saying, "A mistake in a girl's honor" cost her life. The mistake could be saying the wrong word or getting caught in behavior considered immoral. Nevertheless, or at least so he claimed, he believed someone should be convinced of something, not forced into it. "I believed in convincing [them], I wasn't prepared to put pressure on the girls, to do one thing or another, to believe one thing or another, I believed in convincing them, if you're convinced, [then] go do it . . .

"I have faith in [my sisters], they go out here and there. There are women in our neighborhood who don't go out of the house. My sisters go to the university, and I tell them, do what you have to, I speak fairly, I convince them according to our rules. Come to visit me and come and be convinced [not forced], and don't make a big mistake that can influence your whole life."

CHAPTER 4

Dispatchers Are Held in High Esteem: "I'm Considered Someone Who Does Something Good"

Ismail was a "serious" dispatcher who had been sentenced to several consecutive terms of life imprisonment. He worked closely with Yehia Ayyash, known as "the engineer," who was killed in January 1996. Ismail was thin and looked younger than he really was, and had a carefully manicured moustache. His brown eyes were questioning, as though he were curious and interested in everything going on around him. He was wearing pants and a shirt and his head was bare. He didn't look religious. I extended my hand and he shook it fairly firmly. Our conversation was relaxed. We drank coffee together and talked for hours. Sometimes it seemed as though Ismail treated dispatching suicide bombers as just a kind of regular employment.

"I'm 32, single, I've been in prison for the past 5 years, so I didn't get around to marrying. I was born in Nablus and lived in the Balata refugee camp nearby. My father is 69, he works for the Palestinian Authority, my mother is 65, she stays at home. We are ten children, boy and girls. I am number eight. I have been in prison since I was 27. I was in prison when I was 17, too. The IDF took me when I was walking in the street when I was 17, in '84. One of my older brothers is in Sydney, Australia, he's a doctor. One of my older sisters has a BA in mathematics, she lives in Dubai, that's near Saudi Arabia. I also have a sister in Iraq, in Basra.

"I was in my fourth year at Al-Najah University, in Nablus. I was studying life sciences and religion. Now I'm studying political science and Middle Eastern Studies at Everyman's University.

"My father was in the Popular Front [a secular terrorist organization with a Marxist-oriented ideology], but when I was 17 I became more religious . . . I started praying in the mosque, I had religious friends, but I also had non-religious friends, and some of my brothers and sisters aren't religious.

Why did I turn to religion? The world has problems and religion is the solution. It makes me stronger, the religious viewpoint on life, on society and economics and politics. I feel that religion influences politics. In your society too, [the religious parties have] influence."

He stopped for a minute to sip his coffee, and then started talking about other things.

"I'm here in prison, it's a life sentence because I dispatched suicide bombers to carry out attacks. The first dilemma is the occupation. I was one year old when they took my father to prison the first time and he stayed there until I was eight. They tried one of my sisters and my whole family . . . what do you expect from me? The occupation exists, there are weapons, there is shooting and that whole mess, I didn't choose it. One of my cousins was killed in a disturbance in the territories, three of my friends were killed 10 years ago in the [first] intifada. That influences me. A person is not a machine, a person is influenced . . . Friends of mine threw rocks and got killed for it. That influences me. Why did they do that? Why did they take my father? I have a lot of questions.

"Before I was sentenced to prison I hadn't spoken to Jews. I knew Jews only from soldiers and weapons, Jews that shoot at people. Meeting Jews gave me different feelings. There are people who deserve to be treated like me, like you, like all people. Imagine that you know a group of people, you know them because they shoot and kill other people, how would you treat them, you certainly wouldn't feel good about them. If I knew Jews who talked and didn't shoot people, I would have different ideas.

"When I was a child, when my father was in prison, I would visit him every other week, from the time I was one year old until I was 26. I had to do something, I wanted to feel I was as good as my father, he did something for his country, he was in the Popular Front. But he didn't want me to go through what he had gone through, he told me that many times."

Like many of the dispatchers, Ismail suffered from paternal deprivation. On the other hand, his father was a role model, in that he was in prison for security crimes and had been sentenced to a long term. Ismail seemed to need to prove his masculinity and his ability to do things against the Jews, as his father did, and even to outdo him.

He spoke of his mother with great love and affection, and said that he waited for her visits. "My mother came 2 weeks ago. It was a very emotional, very good meeting. My mother simply . . . She asked, 'Are you eating? Do you sleep?'"

However, he changed the subject and his tone of voice, and said decisively, "The path before me was clear: there is the occupation and those who live under it, and something has to be done, I think everyone has to do something. When it came to that there was no dilemma, that was clear. I felt that crimes had been committed against me and that was my reaction . . . every person . . . it's not natural . . . they did a lot of bad things and I couldn't sit quietly [and watch it happen], because I saw my father and mother and my friends, and all of them were harmed."

Ismail, like Mahmoud, felt he had to sacrifice love and marriage because of his involvement in terrorist activity, the goal to which he sacrificed his life. "When I was 25 I got engaged and I asked myself if I should continue or not. It was a difficult decision but I made it. Was I at the end of the road or [was I going to go to] prison. There were people who got killed, my brother was killed, I didn't want to get killed. But that is the path of a soldier ... He has chosen his path and his life is in danger.

"In the end I cancelled the wedding for her sake, not mine. She was my cousin, studying at Al-Najah University, she didn't understand. I didn't explain to her. She understood after I went to prison. I didn't want her to spend all those years waiting for me. She got married 2 years ago. It was hard [for me], but it's her life. I thought about it and decided to cancel the wedding. I thought about it a lot beforehand ... When you're married, you have to take care of your family. My sisters visit me in prison. They let my mother visit just 2 weeks ago, it was very hard. My father—it's been five years since he visited me, and then only once. My mother doesn't feel well, and she has changed. Older, more tired."

Ismail kept switching from his private life to the Palestinian–Israeli conflict.

"The situation, especially the security situation, influences my decisions ... I was in prison four, five, six times. The last time, when they came to arrest me, I managed to slip out of the house, in the Balata refugee camp. I didn't know what to do, I didn't want to go to prison and I didn't want to keep running away. In the end I decided it was better to be free than in prison, to get away for 6, 7 months ... and in the end, life imprisonment.

"For 10 months I was involved. There were attacks that Ayyash and I were involved in. I don't know how they got him. The attacks in Jerusalem, I don't know exactly what the target was, and in Ramat Gan, on the bus. I helped prepare attacks, I didn't know what the target was. The suicide bombers are more prepared than I. They ask [questions] and are insistent about it. It's a dilemma, he has a father and mother, but on the other hand, something has to be done. It was a reaction without a lot of thought. You want to do something because they did this or that to you.

"Now [2000, before the outbreak of the second intifada] I think differently. I think there are people who aren't to blame for the situation. Some of the Jews aren't to blame for the situation now. My parents were surprised ... 'Why did you do it?' They are my mother and father, they want me close to them.

"I did something, not the best thing, but something for the good of the [Palestinian] people. If I had known it would be mostly children, I wouldn't have done it. Sometimes my friend Muhi a-Din Sharif [a bomb-maker and planner of suicide bombing attacks], he came after Ayyash, he was killed in Ramallah. Once I talked to him. He said he went to [blow up] a bus and saw there were only women and children on it [so] he didn't carry out the attack, he came back."

Suddenly he changed his mind and said the exact opposite: "We aim specifically at women and children, this is war and that kind of thing is going to happen. On the other hand, I wasn't a soldier, I saw Arab children, women too, killed and wounded, [and] I did the right thing.

"Someone who trains [as a soldier] knows what he's doing. People who have a country are trained better than people who don't have a country and haven't made a decision. Before people make decisions, if they have a country, they think more, we do this or that in an orderly way. As far as you're concerned, it doesn't matter too much, but there is a difference."

He spoke rapidly and with great intensity. Clearly he was claiming that when a regular army kills women and children, the moral crime is far greater. Actually, he was trying to claim that the fact that the terrorists don't operate under the aegis of a specific country means they can do anything they like. I heard the same sort of thing from another security prisoner, who said, "We can do terrible things that a country cannot permit itself to do, so that ties your hands, the hands of the Israelis." However, not only Israel's hands are tied, but also those of the Western democracies, which sometimes want to answer terrorism with terrorism, but cannot.

To make his intentions crystal clear he said, "When [Shimon] Peres was Prime Minister the Israeli army killed more than 100 women and children in Lebanon [on April 18, 1996, in Kafr Kana, during the first war in Lebanon. The war was waged to fight Lebanese-based terrorist attacks against Israeli civilians.] and Peres took responsibility. I did it with a few friends . . ."

That is, while Peres had to apologize for a mistake that harmed civilians and even stop the campaign, Ismail, as a suicide bomber dispatcher, was responsible for the *deliberate* murder of a hundred civilians for whose deaths he saw no need to apologize.

Thus in 2006 Hezbollah and its leader, Hassan Nasrallah, aimed their long-range rockets at Israeli civilians with the intention of killing as many as possible. Nasrallah apologized for the deaths of Israeli Arabs and asked them to leave their home in Haifa and the Galilee so as not to be harmed. His rockets, he said, were only intended to kill Jews.

Ismail changed the subject again, and returned to his family, and spoke about his experiences as a refugee. "My parents lived near Rosh Ha'ayin. Now they call [the village] Tirat Yehuda. In '48 they fled, some to Jordan, some to Lebanon and Iraq. You see a lot of things, you can't say you don't care. A person has to be active, not to surrender, that's from the religious and nationalist way of looking at it. Hamas was only founded in '89. It was the Islamic movement, at the university and at school as well, [I was 17, and] at the age of 17, religion was influential. Elementary school was religious, so was high school, it had an influence.

"In the beginning there was no violence. I was on the receiving end of violence but I never did anything. Only during the intifada was I active, in '89. The first time, 17 years old, they picked me up on the street. I wasn't doing anything, I wasn't involved. They took me and beat me, me and three, four friends ... Even though I wasn't involved, I was in prison, they left me there for 20 days, and then the process started. Now I don't think there should be attacks on buses, but there should be something."

A story about the trauma of being arrested for the first time and being beaten was a recurring theme for most of the terrorists I interviewed.

Although Ismail had been sentenced to several terms of life imprisonment, he thought about the future, and even in positive terms. "The positive thing I see is studying. The big problem I deal with all the time is, what about the future? A future inside or outside prison? But the last decision I made was to finish my studies, that's what I think. I tried to be something a couple of times, I thought a lot about being released, but thinking didn't bring results. Studying is a positive thing, and waiting isn't easy. I don't know what's going to happen, what the results will be. If I think a lot about what's going to happen, I get tired.

"I have a year and a half, seven, eight, nine, ten hours a day of studies. I signed up for courses at Everyman's University: Jerusalem Through The Ages, Introduction to Middle Eastern History, Jews in a Time of Change."

(It is interesting that a Palestinian prisoner chose to enroll in an Israeli university and take courses about the lives of the Jews.)

"You asked me before if it was worth it. Of course not, but that's the situation, and sometimes the situation carries you away."

Ismail, like others with whom I spoke, was amazed by the fabric of Israeli society, by the fact that Jews immigrated from different places with different languages and cultures and nevertheless managed to function as a united society.

"I listen to Kol Israel [the Voice of Israel] on the radio and watch television. I learn about the influences and the internal situation of the State of Israel. It helps me to see things, this society. It's something complex. Some of the Jews are from Russia, some from the Yemen. They are all joined together about what happens on the outside, but the internal situation is more complicated: Sephardic Jews and Ashkenazi Jews, you don't have that in any other society."

Israel is a melting pot like the United States, its citizens coming from all over the globe. Ismail was amazed, especially at the shared lives of Ashkenazi and Sephardic Jews who came after the State of Israel was established. At the time of the interview with Ismail the Israeli army was pulling out of Lebanon, which it had entered only because of continued Palestinian terrorist attacks carried out against the northern part of the country from Lebanese territory.

As opposed to many Palestinians (and Israelis), he viewed it as a victory for Israel.

"Lebanon is an Israeli victory. They were there for 20 years and they didn't get anything out of it. Why did you go to Beirut? There are no real reasons, and it is a victory for the Israelis that they got out. The prisoners' great hope is to be released as part of the peace process."

(The conversation was held a short time before Camp David and months before the Al-Aqsa intifada broke out.)

"Now it's studies, an hour or two, three hours of listening to the radio, watching television programs. If I don't keep myself busy like that, I'll get into trouble. I was in a separate wing, kept apart from other prisoners because of relations with people outside. When I'm in prison I think there is no real [peace] process. Let prisoners out, that's the natural thing to do, the first thing to do. If two countries want to end a quarrel, the prisoners are the first thing in the process. But for Israel we are bargaining chips.

"I think about myself, what it will be like if I get out. The process interests me, and now I take more interest in my future. My brothers and sisters, we are ten children, they all graduated from high school, eight of them have BAs, two have masters' degrees even though my mother doesn't know how to read and write, but my father was a school teacher 40 years ago. Now things are different, people know how to read and write, she is 70 years old.

"If I had a child and he said, I want to carry out a suicide bombing attack . . . That's a hard question. I wouldn't want him to be in my situation. I would want [his life to be] better. There is a strong desire to do something. If we knew they would take revenge on the family . . . Sometimes a person wants to do something but he doesn't want his son to do the same thing. It depends, it depends . . . Sometimes I want to do something and sometimes I change my mind after a week, according to the situation and circumstances. That's how it is.

"My father said, learn from me, and I, if I had a son, I would tell him the same thing. Sometimes a person won't learn, only from [his own mistakes], and that is generally not wise. The second dilemma was the matter of the wedding, I had to decide about that . . .

"[But] the main dilemma is the occupation. You want to do something to respond, you want to live, not hurt people and not have them hurt you. You want to live, you want to do something for the country, for your friends, your family, your people. I am considered someone who did something good. If a Jew did something for the Jews he would be considered a war hero like [Yitzhak] Shamir, [Yitzhak] Rabin. He was in the Israeli army and he killed people, he was considered a hero by the people, because the background for what he did was national or religious, but he did something I did: he killed people, children, and in the eyes of his people he is a war hero. If you do the same thing as an Arab it's strange, you killed people, you aren't a war hero. That's natural, for example, Napoleon was a war hero, but in the eyes of the Egyptians he was a murderer and a criminal, because he occupied [their country]. Everyone sees things from his own point of view."

It was time to end our conversation because Ismail had to go back to his cell for the head count. Just before we parted he said, "Usually, the reason, the wars ... every people should have its rights, should live. This situation creates motives and conditions and circumstances, [it makes you] do what you can do, if you have a lot of possibilities, you choose the targets and the way, but if there is no other way, you choose the only one you can. If I could have kidnapped Rabin and asked him, "Why did you do that?" I would have done it.

"When I speak to you I'm honest. Sometimes there is no trust, but nevertheless I talk to you and everything I said was the truth. We are in a very special situation, because my whole life is unnatural, and that is the hardest thing in the world.

"I'm perceived as a problem, a criminal, a person who has to be restrained. It's not a good feeling. We got into a terrible situation and so far there is no solution, what we have left is hope. I hope there will be a solution, and believe ... [But] I have my doubts. I live with hope. If there is no hope there is no life."

One of the most striking facts about the prisons, which house terrorists from the Palestinian Authority, is that dispatchers of suicide bombers, as opposed to ordinary criminal inmates, are accepted as being morally normative. They also view themselves as such. They reconcile the apparent contradiction by viewing themselves as the affronted, as those treated unjustly, and they see their acts of murder as legitimate, while denying the slaughter, convincing themselves that they are the real victims. Part of the process is the dehumanizing of the victims. That is the only way to understand the joy the Palestinians show after suicide bombing attacks, their dancing on roofs and burning American and Israeli flags, particularly after mass-murder attacks like those at the World Trade Center and the Pentagon on September 11, 2001. It is a phenomenon well documented in the literature: the behavior of white supremacists, particularly the Ku Klux Klan, for example, is normative and humane toward whites, but they can persecute, maim, and kill blacks and other racial and ethnic groups with no pangs of conscience, with no constraints of principle or feeling.[1] Thus, it is reasonable to assume that the dispatcher does not relate to his victims as human. During the discussions, refugee status was clearly a cause of inferiority and deprivation feelings. It is a key to the bipolarity of the dispatchers' morality: on the one hand, their moral sense is normative, and is manifested in their central moral dilemmas, especially those concerning their families. On the other, there are the aspects of their lives (refugee status and feelings of deprivation) that lead them into non-normative morality, which is manifested by violent aggression that fulfills their social expectations and allows them to use violence. The dispatchers are led to terrorist activities in the same way they are led to feel hatred and to delegitimize the rights of those whose victims they feel they are.

They direct their feelings of jealousy, inferiority, and deprivation at Israel and the West in general to justify their violent, extreme behavior, which includes the murder of innocent civilians. They create a collective ego, a kind of salvation of tribal honor, which earns the dispatcher and his family respect, status, and the sensation of being stronger. The return to Islam is a catalyst for a moral perception which maintains and supports the barrier between the two elements, and which is reflected in the delegitimization of the rights of Jews, Israelis, Americans and westerners in general, and in their dehumanization.

The ability to view victims of terrorist attacks as human beings, even if they were Jewish, was usually gained only after the dispatchers spoke to the members of their own families and were flooded with emotion and surrounded by warmth and love. Then they could see the victims as human, and the attitude they expressed toward them was more human, and they tended not to justify physical violence as much.

Feelings of inferiority and deprivation are strong among Muslims who live in closed communities and are sometimes isolated from Western countries. Thus only in Afghanistan did Muslim youths who came from other countries feel a sense of belonging and acceptance, of having a place in society. Bin Laden knew how to exploit the energy generated during training in the Afghanistan melting pot. Being there was a kind of healing experience for the youths and they swore they would make the utmost effort for the jihad of bin Laden and his associates. Beyond political-religious indoctrinations, and beyond massive amounts of military training, they were prepared for the carrying out of attacks, especially *istishhad*, against the West and against Muslim countries perceived as moderate and collaborating with the United States.

On September 5, 2005, I spoke with a Palestinian sheikh who asked to remain anonymous, and he told me long stories about his experiences in Afghanistan, and about how he felt after he had been a guest of the Taliban on his journey to instill the *da'wah* among Muslims all over the world.

It was his opinion that Muslim countries were happy to get rid of the marginal individuals (who were sometimes criminal) who had come to Afghanistan to fight Russia. Not only that, but those marginal individuals were very well respected, and if they were Arabs their status was particularly high. He said, "The Arabs are the sons of the *sahaba* [comrades] of Muhammad. You feel valued if you are an Arab there, despite the fact that for the rest of the world an Arab is [considered] garbage. In the Far East an Arab has worth ... Maybe the *mujahadeen* [jihad warriors] were garbage because they were on the sidelines and against the régime and suddenly they were Arab *mujahadeen*, and they were really [respected] like Allah. Their value was exaggerated, it was much much greater than what it was in the places they came from ..."

In his opinion, Al-Qaeda was created by the Americans to counterbalance Russia, the same way, he thought, the Israeli Security Agency created Hamas to counterbalance the PLO.

CHAPTER 5

Dispatcher Macho: "My Father Taught It What It Means to Be a Man and Didn't Allow US to Be Cowards"

While suicide bombers are well respected by Palestinian society, that does not mean that there is no criticism. Mu'in, the dispatcher interviewed in the previous chapter, remarked that the dispatcher does not send his own son to blow himself up. To make his point, he said that his own son, Yussuf, was named after Mu'in's older brother, who had carried out a suicide bombing attack and been killed, and he advised him not to take the same path as his dead uncle. Mu'in often spoke about his mother, who would indulge little Yussuf, thereby finding some relief from the pain of her son's death.

Suicide bombers as well, male and female alike, who for whatever reason did not die, complained that not every Palestinian was forced to sacrifice sons and daughters. This is what Rifat told me:

> "I went to the bus carrying an explosive device on my back. I thought about my family, my child, my wife. It was a difficult decision to make, it was the hardest decision ... I'm paying for it, I'm in prison, but others [his dispatchers] don't ... Only we pay for it ..."

He sat across from me and looked at me suspiciously. The meeting was held in 2000 in one of Israel's highest security prisons. Physically there was something very frightening, very threatening about him. Maybe because he kept looking at a length of wood leaning on the wall behind the chair I was sitting on. I felt he was plotting something. Suddenly he said, "No one ever hit you with a plank. [Well,] that's [what] the [Israel] occupation [is like]."

I raised my head and looked straight at him. I smiled at his glaring eyes and asked, "Why would you want to do something like that? Did I do something bad to you?" Very slowly, he lowered his eyes and I felt the wind going out of his sails. One of the things I always tried hard to do in my conversations was to create the calmest, most relaxed atmosphere possible, with a feeling of openness and even empathy, which would make it easier for them to express themselves.

Rifat was dispatched to carry out a suicide bombing attack on a bus in Jerusalem in 1993. His explosive device, which also contained nails and screws, was in a duffle bag he had slung over his back. He had been instructed to get on the most crowded bus he could find in the Machaneh Yehuda market area, find a seat in the back row, and sit and wait until the bus filled up. When it did he pushed the detonator. Luckily, nothing happened. He was caught with the other members of his terrorist cell only after the Israeli security forces had made a focused effort to find him.

Often a suicide bomber is compared to a smart bomb. This weapon, however, is cheap and there is no need to invest in technology. The dispatcher has to make sure the bomber reaches the target area, but unlike all other smart bombs, the suicide bomber can locate the exact target himself. Actually, the suicide bomber is smarter than a smart bomb, because at any given time he can change the target or the moment of detonation.

For Rifat, like many other dispatchers and suicide bombers who had not succeeded, this was not the first prison experience. At the time of our meeting he was 29 and had been in prison for seven years, four times since he was 17.

He told me about his family, which lived in Abu Tor, a Jerusalem neighborhood. His father was 57, a shoemaker who suffered from severe back pains. There were eight children in the family; Rifat was the third-born. He studied as far as the eighth grade then went to work, starting in a carpentry shop and later laying wall-to-wall carpets. His Hebrew was fluent.

"I love Jerusalem, I've lived there my whole life. For me, a Jew is a person, no problem, but he has settled in my country, he does things that are not acceptable, that's what I grew up with. You know it isn't your country. If someone comes into your house, what do you do?" It was a rhetorical question and he wasn't waiting for an answer. "What do you do if someone comes into your house? Serve coffee? It's like someone came in through the window … It's nothing complicated. A person one year old knows that, a person 100 years old knows it too."

"I got married at 21, I had a son, I lived in my own house, I had my own car, no one had what I had, but there was something in my head and I did what I did. My son lives with my father and mother. I got a divorce five years ago because I'm in prison. My wife's family, her uncle convinced her to divorce me. Her father is dead so her father's brother told her what to do."

When he spoke about his wife and her family, his anger was palpable. He made it very clear that the initiative to end his marriage came from his wife and her family, and he was angry and hurt.

"Why does it upset you so much," I asked. "You wanted to blow yourself up, which by definition is a final separation from your son, your wife, the rest of your family. Didn't you think about your family when you picked up the bomb?"

He did not answer immediately, and perhaps was thinking about what I had said. Finally, in a less aggressive tone, he said, "My son is named Othman. That's the name of one of the prophet Muhammad's companions. I read about his life, I liked the name, and I told myself that if I ever married and had a child, that's what I would call him. I think about my wife and child ... That's my home. I want to help my family, do things for them ..."

Initially he tried to pretend his situation was better than it actually was. "I feel I have a great life ... For me, [if] my relationship with Allah is good, then everything is good. It isn't really important that I'm in prison. Everyone wants to be outside, no one likes prison. But if that's the way it is, so be it, and if that's what happened, so be it, there's nothing I can do about it.

I wanted to know if he were really so religious.

"*Inshallah*," he answered.

Inshallah, which means both "with the help of Allah" and "may it come to pass," is said often, not only by dispatchers and suicide bombers, but also by the general Arab population, and not always in religious contexts.

Suddenly he stopped talking, picked up the bottle of water lying on the table between us and looked at it for a long time. Finally he said, "A thinking person, if he wants to put this bottle on the floor, he thinks about what to do with the bottle. A person thinks about what he wants to do. If you want to drink water, you think about drinking and then you do it. [But] if you want to die, you won't think about it at all."

He tried to explain his automaton-like behavior when he got on the bus in Jerusalem. He said that at one point, when he had decided where he would detonate the explosive device, he stopped thinking. His behavior was automatic with no thought for his own life or for the lives of his victims. If any human thought or feeling had gone through his mind, he probably would not have tried to activate the detonator. That, of course, is the goal of the suicide bomber dispatchers, to prevent them from thinking for themselves, to cut them off from all human emotion or thought, even for those who were closest to them.

❖

"Did you ever hear about Zanoubia?" asked Mu'in, the suicide bomber dispatcher. "No," I answered, "who is she?"

"You have long hair, and when I look at it, it reminds me of the story of Zanoubia. She had long, long hair, down to the floor, black. When she rode her horse, her hair covered her whole body and reached the ground."

Mu'in's making a personal statement came only after long hours of conversations and showed he had opened up to a certain degree. More proof came in our following meeting, when he brought pictures of his children to show me, almost as though we were related. I had heard the story of Queen Zanoubia and her hair more than once. She was the Arab Rapunzel, but not quite the Arab Lady Godiva, because no Arab woman could ride around without clothing. In most cultures, women's hair is symbolic of femininity and sexuality. Women, in Islam as in Judaism, are required to cover their hair to keep the men around them from thinking about them in a sexual context. In eastern cultures, hair is one of the symbols of beauty and femininity. My hair is very long and I keep it tightly braided. Most of the dispatchers I spoke to made some reference to my hair and to the fact that I was a woman, although in most instances they were very delicate and circumspect. Before he would speak to me, Sheikh Ahmad Yassin asked me to cover my hair.

As far as I could see, my being a woman was an advantage and made my interviewees more willing to talk to me. Not only is a woman perceived as less threatening, she reminds him of his mother, sister, wife, or friend, and she is not suspected of being an Israeli security agent, which motivates him to talk about his feelings more freely.

Abdallah, the suicide bomber dispatcher, told me that he had worked in a Tel Aviv restaurant. "I worked on the beach. All the time, meat [i.e., bare bodies], all the time, it was unpleasant to look at things like that. To sit with a girl dressed modestly, like you, that's OK, but to sit with women and men without clothing, well, that's normal for them. I had close relations with Israelis. That's the rule in Israeli society, and no one looks at it as something exceptional. That's what I meant, for you it is acceptable to sit on the beach, but I preferred, despite the fact that I can see that it's usual for you, I can accept that, I preferred to work somewhere else. To do something that was more suitable to my personality even if working in construction was harder physically. In construction you're part of a team. In the restaurant I had waitresses who were friends, and men who were friends too, we had a very nice relationship."

Male suicide bombers do not always have a fully formed sexual identity, and therefore they find it important to prove that they are potent, that they can easily satisfy the 72 virgins waiting for them in paradise. There was one instance reported in which after the explosion, among the remains of the suicide bomber, who was completely blown up, his penis was found carefully wrapped in toilet paper, ready for immediate intensive sexual activity in paradise, although the story may be apocryphal. Both Hebrew and Arabic distinguish between genders, all nouns and verbs are either masculine or feminine, and a female suicide bomber, whose mission had failed and who had been apprehended, sometimes used feminine forms and sometimes masculine when she talked about herself. Another female suicide bomber told me that for a long time she was a tomboy, but when she reached the age of 20 she was told that it was shameful for a woman to behave that way, so she changed her appearance and covered herself in a traditional black Muslim garment.

Rifat expressed his need to prove his masculinity. "My father wanted us to be men. [If] you take things on yourself, take them, be a man."

The expectations from men in Palestinian and Arab society are formidable. The child-youth–man continues trying to please his father in the sense of fulfilling the responsible role imposed on "a man." Often such masculinity demands the adoption of behavior perceived as masculine, even in an exaggerated fashion. Nevertheless, there is a special, extremely strong relationship between Palestinian sons and their mothers, a relationship that might sometimes even be described as symbiotic, and the process of individuation and separation from the mother is problematic. When the father takes a second wife, the son's relationship with the mother usually becomes stronger, while the relationship with the father often becomes ambivalent, and the children of the first wife hold a grudge, often hidden but sometimes overt, against the father who rejected their mother and preferred a younger woman.

When Rifat came into the room he stood opposite me. He was at least two heads taller than I. He kept standing there, looking over my head. Quite some time passed before he sat down. I had the feeling that he was measuring his height against mine, and for a minute I felt as though he was trying to say, "I'm taller than you are, I'm stronger, look at how little and short you are compared to me . . ."

Generally speaking, manifesting masculinity is important in the behavior of male terrorists. It is as if they are trying to tell the world that they have proven their potency as males who can fight and preserve their honor. Dispatchers and suicide bombers all spoke about masculinity, about how they were brought up to be men, principally by their fathers, and about the terrorist act as a realization of their masculinity. That might be a hint that deep within the Palestinian soul, the Israeli occupation is perceived as a form of castration, and only active fighting can return the masculinity snatched from them, and that they are relating to the land as a woman who had been raped and defiled.

For Arab males, masculinity develops along the social, religious, and cultural lines set down by society. The male behaves according to the inflexible role demanded by society of his gender with no possibility of mitigation. Abdallah the dispatcher said, "At home males and females respect each other and each one knows his boundaries. I was free within my family. In your society [the West] there is no difference between males and females, for instance tea and coffee, everyone prepares them and everyone drinks them. In Arab society, the females have to make tea and coffee for the males."

Sexual identity is formed through biology and psychosocial forces. Concepts of male and female exist in all languages, and concepts of masculinity and femininity reflect the distinction in modes of behavior, talents, and feeling expected from both sexes. Perceptions of masculinity and femininity change in accordance with the nature of society and the time period under discussion. In Arab society, however, it is almost impossible to find activities, behavior, feelings, and the like, which are not clearly defined as masculine or feminine. That is in opposition to modern Western society, where in many instances there is no such well-defined distinction. To explain that, one of the dispatchers said, "A husband can be a chef in a hotel and know how to cook really well, [but] at home he would never do that, because it's the wife's job."

Both dispatchers and suicide bombers consider themselves very masculine and believe that terrorist activities make them "more" masculine. The very idea of such activity is perceived as masculine behavior, as opposed to the passive, submissive behavior of women. Mahmoud the dispatcher said, "My father taught us what it means to be a man and wouldn't let us be weaklings."

CHAPTER 6

Sheikh Ahmad Yassin, Hamas Founder: "The Shaheed Doesn't Die, He Lives with Allah"

On December 13, 1996, a cold winter day, I went with my husband Reuven, an expert in Middle Eastern studies and fluent in Arabic, whom we listed as my "research assistant," to a detention facility near Ramla. I was on my way to interview Hamas leader Sheikh Ahmad Yassin. What bin Laden was for the Americans, Yassin was for the Israelis.

I could not decide what to wear. In the end I put on a black skirt long enough to cover my ankles and a turtle-neck sweater: modest, simple attire.

We arrived at the facility's medical center. When we said that we had an appointment with Sheikh Yassin the guard raised his eyebrows and said he had to check.

After a few minutes the gate opened and a prison official was waiting for us. It turned out he was also the doctor on call. He took us to the library, where we were supposed to meet Sheikh Yassin. We asked him about Yassin's health.

"He's confined to a wheelchair," said the doctor, and added as an afterthought, "you will have to cover your hair." They found a hat for me and I twisted my braid up and hid it underneath.

Yassin was waiting for us when we entered the library, sitting peacefully in a wheelchair. At his side was the male prisoner who attended to his needs, a man with a thick black beard and piercing black eyes, full of suspicion.

I took a deep breath and sat down opposite him. There was a table between us. He was wearing a perfectly clean white garment and his head was covered with an ironed white handkerchief. I wondered how he managed to keep everything snow white in jail.

With Reuven doing the simultaneous translation, I introduced myself and said that the interview was research for my doctoral degree. Yassin wanted to know at which university. He said he had no problem being interviewed, his only condition was that when he spoke to women their hair had to be covered, a condition I had fulfilled before entering the library.

I had prepared the questions with my thesis advisors and I gave the page to Reuven. To my surprise, he did not translate my questions. He asked about the relationship between Judaism, Christianity, and Islam. I grew up in an Arabic-speaking household and there was no way I could have been mistaken. I asked him please just to read the questions and not change anything. He said we had an exceptional, historic opportunity of interest not only to criminologists, and he had questions of his own which he felt he had to ask. In retrospect Reuven was right, because the interview presented the opportunity to question Yassin about many different, varied subjects.

A transcription of our interview follows. Arabic is a rich, dramatic language full of picturesque expressions whose exact meaning is sometimes lost in translation. In addition, because a great deal of what he said was related to religion, it might not be completely clear to someone who is not intimately familiar with the Qur'an and other religious literature. I have tried to fill in some of the blanks.

Reuven: I would like to present to you a woman who is researching her doctoral thesis. As ideologue, philosopher and head of Hamas, what do you think we should do about the Jewish-Arab situation?

Yassin: The noble Qur'an says, Oh, men, we created you man and woman and we made you into nations and tribes, and those whom God finds honorable among you are those who believe devoutly, and that is the solution. [Not an exact quotation from the Qur'an].

Author: Is the intention to define or make a distinction between men and women.

Yassin: Between all people.

Author: Do you support the peace process, and why?

Yassin: Of course. Everyone loves peace.

Author: Why?

Yassin: But the argument is over the demands of peace and the foundations upon which it stands.

Author: How can children grow up in peace and tranquility, given the circumstances?

Yassin: If there is justice, everyone can live in peace. There is no life without justice.

Author: How would you define justice? Justice depends upon the individual's subjective viewpoint.

Yassin: No, that is incorrect. Justice is justice all over the world. That is, I take your watch and you say, let's sign a peace treaty, or would you say, good, but first give me back my watch. You hit me, at least say you're sorry, and tell me, let's sign a peace treaty, or you

take my house, even in a conflict between you and your brother,
justice is in the end a matter of the judgment of the truth. That is,
if true justice is not served, it is neither true nor just.

The example of the watch was used by one of the female suicide bombers
I interviewed, who said, "They took my watch, I want it back." It is possible
that it is a metaphor used in the mosques and schools as part of the program
of indoctrination. A watch cannot be divided in two, and at least until a few
decades ago, it was also very expensive. It is also possible that there is some
association between the Arabic sa'ah, which means both "watch" and "day
of the hour," or Judgment Day.

Author: What is the essence of the concept of jihad and its significance in
relation to other religions?
Yassin: First of all, we agree that someone else is always a question mark.
And we all agree that the foundation at the source of the world is
peace and love and cooperation for the sake of good. Islam
decided that jihad would be the response to a hostile act against
Islam or Muslims, whether it was a conspiracy against their
sacred places, or their religion, or their homeland, or their honor
or their property. It is an individual's right to defend himself
against anyone who conspires against his faith and religion, his
land, homeland, property, honor and everything else. That is the
meaning of jihad: let there be peace, but if someone conspires
against you or attacks you, then you have to wage jihad and fight
against him.
Author: So what you are trying to say is that jihad is a term describing an
act of self-defense, not a divine concept instructing Muslims to
fight against those who do not believe in a monotheistic God, but
rather it is a response to those who attack you, no matter who
they might be.
Yassin: That is, Allah says in the noble Qur'an that there is no hatred in
[our] religion. Freedom, worshipping Allah and performing
religious duties, that is, if a person is given the freedom of choice
to worship as he pleases, it means there is no fear [of the duty of
jihad].
Author: You mean that no matter who he is, even a polytheist, he can be
left alone?
Yassin: No. When we say freedom of religion, we mean the religion a
person chooses and whose path he wishes to follow. If anyone
stands in the way of someone's choosing Islam, and they want to
prevent me [from following Islam] or to fight me, that means they
have conspired against religion, against a Muslim's freedom of
religion. As far as polytheists are concerned, we all agree that

there is no God but Allah and that no God is to be worshipped except him.

Author: Can those who worship one God be acted against? In what circumstances would you wage jihad against those who worship one God?

Yassin: I have to defend myself from anyone who conspires against me and wants to harm me or act unjustly toward me, even if he is a Muslim.

Author: In that case, can jihad be waged against a Muslim?

Yassin: Yes, it's a possibility. A certain man said to the prophet, Oh messenger of Allah, what do you think if someone comes to take my property. [The prophet] said, fight him! [And the man said,] and if he fights me? And [the prophet] said, fight him! [And the man asked,] and if he kills me? [The prophet] answered, then you will go to paradise. [And he] asked, and if I kill him? And [the prophet] answered, then he will go to hell! That means, it is my right to defend myself.

Author: What is your opinion of the peace treaties between Israel and Egypt and Jordan?

Yassin: The principle of peace is general and not the right of some people and not others. That is, if I want to make peace, I make peace with everyone and not with some and not others. Peace with Egypt and Jordan is only partial peace, and the conflict is founded on the Palestinian problem, and as long as that problem exists and has not been solved, it means that there is no peace.

Author: What makes Muslims want to commit suicide for the sake of a certain goal?

Yassin: Here your understanding is wrong. The person who kills himself in [one of] many ways, by shooting or taking drugs or to escape from life and its problems, because of personal distress, that is suicide, but the person who goes to fight an enemy who fights him who took his land, his country, or who took his property, fights him and is killed, such a person is considered a *shaheed* [martyr for the sake of Allah] and not someone who committed suicide.

Author: According to the noble Qur'an, is suicide permitted or forbidden?

Yassin: Forbidden.

Author: If the *shaheed* kills other people, does he believe that by doing so the problem will be solved any faster?

Yassin: No.

Author: And in addition to the fact that he dies, after the action, how does he interpret the results, practically speaking? Did he come any closer to achieving his desired goal? And how will he benefit from if he is dead?

Yassin: It is not a question of "dead," since the *shaheed* is not dead, he is alive with Allah. First and foremost, the faith of a Muslim, of an Arab, is that he believes that anyone who is with Allah is in better circumstances than if he were in this world. And this world, when the faithful Muslim weighs it up, lacks value, and the many *mujahadeen* [the jihad warriors who, if they die, become *shaheeds*] who choose death . . . In the eyes of the faithful, this world is nothing, and the prophet says it is like a traveler who sits under a tree and rests and does not rise. That sort of person [the suicide bomber] is not interested in this world . . . He is waiting for Allah, who is good . . . and death for him is enjoyment, and the *shahadah* is not a burden for him, it is good, preferable. Let me use a parable: you live in a house with two or three rooms and a yard, and someone comes and tells you, I will give you 100 dunams [about 25 acres] and villas and gardens [within the 100 dunams], would you be happy or angry?

Author: If that's a serious question, I'll answer. If I'm alive to enjoy them, I would choose the 100 dunams, but if I have to die for them, that's something else again . . .

Yassin: Our understanding of death is incorrect. Death is a time of passage for man. As a human being, a man was in his mother's stomach: life. After that he lived in this world: life. And after that he passed over into the next world: a different life, and therefore he is alive and not dead.

Author: How do you allow a child to choose that option? Would you allow a small child who wanted to carry out such an act to become a *shaheed* to do so?

Yassin: Yes.

Author: Is it dependent upon age?

Yassin: Of course!

Author: How?

Yassin: For us, in our religion, a person—someone 15 years old can consider such an action. When he turns 15, if he makes a mistake, he can taken to account. Before that age, if he makes a mistake, he is not taken to account.

Author: Does that mean the responsibility and the ability to choose begin at the age of 15?

Yassin: Yes.

Author: So someone who is 15 can choose *shahadah*?

Yassin: Even before 15. There is no problem . . . But if he is taken to account for his decision or not, that is, if he made a mistake when he decided, Allah will take him to account for it.

Author: What is your opinion? How do you feel about a child who wants to make such a decision?

Yassin: A person, fundamentally, as long as his intelligence is not complete, is not judged by his decisions. Even when an insane person wants to do something, his decisions are not judged. If he has reached the age of 15 he can reason, his fate is measured and he can be taken to account for his decisions.

Author: If someone close to you came to consult you, a brother, a relative, and said, "Honorable sheikh, my 13-year old son wants to get on a bus and blow himself up," your nephew, for instance, and he wants a *fatwa* [Islamic religious edict] from you, or some other type of permission, or if he were 14, what would your answer be?

Yassin: That is not something required of him. It is required of someone who has reached the age of understanding, and when he has reaches the age of maturity—it means he goes . . .

Sheikh Yassin was trying to make a distinction between physical–sexual maturity, which according to Islam begins at an earlier age, and mental maturity, which begins at 15. Some of the dispatchers ignore even the minimal criterion of the young age of 15. Abdallah Karan, an 11-year old child, was sent with a schoolbag full of explosives to the Hawarah checkpoint near Nablus.

Author: Does that mean maturity is physical?

Yassin: Yes, but of course for children under the age of 15, we advise them not to carry out actions that are not required of them, especially when there is some unusual circumstance or they endanger him or his property. Even if someone younger than 15 has property and acts incorrectly, we hand him over to a guardian who will watch over this behavior . . .

Author: What is your opinion of someone who decides to become a *shaheed*, if he is already 15?

Yassin: That is only his business . . . I am not willing to stand between an individual and his desire to carry out [an action] or present [something] to Allah, may he be exalted, or to perform an action that will bring him closer to Allah when [his] religion gives him the freedom and the decision. He is free. He has freedom of choice. We tell him, you don't have to do this thing, and if you have decided and you have the reasons for it [then it is your decision], but you don't have to do it, that is, Allah is not directing you to do this thing.

Author: Do you view such a decision as coming close to Allah?

Yassin: As long as the person wants to defend himself, it is his right.

Author: How do you explain suicide or an action for *shahadah*, or an action as you have described? Is that jihad in your opinion? Especially if it means blowing up a bus with 30–40 people, among them old people and children, babies and generally speaking, civilians? What is the socio-economic background of the suicide bombers? Do you have any kind of general description about people who carry out such attacks?

Yassin: According to our religion, a man must make sure to distance himself from innocent children and women and old men. It is forbidden by Islam to kill them or harm them, but in war things happen that contradict [religious] principles . . . [Sometimes there are] mistakes, for example, Israel in the [first] war in south Lebanon killed 100 people, and weren't they civilians? That is, either by mistake or in retaliation, one thing for another. You kill children, you kill women, I take my revenge and by defending myself I pay you back, an eye for an eye, a tooth for a tooth. That's what happens in war and that means that for us a warrior kills his enemy to settle the score, not to kill women and old men, but the minute he sees his sister was killed, his mother or his father, he wants to cause the same deaths the enemy caused him.

So, according to Ahmad Yassin, the response to an Israeli mistake is the deliberate, premeditated murder of civilians, a paradox since killing women and children is specifically proscribed by Islam.

Author: So then he is not obeying a religious commandment, he is taking revenge according to his own private criteria?

Yassin: No, not his criteria. Islam gave him clear instructions, but if you conspire against me, then I conspire against you. Allah said, if someone does something to hurt you, respond in the same way and hurt him.

Author: Is that written in the Qur'an?

Yassin: Of course. If you are injured, respond in the same way you were injured. But there is a stage higher than that where the Qur'an says it is preferable to be restrained and patient, etc., and leave the matter in the hands of Allah. That is, patience and leaving the matter to Allah is a higher level.

Author: Honorable sheikh, we have seen the recent attacks, which were carried out on buses and were not the response of a victim who sought revenge the same way he was hurt, but of people who planned a series of attacks which were similar to one another. Isn't that a well-thought out policy, a policy of premeditation, of people who didn't choose the option of patience and waiting, but decided to attack civilians on buses? In your opinion, is that the proper response, to kill civilians on public transportation?

Yassin: That goes back to what we said before, because during the intifada, you see your mother die, you brother, you sister, and you control yourself, you are restrained, for a year, two, three, and that's enough. Your heart awakens and suffers more and more and then it's enough, your heart can't bear any more, it's the chain of behavior of the Israeli army and the occupation, the accumulated response of actions against it.

Author: That is, those actions are the correct response, ideologically and religiously, to the series of Israeli actions against Arabs, which in your view was the justification for the attacks carried out in Israel.

Yassin: You call it "the correct response." You are not speaking the truth. It is not the correct response, but rather an extraordinary response. That is, an exceptional situation, an emergency in view of the existing situation. That is not the source, because [the act] is forbidden at the source, because children and women, old people, civilians, conspiring against them is forbidden at the source, and if you act against them it is an exceptional act, and not genuine. It is not the correct solution, but rather an irregular action. [Calling a suicide bombing attack on a bus "an irregular action" does not mean that Sheikh Yassin had any reservations regarding them.]

Author: Generally speaking, you call such actions, which we called terrorist attacks, "jihad actions?"

Yassin: When we started I explained jihad to you. Jihad is aimed against someone who fights you, who takes your property or conspires against your religion and homeland, and every action you take against him is jihad! And have no [reservations] about calling it jihad, for it is a war. We are not in a state of peace, and so everything that happens between the two sides is jihad.

Author: How would you describe the *mujahad*, the *shaheed*? Can you think of general characteristics?

Yassin: Religion [i.e., Islam] forms their character.

Author: According to your experience and knowledge of them?

Yassin: In principle, to receive the title of *shaheed*, the *mujahad* must be first and foremost a Muslim. In that case, his prayers to Allah, and his fighting and death against his enemies would make me call him a *shaheed*.

Author: Does he commit suicide?

Yassin: If it happens during jihad, then he is a *shaheed*!

Author: According to your knowledge of the *shaheeds*, what characterizes them? Where did they grow up? What kind of education did they receive?

Yassin: The *mujahad* must undertake jihad for the sake of Allah and not for his own sake, for the sake of becoming prominent as a leader or for money or respect. And the prophet was asked who a *shaheed* was, and he said, he who fights so that the word of Allah may be supreme is on his way to Allah. That is the *shaheed*, not

he who is brave when defending his family or tribe, but rather he
who falls to realize the supremacy of the word of Allah.

Author: That is, the jihad actions they carry out, the *shaheeds*, they are
on that plane, of "realizing the word of Allah?"

Yassin: Of course. But there is other significance. Allah said that a
Muslim who fights his enemy and dies is a *shaheed*, but the
question of whether Allah considers him a *shaheed* or not goes
back to Allah.

Author: We are speaking in practical terms about a number of *shaheeds*
whom you had the opportunity to meet in the past. Can you give
me a general description, for example, someone who grew up in
a rich neighborhood, a refugee camp, to describe their personal
backgrounds, their economic status...

Yassin: No. No.

Author: Have you found any connection between place of residence,
place of birth, etc., where they went to school, the number of
people in the family? You said [the suicide bomber] was
desperate, that his motive was having his land stolen and you
implied his family's economic background... Was he educated in
a religious or secular school? In your opinion, is it possible to
paint a general picture from the various backgrounds which
contribute to making a *shaheed*?

Yassin: The factors motivating fighting and becoming a *shaheed* vary from
one person to another. There are Jews who pray and Jews who
don't pray, it varies from person to person. There are rich people
who pray and poor people who don't pray and poor people who
pray all the time and rich people who don't, and the Islamic aspect
has to do with the degree of a person's faith, his devoutness and
love of his religion. That is the first level. The second level is the
circumstances he lives in. One man lives in the city and another has
his own house and land, that means his situation is good by about
60–70%, and not someone who was expelled from his home and
country and land and he lives in a house with three rooms, he and
his sons and his daughters and a toilet and a kitchen and nothing
else. Circumstances like that [create] completely different factors,
and someone who feels oppressed is different from someone who
doesn't. That is, the problem, the condition is that you feel oppressed, and unless you do, it is very probable you will be relaxed
and won't do anything. It may happen that everything is taken
from you and you don't feel anything. If a person feels oppressed—
that's what created problems. When you continue, pay attention,
because among those who carried out actions you will find some
shaheeds who were rich, among the richest in Nablus. There
were some from the villages of the West Bank, resident civilians

[i.e., not refugees] who carried out actions which people from the refugee camps did not carry out, that is, the source is how strong a person's faith is and how much he loves Allah, may he be exalted.

At this point Sheikh Yassin's attendant interrupted to say that the first *shaheed* killed when a car bomb blew up was Fahed Kna'an from Nablus, whose father owned a tehini factory and who was one of the richest men in the city. Yassin asked his attendant about a *shaheed* who belonged to the Popular Front, and was answered that they "shouldn't talk about that here." Apparently he had reservations about the relationship between someone from the Popular Front, a Marxist-oriented secular organization, and *shaheeds*. In any case, it was obvious that Yassin did not think the names and identities of the suicide bombers were very important.

Author: Is it possible that the suicide bombers were people who were suspected of collaboration with Israel, they or their parents or relatives, and to allay suspicion and deflect questions they were willing to sacrifice their lives, and that there were those who were on one side and then repented and became loyal?

Yassin: Every person has his own nature, and an essence of religious, social, spiritual faith, and every person has virtues that distinguish him from others, and abilities that distinguish him from others, and experience that distinguishes him from others. A person who failed by collaborating [with Israel] or becoming a traitor is the victim of the special circumstances that occurred, whether it was a threat or temptation or fear . . . And he reached such a state that he went from the ranks of nationalism to the ranks of the enemy. He did not do so because of faith or freedom, but it was the product of circumstances and the situation he lived in and because he was forced to do it, and the result of the conflict in his mind was that he was forced to work for the other side . . . It isn't enough for it to be just an internal conflict, but his home as well, his children and wife and brothers, his whole family are part of the conflict, because when they found out that he had gone to work for the enemy they turned against him, and he found himself besieged by his family, his people, his relatives and those closest to him, they washed their hands of him, and then he got to the point where he regained his self-control and came home to his family, his children, and lived like one of them the way he did in the past. Our program is good and suitable and excellent. He is willing to pay anything, even with his life, to get rid of the ugly image people have of him and his family. And don't forget that they label his wife "wife of a traitor," and his son "son of a traitor," which means that his whole life and family are in a very difficult position in society. [As a result] he goes to sacrifice his life... That's one. And it is possible that he is persecuted and threatened by groups of Palestinians who want to kill him, and then he weighs [his options], to die as a collaborator or to die faithful to his nation, and it is preferable to die faithful to his nation... And then he [carries it out,] and kills or is killed to become faithful to his nation, so as not to be [considered] a collaborator. In both cases he does what he does to purify his soul.

There can be other reasons for such absolution, for instance to "preserve the honor of the family," which very often means a woman has had an extramarital affair or premarital sex, or has been suspected of doing so, sometimes with no basis in fact.

Author: Are there many such cases?

Yassin: Of course there were many, why not? I remember one person in Gaza who went to work for the [Israeli] authorities in 1970, with the occupation. His brother was a friend of mine. He worked like that until 1990 or 1993, I don't remember. He had sons and daughters who grew up and wanted to get married, but because he was under such emotional pressure, because his sons and daughters and his whole family ostracized him because of what he did, he went and killed a Jew in Tel Aviv to purify himself, and of course he was sentenced to life imprisonment, after having worked 20 or 23 years with the Jews.

Author: And did he really absolve himself?

Yassin: He considers himself as having changed camps and returned to the ranks of the nationalists and is now fighting against the Jews, those he worked for before.

Author: Does such an action really absolve him?

Yassin: We consider that kind of absolution "returning to oneself," that is, repentance. Not with me or with you. He has repented before Allah. If you are honest with Allah and have stopped sinning against your family, your nation or Allah, then you have repented, for Allah keeps the gates of repentance open for a man as long as he hasn't died. If he repented before he died, he is forgiven even if he killed a hundred men. No matter what he did, the important thing is that he repented. If he has really repented in his heart, Allah knows. We look at external things, but if they are true or not is for Allah to decide, may he be exalted.

Author: Does such a person have to prove that he has really repented, does someone check on him, or is it between him and God?

Yassin: Repentance is between him and Allah before it can be between him and other people. He proves to Allah that he has repented, but it is people who decide if he has or not. If they see that he is sorry for everything he did in the past, he is considered as having repented, but if they find that he has gone back to his old ways, they call him a liar.

Author: Sheikh Ahmad, not everyone prefers death to life. Some of them have been hurt by Jews, but only a minority choose death.

Yassin: To be called true believers they have to prefer life in the next world to life in this world, to believe that what Allah has is better than what there is here. That is, if he has 100 dunams in this world, and if he is convinced that if he meets Allah then he will receive 1000 [about 250 acres], then what Allah has is better than what there is here.

Author: In your opinion, did God create man with specific traits, that is, to be evil, or a miser, or a criminal? Was he fundamentally created that way, or did he adopt such characteristics in the course of his life?

Yassin: It's like this, man is born with a clean slate, but you can write on it with any color you like, white or black or red, whatever you choose. If you have a squash [the light-green Middle Eastern variety of which is, generally speaking, fairly tasteless], for example, you can cook it and make it into a delicacy. A person is born like a squash, and he chooses the path he takes, and he is taken to account for what he has chosen to do.

Yassin used metaphors and similes to express a concept that appears in many cultures, but essentially he was mouthing the sort of platitude that is always perfectly acceptable while being virtually meaningless.

Author: It is permissible to kill a drug dealer?

Yassin: Basically, a murderer and a pimp and someone who has abandoned Islam may be killed. We can put someone who kills with drugs on the list of murderers because he has killed thousands of people indirectly.

Author: Should he die? It is permissible to kill him?

Yassin: He can be judged and executed, if it is accepted that he harms society. If there is a drug dealer and he has a thousand, two or three thousand addicts, and every day five of them die, six even, then he killed them.

Author: Looking at it from another angle, someone who deals drugs is a murderer. And what about someone who deals drugs to the enemy, how would you describe him? And is it permissible to use the money from his drug dealing?

Yassin: Islam has forbidden him to deal drugs, even to the enemy.

Author: I mean infiltrating drugs into the ranks of the enemy, not selling
            them.
Yassin: It is forbidden. All drugs are forbidden, possessing and selling
            them are forbidden.
Author: And if it were to have an influence on defeating the enemy, then . . .
Yassin: It is forbidden by [the Muslim] religion to purchase and possess
            drugs, so how could I sell them to the enemy?

According to various sources, what the sheikh describes as forbidden
is standard operating procedure for Hezbollah in Lebanon. According to
available sources, the organization deals drugs and uses the money to finance
its terrorist activities. In addition, the drugs are smuggled into Israel and used
as a weapon to corrupt Israelis. The connection between drugs and funding
terrorism is well-known in the West.

Author: How do you explain the fact that Islam has adopted technology
            and other aspects of Western life—cars, telephones, missiles, etc.,
            all originating in the West, and at the same time it rejects the
            West as an idea? Do you see Islam as one side and the progress
            and modernism of the West as the other side? Is there a gap
            between them?
Yassin: No . . . no . . . no . . . Islam is progress! Everything an individual
            can acquire that is a product of ideology, anything material, a
            product of industry or technology or commerce is fully supported
            and loved by Islam. There is no gap between them. Islam is
            scientific progress.
Author: We see new inventions in the West, new means of doing things, a
            new way of thinking.
Yassin: That's wonderful, but who invented the first clock? The Muslims.
            Astronomy [was also developed by Muslims] . . . Scientific
            progress? Islam preaches it, loves it and commands it.
Author: What in Western culture does Islam reject?
Yassin: Islam rejects all the cultural and social aspects which contradict it
            and the Shari'a [religious Islamic law], for example, the life of
            whoredom of unveiled women—all the immoral factors in the
            [Western] world are rejected by us.
Author: Are not Western inventions and achievements the product of its
            openness, life styles and ways of living?
Yassin: Absolutely not! You can find many examples of Westerners who
            were in the east, many great scientists, many who went from the
            Arab states to the West because of problems and difficulties in
            the Arab and African states and who began in the West and
            became famous as inventors. If a woman removes her [traditional
            garment which covers her entirely], it does not necessarily turn

her into an inventor in a progressive culture. And does exposing her body make her an inventor? That is, invention is a function of thought, of the mind.

Author: If we compare the achievements of East and West we find an enormous gap. What explains it?

Yassin: Truth! Life is a cycle. For example, during the Middle Ages the East was the center of progress and invention, of culture, and the West lived in ignorance. There was slavery, exploitation... When the West lived in darkness, the East lived in light, with industry and progress and astronomy and chemistry and the natural sciences. There was a great deal of progress, and the West built its Western culture on the foundation of what went before, what was offered by the East, and now the West progresses because the East lags behind, the result of colonialism, poverty, etc., which prevent it from advancing. It does not have the ability to do so, and the wheel turns and goes from West to East... and thus ...

Author: The fundamentalist Muslims, including Hamas want to go back to the "sources," that is, to the days of the prophet. The West lives according to a new model. It has its drawbacks, but as a model, should we look at it and perhaps aspire to it, strive to reach its level of cultural development? Does Islam want to adopt its achievements, or does it reject them completely?

Yassin: Islam calls upon its sons to adopt and develop all the achievements of humanity. We relate to Islam like a bee which takes nectar from the flower and turns it into honey. But others relate to cultures like locusts—they eat and destroy. We do not imply rejection of the West, but rather take what is good from it and develop it.

Islam may take the nectar, but does it turn it into honey? Or like the bees in nature, does it sting and die, like the suicide bomber who blows himself up along with his victims, or even like the danger of a swarm of bees? Sheikh Yassin in effect presents a certain self-defensive tension to ward off the locust, and feels the Muslim world has been exploited by the West. However, the essence is aggressive, spreading "the message" to the world.

Author: What is Islam's position on the place of women?

Yassin: Read the Qur'an and you will know about women. In the first place, Allah created a helpmate from man's own self, that is, she is part of a man's existence, and the connection is one of good will and mercy on both sides.

Author: Do you believe in full equality?

Yassin: Islam believes in justice, not equality.

Author: Do you mean the justice a man gives to his wife?

Yassin: No, not at all. In a company there is the head, the deputy, the head of a department, the worker, etc. Is there equality or justice between them at work?

Author: Here is a personal question for you. If you have a son or daughter, and you see that your daughter is more talented than your son, do you allow her to develop and attain achievements higher than his, despite her gender?

Yassin: I have 11 children, eight of them girls. One daughter is the only one with a matriculation certificate. The boys don't have them.

Author: Did you encourage her?

Yassin: Of course.

Author: Can girls get ahead if they are more talented?

Yassin: Why not?

Author: Even if it means she will have to travel out of the country and study in Europe?

Yassin: We will send her out with limitations and under certain conditions. There is no disagreement over the issue of her needing to study and to be responsible, but over how she does it. That's the question.

Author: Can she be a director, a prime minister?

Yassin: Why not? She will do whatever she is able to. Allah who created man and woman created each one with different potential. Women have no fewer abilities than men, but only women can give birth. And if she has the potential to do something else there is nothing to prevent it. If you have potential, you need to deal with it and to create using your special ability.

Author: In your opinion, did the Creator have something specific in mind for women?

Yassin: If not, why did he make her the way he did?

Author: That is, the Creator gave women a number of capabilities that only she has?

Yassin: Women have a number of advantages men do not have, and vice versa, and they complement each other.

Author: I have a question about Islamic law: In the Qur'an, where the Israelites are held in honor and respect by the prophet, he calls them "Allah's chosen people," and gives them the land. [According to the Jalalayn commentary, "the land" is greater Syria, which includes present-day Israel.] After the people of Pharaoh were destroyed in water he says, "and we have bequeathed to the oppressed people the land which we blessed," and elsewhere, "we will bring the Israelites here [to the land promised them] from the far corners of the world," and there are a number of verses which show beyond a doubt the divine intention of returning the Israelites to their country. What is your opinion?

Yassin: First of all, we know that all the land belongs to Allah. Every land is different, and there are certain which are more noble because of the ruling régime. And if the régime follows the religion of Allah and is led by the prophets and [Allah's] messengers, following his law, then the land is the land of Allah, that is, the land is for the worship of Allah and for obeying him. Allah, may he be exalted, did in fact prefer the Israelites at a certain time, when they were led by the prophets and the messengers and they raised the status of the Israelites, and he promised them forever because they were following his path and his faith, and when they violated the command of Allah on Mt. Sinai he punished them. He left them to wander in the desert for 40 years.

Author: And what about the return of the oppressed [the Israelites] to the land of Eretz-Israel?

Yassin: Allah, may he be praised, lifts up nations if they glorify their religion, and he calls them to account if they stray from his path . . . There were two historical eras of the Israelites: when they were the people of the prophets and Allah lifted them up and stood by their side and saved them from Egypt and helped them take over Palestine from the nations who were here, and they were a "nation of heroes." But when the age of the prophets ended and others came among them and they strayed from the path, Allah punished them and scattered them.

Arafat claimed several times that the Palestinians were the direct descendents of the "nation of heroes" who lived in the region before the Israelites. His aim was to prove that they were the first possessors of the land. He disregarded the fact that if there were any basis for his claim, according to the Qur'an the Palestinians would be infidels and pagans who were expelled from the land of Israel by the Israelites under Moses, with the help and blessing of Allah. Sheikh Yassin's interpretation is similar to the familiar Christian interpretation, which says that God made a covenant with the Jews in the Old Testament, but they violated it, after which he entered into a new covenant with those who recognized Jesus.

But after the prophets, after the Israelites strayed, Allah became angry with them and scattered them in every direction, and took the land from them which they had held, the land of Palestine. And now the Israelites do not follow the path of faith in Allah. I believe in Adam, and after him in Noah, Abraham, Ismail [Ishmael], Isaac, Jacob, Issa [Jesus], Musa [Moses] and Muhammad. In Islam, if I say I believe in Muhammad and not in Musa, I am an infidel. That is, I must believe in all the prophets, and if I deny one, I am an infidel. We rule that all those who do

not believe in all the prophets are subject to the same decision we
are: they are infidels.

That is the classic Islamic approach, prevalent since the days of Muhammad. He recognized the founding fathers of Judaism and Jesus, but claimed
that he was "the last of the prophets," and demanded that everyone recog-
nize him as such. Anyone who refused was labeled an infidel.

Author: The question for the believer is whether the Qur'an mentions
            that the return of the Israelites, the Jews, to their country
            depends on their behavior? Is that true?

Yassin: Not only their return, but their survival as well depends on their
            taking the path of honesty and incorruptibility... The truth in
            Israel today is that it relies on force: we are strong, period. We
            can do what we want... But existence on earth is permissible
            through justice and truth. If there is corruption, then it's
            over... a few years... and they will be gone.

Author: Can Israel correct itself to be able to follow the commandments
            of Allah and not be considered corrupt?

Yassin: Allah, may he be praised, gives and takes. He gives to whoever
            follows the path of righteousness and takes from whoever strays
            from it. And he punished the Israelites for a time, and then raised
            them up and preferred them above others, and confiscated their
            property for a certain time and was angry with them for a time
            and cursed them because they strayed. Israel now... that is, I'm
            not going to tell you what Israel is, you know... And I admit,
            you see that there is a religious process, but in the eyes of faith it
            is not complete, it is a religiousness that believes in some things
            and denies others. If it were true religiousness, it would be
            committed to believing in all the prophets and messengers and
            books. I believe in the Torah and the New Testament, in the
            Psalms, I believe in them, that is, religiousness [in Israel] is a
            perversion, that's one thing, and then there is the secular side,
            morally things are bad in Israel and there is corruption... there is
            corruption and its result will be the destruction of the country.

Author: So, what you are saying is that if the Jews accepted Islam, it
            would be the right thing. That is, in your opinion they cannot
            remain Jews.

Yassin: They could not possibly remain Jews unless they believed in all
            the prophets. Originally the Jews were Muslims, and whoever
            believes in Musa is a Muslim. Now [the Jewish people] have
            taken the rights of another people, that is, the right of the
            Palestinian people to exist, and there are two factors for the
            Palestinian people: the Islamic factor, and the factor that
            determined that this land is blessed by the noble Qur'an and

linked to the holy mosque [Al-Aqsa]. The Palestinian people lived on its land for thousands of years before the Israelites and [will live on] after the Israelites, and want to follow the path of righteousness, with faith in Allah and in the messengers and books, and they have the right to this land.

Author: The last question, with your permission. How do you view the Islamic Movement [a movement operating with the State of Israel] and the peace process? How do they join and go together?

Yassin: Our starting point is politics, which is an inseparable part of religion. Political policy is built on religion, and therefore we say that as far as the land is concerned, it must be controlled by the rule of Allah, may he be praised, and the ruler must be Islam because it is the rule of Allah. If the rule is not that of Islam we reject it because it is not divine rule, even if it is an Arab state and not just Palestine. Every Arab régime or other in the world where the rule of Allah and the religion of Allah do not exist is a rejected régime. [One often hears from Muslim clerics that with regard to the sanctity of the land and rule over it, there are lands in Europe which are included, for example Spain and Britain.] But the force of confrontation changes from place to place according to circumstances. If you enforce your rule over me by force and oppression, I am required to fight against you the same way you fight against me.

Reuven: The lady [the polite Arabic form of address] thanks you, and would like to ask if you are willing to meet her again.

Yassin: I have never refused anyone who wanted to meet me.

Author: Even in the Gaza Strip?

Yassin: Even on the moon ... Women journalists have interviewed me and I made their visits conditional only upon their covering their hair. It's against my religion. I am willing to meet any woman on the condition that her hair is covered.

Author: We thank you for this pleasant and very beneficial meeting.

❖

Sheikh Yassin was a cripple and confined to a wheelchair as the result of an accident. He resided in the Zeitoun quarter of the city of Gaza and was incarcerated in Israel for the first time in 1984. In 1989 he was sentenced to life imprisonment, but Israel was forced to release him after the Mossad botched an assassination of Khaled Mashal, as of this writing, head of Hamas' "political bureau" in Syria. After his release Sheikh Yassin continued to lead Hamas and was accused by Israel of being responsible for terrorist attacks, which caused the deaths of hundreds of Israelis. On March 22, 2004, on his way to a mosque in Gaza, he was killed by a missile fired from an Israeli helicopter. Murad once said, "Yassin was a religious man, and we [Arabs] always have respect for a religious person who has faith and values. He was not a great scholar or anything like that. There were two things . . . that influenced the way Palestinian society regarded him. In the first place, he lived a simple life. In the second, his external appearance. People saw something of the divine in him, as though Allah wanted him to be a cripple on one hand and a leader on the other. People admired and were attracted to the little man who sat in a wheelchair. He was a source of inspiration because even though he was a cripple, he was a great leader. He symbolized the Palestinians as victims. He came across as a victim of the occupation. "People loved Yassin for the same reason they admired Arafat. Their external appearances made them symbols, and that's important. Arafat had a beard and a *kafiyeh*, and a kind of simplicity . . . they were simple leaders and the way they looked wasn't important as far as they were concerned, as opposed to Mubarak, the president of Egypt, who always wear a suit. It reminds me of the great Muslim leaders, who lived simply. Muhammad also dressed simply, even in torn clothing, he was a simple man. Simplicity is regarded as a value and that's important, especially if you live in a slum like Gaza." One can relate to bin Laden in the same context, as an individual perceived as modest, living in a cave some of the time and wearing simple, traditional clothing. It is said that he speaks little and can hold a wordless dialogue with those close to him simply by looking at them.

Professor Shaul Mishal from Tel Aviv University said that "we were the ones, to a great extent, who turned Yassin into a symbol. His devoutness, devotion, affliction and firmness also strengthened him. His record of struggling against Egypt with his disability and his struggle against the military authority in the Gaza Strip raised his status more than his objective measure. He was in the right place at the right time. He was not a scholar or a member of a strong military faction or a politician. He had no relative advantage in any field. He knew how to repeat mantras and his intuition was formidable, as was his ability to grasp a situation, but he was far from being well educated or authorized to issue *fatwas*. Israel gave him more credit than he deserved, as though he were a religious leader, but he was only a symbol, and there was general agreement that Yassin was suitable to be a symbol. People were attracted to him. His disability symbolized Palestine, he was an invalid and Palestinians also don't realize their dream . . . The Israelis made him famous when they put him in prison and when they killed him, and he has gone down in history as a hero."

CHAPTER 7

Women in Prison: "She Poured Boiling Margarine on My Face"

On the ground, sparrows pecked at a loaf of bread someone had deliberately left there. They came in through a hole in the metal mesh covering the prison yard. Woolen blankets were hung on the cell railings, some of them patterned with flowers. The colors were strong, pink, purple, and green most prominent. Some of the green blankets also had Arabic inscriptions. Samira told me that the inscription said the blankets were a donation from the kingdom of Saudi Arabia, a contribution to female prisoners who were not allowed to have visitors. The other blankets were brought by visiting relatives, which the women preferred to those handed out by the prison.

Samira and I sat on stools in the yard, a small round table between us. "How did the birds get in?" I asked.

"From up there," she answered, pointing at the mesh of the exercise yard. "You should see what happens here in the evening. There are lots and lots of birds all over the yard, eating the bread the girls leave out for them."

"How are you?" I asked. During my previous visit Samira told me she had medical problems.

"My feet are swollen," she said, pulling her pants legs up. "Maybe I have a kidney problem, like my aunt . . . But I feel a lot better now."

Shouts came from one of the cells on the upper level. A face could be seen through the grille covering the small opening in the door.

"Zinab wants to talk to you," said Samira.

"OK," I said, "is that the same girl who got boiling margarine spilled all over her?"

"Yes."

For a long time two groups of female security prisoners had been at each other's throats. Samira, spokeswoman of one group, claimed that the quarrel broke out because of Huda, the spokeswoman and central figure of the other group. "Huda decided she would read all the letters we wrote and it was very unpleasant. If I have secrets I don't want her to read about them. And besides, she handed out punishments."

The silence was broken by a warbling voice calling the faithful to prayer. I knew immediately that it was not the voice of the regular muezzin.

"Is there a different muezzin?" I asked.

"No," answered Samira, "Someone came to visit the muezzin and Samiha has taken over the call to prayer."

I listened to Samiha's contralto, full of emotion and direction, calling the faithful to prayer, and I looked at the delicate face of the woman who looked out from behind the iron grille covering the small opening in the door. She was wearing a light gray head covering that swayed with the rhythm of the song. "It's the same woman," I thought, "who escorted the suicide bomber to the attack at the Sbarro restaurant in Jerusalem in 2001, but then she was wearing Western clothing . . . "

On the way to the attack, according to the story, she was wearing a blouse that exposed her stomach. Here in jail she was covered from head to toe in a *jilbab* (traditional dress) and a *hijab* (partial head-covering).

Samiha was the prisoners' deputy spokeswoman and did a great deal for the welfare of the wing. The security prisoners were divided into two groups. One was composed of members of Fatah/Tanzim, a secular organization, and the other of Hamas and the Palestinian Islamic Jihad, whose ideology was Islamic fundamentalist. A fierce rivalry had developed between the two, which sometimes deteriorated into overt hatred. Nevertheless, some of them claimed that the conflicts were personal in nature and had nothing to do with organizational rivalry.

A tall woman came into the office close to the exercise yard. She had long, black, slightly frizzy hair and was wearing pants and a loose white cotton knit shirt. She was an Israeli citizen and spoke fluent Hebrew. "I passed the matriculation examination in Hebrew," she said proudly. "They arrested me when I was 19. Two years have passed since then, but I'm still 19 . . . I live in a village in the north." Her name was Zinab.

Zinab was pretty. Whenever she smiled, dimples formed in both cheeks. "Are you one of the girls they spilled boiling margarine on?" I asked.

"Yes," she answered. She exposed her arm to the shoulder and pulled back her hair to reveal her neck. The skin was covered with deep pink scars. "I will always have these scars. They did it to me a long time ago but it still itches and I can't feel heat where the scars are," said Zinab.

She accused Huda, the spokeswoman of Wing 2, of having abused her. "The prisoners who attacked me said it was a shame that only my arm was injured, because they wanted to scar my face. It happened more than a year ago, and the newspapers called it a quarrel between members of Hamas and Fatah/Tanzim, but it wasn't really like that." Her remarks are interesting in light of the violent clashes that took place in January 2007 between Fatah and Hamas in the Gaza Strip, between Hamas prime minister Ismail Haniya and Palestinian Authority chairman Abu Mazen.

"Huda has been here for three years and she is the Tanzim spokeswoman. She hits her girls [the prisoners who obey her], punishes the girls in her cell, only lets them eat once a day, and says, 'only make one cup of tea a day.' No one can say she doesn't want to [do what Huda tells her]. She has authority and they are afraid of her.

"Once Huda threw chlorine bleach through the opening in the door. We were sitting down and eating dinner and it got into our eyes . . . From the beginning she told us that she had a lot of rules . . . For example, if you want to send a letter to your parents, you have to give it to Huda to read. She says it's for the prisoners' security . . . I can't understand that. She wanted all our commissary money . . . The prisoner signs and says that Huda can do what she wants with her money. According to her rules no one can speak to the guards, even if she needs a nurse or water.

"I don't even behave like that at home. I don't ask my mother for everything. I want to talk to the guards and I need to talk to them. She laid down a lot of rules and in my opinion they're stupid. And another thing, if your lawyer comes, she has to agree for you to see him. She can say, 'Zinab isn't going anywhere.' There are girls who have been here for four years and haven't seen their lawyers because of her."

Zinab put her elbows on the table and brought her face close to mine, as if she wanted to tell me a secret. "It took me four days and then I refused to accept her rules. I was the first one to refuse, because she thinks she is above everyone . . . She started convincing us . . . I didn't leave my room, I didn't want to go into the yard with the group because in the yard they used to have meetings to discuss Zinab, and about how Huda had to be obeyed . . . I asked to speak to the warden, and that's how the conflict began.

"Huda said to me, 'You can't destroy everything I've built. Let's think about it again and get together.' Her tongue is dipped in honey when she speaks to you. I told her that I would give her my answer in a couple of days . . . We didn't speak to each other for five months. Then my parents came to visit my sister [who was also in jail but has since been released] and me. I told my father and mother about Huda and how she treated the girls. Around that time Huda's parents visited, and she cried, and then she started saying nasty things about my parents. I couldn't stand it . . . I told her to stop . . . I told one of the senior guards, 'You hear what she is saying and you don't say anything,' she wanted to talk . . . In situations like that I can't control myself, and I hit Huda. She bit my sister, she took a bite out of her leg. I struck her hard and she attacked my sister . . . She's 25, older than I . . . She [Huda] started biting and four prisoners couldn't get her off. I asked a policeman to help my sister, to take her into the visitors' room. My sister had flesh caught in her pants leg. I couldn't really grasp that someone had bitten her leg like a dog...Not even a dog behaves like that. My parents were still here, and I went into the visitors' room and told them, it was a shock for them. My sister was on the floor and they saw her leg."

Zinab spoke without stopping and I nodded every so often. Suddenly she stopped and said directly, "You listen and you pay attention, but no one else listens ..."

Then she said, "Samiha was in Huda's group, but then she left it because Huda punished her and she didn't want to keep being with her, because she was too smart for the group. Samiha saw that our group had more education. The girls in our group were brought up better. [We were] religious. Religion is the first thing that interests security prisoners... Security prisoners have to maintain their self-expression, and they do that by the way they dress. I fast during [the Muslim holy month of] Ramadan, [but] I don't have the right clothing... I was convinced the way I should be... I thought of being like all the other girls, wearing religious clothing, it's nice to be like everyone else."

A Western woman who arrived at a social event and found another woman wearing the same dress would leave immediately. For Zinab the opposite was true: before she went to jail she wore jeans and a T-shirt, but once she was imprisoned she decided to wear traditional clothing to feel closer to the other girls, and because it was an obvious manifestation of being a security prisoner.

She continued talking about how she had been hurt and about Huda. "Even though there was a quarrel between the two groups, there were girls [in the other group] I spoke to. I don't even hate the Jews, only those who kill. I hate Huda's leadership and what she does, but I don't hate her whole group. I spoke to Hana... she's 17. We had a relationship, but not a strong one, 'Hi, how are you,' that kind of thing. I said hello to her, but quietly, so that Huda wouldn't punish her ...

"The day they attacked me I was praying in my room. There were two girls handing out food in the corridor. Hana was one of them and she said she wanted to talk to me about something interesting. She was the one who burned me, and Fahima was the one who burned Fatima. I asked Hana how come she was talking to me in front of everyone. I knew that Na'ima, who was the deputy spokeswoman and Hana's sister, would punish her for it. Na'ima was sentenced to 15 years, she tried to stab a soldier ... She punishes the girls and her sister as well, to show Huda that everyone is the same, that everyone is afraid of her [Huda].

"Hana wanted me to stand up while she was giving out food, so that she could suddenly spill boiling margarine on me. I asked her how come she was talking to me in front of the whole wing, and they called her to Huda's room. That's when they were heating up the margarine, and they pretended to yell at Hana for talking to me. I sat back down and continued praying. Suddenly Fahima said, 'They want to talk to you, it's urgent.' Hana was standing by the opening in the door again and she said, 'Come here, a little closer, I want to talk to you, stand right by the opening, I want to tell you something interesting, I want to tell you what one of the male prisoners said . . .

"At the last minute I saw she was holding the kind of [plastic] box chicken soup [powder comes in]. Praise to Allah, I moved away, because she threw what she had in the box at me just as I moved. It hit my arm. At the same moment Fahima threw boiling margarine at Fatima's face. It was as though someone had struck the girls in my room . . . In such a situation, how could I even speak at all . . . Samira, who is our spokeswoman now, ran over to hug me and take me to the infirmary. Everyone in the whole jail was yelling, and prisoners were chasing the girls who did it, and then they put them in solitary confinement . . .

"It was a long time before I left for the infirmary, and then it all stuck to my arm . . . Fatima was crying all the time, her condition was much worse, her eye, her whole face, everything was burned. They took us to the infirmary and put cold water and ointments on us. We went back to our room and took Fatima with us so that Samira could take care of her. I lay on my bed and looked at Fatima, at her face. She would wake up and cry as though they were pouring boiling margarine mixed with sugar on her. She was afraid it would leave a mark."

Huda made sure to tell Zinab that she had received her "punishment" a year after the time she bit her sister, and promised her that every year, on the anniversary, she would make sure to remind her of what had happened. "After Hana burned me, Huda called to me from her room and said, 'Every year on this date you will get a present from me' . . ."

Palestinians attach a lot of importance to anniversaries, sometimes even ascribing magical powers to them. Many dates were sanctified by Palestinian society: May 15, the Day of the Catastrophe, the day the State of Israel was established in 1948; March 30, Land Day, when land was expropriated to build settlements in 1976; and various dates set aside as Days of Rage by the terrorist organizations, etc. Al-Qaeda as well has a particular sensitivity for certain days, the anniversaries of its mega-attacks, for example.

After Zinab had finished recounting her story about violence in the prison, she said, "There is a picture I have always wanted to draw . . ." I gave her a piece of paper and a pencil. She drew an eyebrow, an eye in profile, and opposite the eye a vine leaf, saying as she drew, "The vine leaf is what separates this part of the picture from the other, like a face," she said, pointing at what looked like a broken line. "For us, the vine leaf," she said pointing, "symbolizes life outside prison . . . everyone has something that hides him, prevents him from seeing what he should. I'm a prisoner, [and] there are certain things inside me that no one can reach, not easily . . ."

Lower down on the page she drew a terra-cotta jug and through it a line to symbolize breaking it into pieces, and said, "We buy a jug and put it in the living room. When it breaks, it will never be the way it was before, and if you put it together again, you will always be able to see it was broken. That's a person, that's honor...If a person breaks something he can never make it the same as it was. If he manages to fix it, with Allah's help, for the rest of his life it will be obvious that at some time he broke it. It's the same thing with a girl's honor...You have to preserve everything you have so that you never have a reason to repent. If I have freedom, honor, [I have to] preserve that freedom, because if I ruin it, I'll never be able to fix it."

It is fairly certain that she was speaking about premarital sexual relations, which Arab woman are absolutely forbidden to engage in.

Regarding her life, she said, "I passed all my matriculation exams and registered at a college in Safed [a city in the north of Israel]. I wanted to become a registered nurse or study nursing as an academic subject, and for that I had to take the psychometric exams. In the meantime I worked in a clothing factory. I worked there for a year to make money to pay for my tuition. My life was like the life of any other girl my age who dreams about the future all the time.

"I liked to surf the Internet, and that way I met someone from Hebron, in a chat room. It took three months, all I did was talk to him in the chat room, just a few months...We had a strong relationship, private. We talked about his situation and about mine...I write nationalist poetry, love poems ... We talked about the fact that he liked my poems and he asked me for my cell phone number, and after three months I gave it to him and we started talking on the phone. My sister knew I was talking to a boy on the phone, but my father didn't. At first I didn't ask anything, but then I got curious. We talked and then he stopped calling. He said he was leaving his house, that the security situation was bad. He told me how bad life was under the occupation, how they didn't sleep at night because there were soldiers, and then they arrested me. Before that he told me that he had to see me, to strengthen our relationship. It wasn't a romantic relationship, a love relationship...An ordinary relationship like having a boyfriend ..."

Zinab blushed bright red when she spoke about "the boy from Hebron" and her secret relationship. Actually, she was one of many Arab women who have been exposed to the world through Internet chat rooms. It is incidentally also easy for the terrorist industry to manipulate and exploit such women by creating romantic unions, an area in which they have no experience, and which, because of the circumstances, they have to hide from their parents. The chat room relationships formed between Arabs and other Muslims all over the world, including those between Israeli Arabs and those living in the Palestinian Authority, increase the connection with and exposure to what occurs in the territories, and creates dilemmas for some of Israel's Arabs, as Zinab's story showed. The terrorist organizations' use of the Internet is well known. Their sites appear and disappear, making it hard to track their activity. It is quite probable that the exploitation of Arab women via the Internet will increase, because in many instances it is the only way romantic relationships can be formed, relationships which are often manipulated for terrorist activity.

Zinab continued, "I used to talk to boys . . . my sister and mother knew, but my honor had to be preserved, that freedom . . . They arrested me because the boy from the chat room was involved in attacks. Not everyone from chat rooms meets and gives out their telephone numbers. Boys from the territories want to meet, but in such a situation it's impossible. I watch the news and I know what's going on, we talk about the conditions they live under, that there is the occupation, that a *shaheed* fell . . . After they arrested me he said he was going to carry out an attack . . .

"I didn't have any problems before, I was responsible for myself, I liked working and didn't ask my parents to buy me anything. I felt like a responsible person, I went out of the house and I came back . . . my family, well, it wasn't like I had a father I had to be afraid of, we were like friends, my mother and father [and I] . . . My sister pities me because I got sentenced to [so many] years in jail . . .

"Even now I still dream, I write poetry and I read a lot . . . Guards and jail won't destroy my dream. My family always tell me to go on, and in spite of my situation I keep going and I want to study."

At that point, as if confiding a secret, she lowered her voice and said, "I want to tell you the real reason I asked to speak to you. I would like to study at Everyman's University, I would like to study sociology and maybe continue to psychology, and I wanted to know how you ask . . . I mean, ask a question, and the answer is part of the words, not the words themselves." That is, she wanted to learn the interviewing technique for the time she would apply to be accepted for academic studies. I smiled.

Then she changed the topic and said, "A couple of times I went into chat rooms on Nana [an Israeli portal that operates in Hebrew, English, Arabic, and Russian] to talk to Jews, to find out what they think about us, to speak Hebrew, to find out about them close up . . . I didn't want to talk only to Palestinian Arabs from the territories. I had friends, I like having friends, I have a lot of them.

"I want to study . . . 19 is the age when you start studying, when you start living. I see getting married as the end of life . . . You have to study something interesting. I wish there were someone who would talk to me about it . . . I want to leave here with a university diploma, there are other prisoners who did it."

She asked for my advice as to what to study, and then went back to talking about the burn. "Samira, the spokeswoman of my wing, asked me, 'If you could burn Hana, or Huda, who sent her . . .' And I say, something in my heart was burned, not my arm, that a Muslim Arab woman could do such a thing . . . If they let me do it, well, I'm a Muslim and my religion doesn't force me to be evil to people like that. Not the religion, the culture, my parents, I wouldn't do it, I would keep my distance from her, from Huda, do the accounting with myself. You know, as much as it hurts, I don't [want to] give my pain to someone else.

"Huda is really mentally ill. Sometimes she's OK, [when] there's no pressure on her, and [then] suddenly she explodes and hits the other girls, that's not normal behavior...Huda has [some kind of] remote control and she controls the girls. Sometimes she grabs their hands and hurts them...She invites a prisoner into her room and the prisoner talks to her and tells her everything, what she did and what she didn't do."

As a result of the bitter quarrels and violence, the prisoners were separated into two wings, and Zinab thought it was the right thing to do. She kept repeating her desire to use her time in prison to study. "It's a tough situation but we try to do it, [it's] something nice, we study in the yard. I teach the other girls Hebrew. Samiha taught us about politics today. She went to university, she teaches us about the relationship between prisoners and guards, how security prisoners are treated in prison. Relationships with the guards are good...There has to be respect in every relationship...Forget about the fact that she is a guard and the door is closed, she didn't bring me here, even if she is Jewish and I'm Arab, it doesn't matter, I want a smile. The guards are fine...they say 'Good morning' when they open the doors. What I want, the whole group wants."

Zinab looks like a sportswoman, and it is obviously important for her to preserve the image. "My hair is OK," she said, running a hand through her long black hair, "but I've gained a lot of weight here. I used to engage in sports a lot before, even basketball...Sports are good for your body, and it's also important to be strong and healthy. I exercise for two hours, I want to see the other girls and I want to study as well. I don't eat a lot, but I gain weight from everything I eat and that's not good for me. The same is true for Samira the spokeswoman, she likes candy. I just had a glass of milk, at five they cook dinner and you get fat from it. Sometimes they bring us chicken and rice, peas and carrots and potatoes all together, and cook it all with tomato paste or chicken soup powder...We have an electric kettle and a hotplate in our room. At night we make instant coffee, hot chocolate, something hot with cookies and cake."

She talked about playing basketball with a team of Arab girls after overcoming her parents' objections. Then she said, "I smoke. My parents don't know...My father always said, not out of fear, because of a girl's honor. There are six or seven girls who smoke here. In Huda's group they all walk around with cigarettes as though it makes them look more sophisticated. Arab women who smoke do it in secret because it doesn't look nice in public, but men smoke freely. If a woman is respected and gets caught with a cigarette, she isn't respected as much.

"Karina, one of the Russian prisoners, told me that kissing a woman who smokes is like kissing an ashtray...Originally she was Christian, but she married a Muslim and now she is a Muslim too."

I asked one of the staff to let me meet Shafiqa, who was one of a team of suicide bombers. The other, a boy, blew himself up. At the last minute she decided not to press the detonator and left the site. Sometime later she was caught.

She walked confidently into the office I was sitting in, looking like a raven. Her entire body was robed in black, even her head covering. There was something clumsy about the way she walked, and her face looked older than her 22 years. I wondered whether she was heavy under all that clothing, "I have no problem about talking to you, but there are rules and we have to obey them," she said after I explained why I wanted to interview her. "People without rules don't live human lives. I'll call the deputy spokeswoman and tell her I'm going to talk about my life. I wish other people would ask me about my life... I'm sure the girl responsible for me will agree to my talking to you."

In the meantime, until the deputy spokesman arrived, we began talking in Hebrew and English, the discussion interlaced with polite phrases in Arabic. Shafiqa spoke English well and she could also communicate in basic Hebrew. Her gaze was direct and confident, as was her handshake. Nevertheless, she didn't want a long conversation lest she be suspected of collaboration.

"My life is not a movie... I think it's something special. I'm willing to tell you my name, my age and why I'm here... Like you said, it's my life... No one has the right to ask about my life," she said.

"You know," I told her, "I've spoken with a lot of security prisoners. They didn't have any problems when it came to talking about themselves. Women are cowards," I said, and looked at her eyes.

"Yeah, all right." I could tell by her tone that the use of the word "cowards" had offended her. Maybe she felt challenged to contradict me. In any case, she began speaking.

"I'm 22 years old. I was born in Amman, in Jordan. In 1991 I came to Israel, to Beit Sahour. My father died in a car crash when I was six months old. When I was 10 my mother remarried and I had to go live with my aunt, my father's sister, and my grandmother, my father's mother. I didn't want to stay with my mother. It was very difficult."

"It must have been hard for you to be separated from your mother."

"I don't want to talk about that," she said sternly. "I decided to leave my mother... I have a secret, and it's only my business."

"I have a daughter about your age," I said, "and for both of us, separation is the hardest thing in the world."

Shafiqa's story is not exceptional. In Arab society, when the father divorces the mother, the children usually live with him. If he dies, they move to his parents' house, thus they are often separated from their mothers. One divorced terrorist (who was apprehended on his way to carrying out a suicide bombing attack) told me that his young son had been placed with his parents. The child ran away to the mother. The father, serving a life sentence, was quite angry that the child had dared to want to be with his mother.

Shafiqa made it clear she would keep her secret and we continued our conversation. It is not unreasonable to assume that her father's family was unhappy about the mother's new marriage. They might also have grumbled about the widow's moral conduct. An Arab woman is not expected, like an Indian, to perform suttee or throw herself into the grave but she is expected to bury herself at home. It is especially complicated if the woman has children. Her husband's family watches her and her conduct is generally open to criticism. Under no circumstances will they agree to the children's being raised by another man. Needless to say, it is considered normal for a widowed or divorced father to bring home a new wife.

Shafiqa, apparently, had already seen that "movie." The trauma also certainly fashioned her life and it most likely influenced her decision to end it in a suicide bombing attack.

"I fast when I want to, to be close to Allah," she said.

"I have no desire to speak about prison, so don't ask me . . . I'm not afraid of anyone, only of Allah . . . There are all kinds of things running around inside my head."

She tried to project strength and perhaps even apathy, but her eyes were full of profound internal pain.

"My grandmother was like a mother to me . . . We're friends," she said, trying to say that a 10-year old child can live without a mother and that it wasn't so terrible. "I had a better life in Beit Sahour than in Jordan, because this is my country, not Jordan. I'll live here when I get out . . ."

Shafiqa said there we could easily talk about topics unconnected to military action, and then she left to call Na'ima, the deputy spokeswoman. Na'ima was about 30 years old, heavy, wearing a scarf to cover her hair and a worn sweater and tight pants. I extended my hand; hers was damp and her handshake feeble. In Arabic Shafiqa told her what had been said so far. "That's what I've said . . . the story of my life . . . beyond that I didn't say anything, right?" Her eyes sought mine, asking me for verification.

Na'ima did not seem to be charismatic, nor of being capable of acting as deputy spokeswoman. She seemed to be living in the shadow of Huda, who had been removed from the prison for a certain period of time. Huda's status among her supporters remained strong and unshakable. Na'ima was incapable of making decisions, not even those relating to the welfare of the prisoners in her wing. Every communication, even from the Red Cross, was automatically rejected.

I was surprised that she had been chosen as substitute spokeswoman. Shafiqa gave the impression of being charismatic, fluent, and full of self-confidence and determination. Nevertheless she seemed uncertain in Na'ima's presence, and she was obviously afraid that the latter would suspect her of having said something to "the Jew."

"Shafiqa's life is like all of ours. We are all together," said Na'ima, facing me. "We are all here in prison, and what goes on outside, goes on outside. We hear one or two things. Huda, the spokeswoman, is everyone's friend, and the spokeswoman's life is like everyone else's." Huda's reign of terror made itself felt and her spirit still ruled, even if she wasn't there. I knew how she had achieved it: by telling two women in her wing to spill boiling margarine mixed with sugar on two women in the other wing. And I couldn't help thinking that mixing sugar with the margarine was like putting nails and bits of metal into the suicide bombers' explosive devices, to cause the worst possible and most painful wounds possible.

CHAPTER 8

As Machiavelli Said,
"The End Justifies the Means"

Huda, who was serving a life sentence, was finally returned to the wing, but only after prisoners under her thrall had attacked prisoners from the other group. I asked to be allowed to meet her. Murad (the journalist) said, "She has a bad reputation, and people say that she has been with a lot of men."

Huda turned out to be a young woman, 27 years old, nice looking and wearing a white cotton knit shirt and wide sweat pants. Dimples appeared in her cheeks when she smiled. There were faint stains on her face. She had lovely brown hair falling all the way down her back, carefully arranged and styled with a hair dryer. She was mature, intelligent, and fully capable of expressing herself in Hebrew. But when I asked her about the half-heart she wore as a pendant, and wanted to know who had the other half, she blushed and smiled with embarrassment.

During our first meeting she was suspicious but nevertheless spoke freely and with evident self-confidence. She was considered the most charismatic of the security prisoners, for good and for evil. She was also famous enough to have had the Israeli media devote a lot of time to her. They usually described her as manipulative, sophisticated, and an uninhibited murderer. She was often in trouble for infractions of prison discipline and found herself separated from the other prisoners and with her visitation rights revoked. There was a certain childish stubbornness about her, and a perverse insistence upon doing the exact opposite of what the prison authorities wanted.

Once she started talking it was impossible to get her to stop. "Whenever someone talks to us, in the end we wind up looking like murderers. [They say] we have problems with our families at home. They never talk about the fact that we have feelings and do things for our families. They never make us look like human beings. Don't forget that we are security prisoners, and that's the goal, to make it look like there's something wrong with us. They always turn me into a murderer. No one ever tries to understand me and to get to know me, and I'm exactly the opposite. You can ask any member of the staff here ... It's a problem, so we decided we didn't want to talk to anyone."

I found it hard to understand why Huda thought she would get a good report card from the members of the staff when quite the opposite was true.

"I studied psychology ... I know myself and I know what I'm talking about ... I'm more famous here in prison than outside ... I had friends at the Hebrew University. One of them works for Meretz [a left-wing, citizens'-rights-oriented Israeli political party]. I explained [to him] that I wasn't like [the way they portrayed me] on television ...

"At first I thought that the Jews only knew how to be soldiers. They stand at the roadblocks and curse us. In jail I got to know the guards and the [non-political] criminals and I saw that they were all the same. I heard how they suffered, the guards and the prisoners, and we talked about our lives. We didn't talk about why we got life sentences ... I thought that if I were outside, I could be friends with one of them, we could do things together, go places together."

Huda lived in Jerusalem, in the Old City, and had an Israeli identity card. When she was 13 she moved to Bir Naballah, a village between Jerusalem and Ramallah, but came back to Jerusalem because she wanted to keep her Israeli identity card. "Like they keep telling me, I was a smart little girl, I wanted to know everything. I don't remember a lot, but I remember that I started reading the newspaper when I was young. My father gave me money to buy candy and I bought the newspaper. I loved knowing things. All the neighbors liked me. They knew me, I used to talk to everyone and if someone had a problem they would tell me about it. They told me I had a 'white heart.' I could listen, help ...

"My father died three years ago. I was already in jail ... It's very hard ... He fell off the roof of our house, they were building another story, and he wanted to leap from one place to another and he fell [It is rumored that he committed suicide.] ... Everything comes from Allah ... I didn't go to the funeral ... We are two sisters and two brothers, we all went to university, my mother went to university too, in Iraq ... She came from a family with a lot of money, very rich, so her father sent her to Iraq with her brother and both of them studied there. She studied economics but she never worked outside the house, and she married my father when she was 25 or 26.

"For me, my father isn't just a father, he's a friend, everything [he does] is for me ... He gives me everything I ask for. He looks at me and he knows what I want, and gives me everything I want ... He raised me right, we trusted each other, he brought me up knowing he wouldn't be afraid of what I would do. He always relied on me. I used to buy him presents even if there was no reason, clothing, I liked to see him dressed nicely, wearing nice clothing, nice shoes, a watch. Every month or two I leave a note on his pillow telling him that I love him, that he's the only person in the world I love ..."

Huda's father died while she was in jail but sometimes she still speaks of him in the present tense, as though he were still part of her life.

"My mother loves me a lot so I did everything she wants, at home and outside. I do all the household shopping. We all went out to work ... She's at home all the time, so I took her out to restaurants. If I have a problem I talk to her about it, and if she has a problem she tells me about it and asks me what to do ... I look older than I really am and I learned that it's a help ... I would tell her about my studies and give her books to read ... I got a BA in psychology and communications from the university ... It was 50% girls and 50% boys, although they thought there would be more girls than boys [in the department]."

"None of my brothers or sisters is married, all of them are at home. They come to visit me and bring me a lot of clothing ... Being able to change your clothes in jail makes you feel good. If you wear something new, it makes you feel you haven't gone too far away from freedom."

The articles written about her in the Israeli newspapers disturbed her a lot.

"As far as I can see, the newspapers print an article about me every week. What they write annoys me because there's part of the truth they don't write. They always make me out to be a problem ... They write that I'm smart but evil, like a criminal ... That's the image they give of me. You're the first person I've spoken to about how I feel inside ..."

I asked her about the other prisoners.

"We talk, the girls talk, we have conversations once a week, once every two weeks, and everyone says something about how she feels now and what it was like outside ... Everything is so hard, you have to get things out of your system. I talk to everyone alone, too ... For instance, they're painting the wing now, doing good things, in the rooms, pictures, they want to have exhibitions, they want to have a campaign against smoking ..."

"So maybe you'll stop smoking, Huda, what do you think?" I asked.

"Maybe," she answered, but a few minutes later she lit a cigarette. There was something masculine about the way she held it between two fingers close to the filter.

"I really really liked studying ... I liked everything I learned and I was willing to study a book from morning till night and just learn [things]. I was always at the head of the class ... I liked to sing all the time, people tell me I have a good voice. I liked everything that had to do with school. At first I went to a coeducational school, then when I was 11 I changed schools because we moved from place to place.

"There is one thing I have always talked about and is hard for me to forget: in '82 there were the massacres in Sabra and Shatilla, and I still carry everything I saw and heard inside. I saw people on television, they were screaming, and then in the next picture I saw how they died. Some of the Lebanese carried out the massacre, Lebanese soldiers were there too. The Jews who were there opened doors, they let the Arabs kill their friends. It is very hard for me to forget everything I saw and heard."

Actually, Huda's version of the Sabra–Shatilla massacre is basically similar to the Israeli version. She did not blame the Israelis, and it was clear to her that Arabs killed Arabs, but she had a problem with her anger at the Jews who did not prevent it. Suddenly she moved to a different topic and said, "Someone I know, from the time he was 15, when he saw a soldier kill a little child, he wanted revenge, and the Jews who see attacks want to do the same thing."

"But," I said, "when Israeli soldiers harm children it is not done deliberately. It's the terrorists who hide behind children."

"When I was 12 or 13, we went to my grandmother's house in Jericho, and at night I was outside the house and I fell and hurt my knee. There was no one at home, just me and my brothers, and the older ones were away. There is a restaurant [and I went there], and a Jewish soldier who was there helped me—I always tell the girls this story—he bandaged my leg and took me to the hospital and then brought me back. That's something I don't forget."

Huda tried to sound humane and definitely not militant regarding Jews, but sometimes she was aggressive and uninhibited.

"When I see things on TV I always tell the girls about them, even [terrorist] attacks, and I start crying and I tell the girls I cried, I see what they did to a little [Jewish] child, I see it's a person."

It is hard to reconcile what Huda said with the murder she committed. Not only that, but according to the guards, when she was arrested, at night in her cell, she used to imitate the pleading and cries of the boy she helped kill. She uttered heart-rending screams and pretended to cry bitterly to provoke the Jewish guards. "A cold-blooded murderer, that's what she is," said one of the female prison officers who knew Huda well. "She knows how to be charming, especially around men, and to pretend she has human feelings, but it's all pretense . . . She's full of evil, she's a devil, a child-murderer . . ."

Huda kept talking about her human reactions to Jews. "There was an attack, I don't remember where, and there was a little Jewish child . . . I had this feeling when the mother cried, how she was praying to the whole world . . . I wanted to write to her. It doesn't make any difference, Jew, Arab, it doesn't matter what religion, if I see a person crying, it makes me want to cry, too."

The child Huda was referring to was Hadar, an infant hurt in the suicide bombing attack at the Maxim Restaurant in Haifa two days before Yom Kippur, 2003, when a female suicide bomber, calmly ate lunch and then blew herself up. His father was killed and Hadar hovered between life and death for weeks. However, it is interesting to note that suicide bombers often eat a good meal on their way to carrying out the attack. Even Palestinian terrorists who kill a suspected collaborator and throw his body into a ditch later go out together to a restaurant to eat hummus, apparently finding murder a banal activity which does not prevent them from going on about their business.

"Tell me something about love," I asked.

"I had a friend, [but he was] not a boyfriend. We didn't think like that ... It was love. As I see it, I'm from a well-educated family and I have my own life. [My family] trusted me, a lot of boys called me on the phone at home, they used to come to my house and sit with my family. During the intifada there were no movies in Ramallah, so we used to go out to restaurants.

"I knew him for about two and a half, maybe three years. I was 21. When I came home late he would bring me from Ramallah or from wherever we had been, right to my house. I know who I am and I wasn't afraid people would talk about me, we weren't alone together all the time, he had friends and I was with some of my girlfriends. I never cared about what people said about me, not only about him, about everything else that concerned me.

"If there was 'a thing like that' [behavior considered inappropriate or wanton] I would have thought about it, but I don't give an accounting of myself to anyone. I know that I don't touch anyone, don't hurt anyone, there's a limit to everything ... The boy was from Ramallah and he was one year older than I. He didn't study with me at the university but we were in the same field. I worked for a newspaper, another girl and I, we produced the whole newspaper, it was local. I wrote the articles, we distributed the paper, people took out ads, that's how we financed it. I did it all with just one other girl.

"It wasn't something ordinary, [an Arab] boy giving [an Arab] girl a ride, but it's the same thing, you [Israelis] do the same thing, but [but we don't do it] where everyone can see ..."

Relative to the way Arab girls usually behave, Huda's behavior was very free. It is most unusual for a girl to ride in a car with a man if she is not his wife or a blood relative. It could start a whispering campaign and, under certain circumstances, cost her her life.

She said, "When I left home and went to university, my father told me, you have to do thus and such ... You know our religion ... He said, 'Don't disappoint me,' those three words. They always used to tell me they were proud of me, and I wanted to keep their respect. If there were problems, if they misunderstood something, I would sit with them, my parents, and say, 'Let's talk about it. If I'm wrong, convince me, and if you're wrong, I'll convince you,' and that way we would solve our problems. I used to go to political meetings, I sat with everyone, even with [Yasser] Arafat, and I explained to my father that it was something inside me. I want to understand everything and talk about it, it's part of my life, so enough, let me do what I want, I promise not to do anything bad. In the end my father agreed."

Huda's family was obviously very liberal by Arab standards, but reading between the lines, she exploited the freedom they gave her. Murad, the journalist who had dated her, said, "Bad reputation, she has the name of someone who goes around with a lot of men."

Huda said, "As far as honor goes, I don't mean 'that' [i.e., sexual relations, but even the most liberated Arab woman would have a hard time explicitly saying the words], but all my conduct, and even if I went [out] with a boy or a man, it didn't damage my honor. I know what the limit is. Most people knew me and knew that I didn't make mistakes.

"Sometimes I have trouble explaining myself. That's because of the language, sometimes I feel shy. I know I have self-confidence ... You can be shy when you have self-confidence ... I use makeup, but only a little. I like to be natural. I know I'm not so pretty, but I have a beautiful soul ..."

She stopped talking for a minute, waiting. "You are very pretty," I said. Her face lit up, and she continued, "I like to laugh all the time and make other people laugh ..."

There are people in Israel whose lives Huda destroyed, and they don't laugh at all when they think about her, but she doesn't relate to them. She never mentioned why she was sentenced to life imprisonment and said nothing about the injuries she had caused to her fellow prisoners. Quite the opposite: she tried to present herself as a normal girl, friendly, liberal, sensitive to other people, but apparently she had no conscience.

She enjoyed talking about herself. "I like to go to places where everything is green. And like I told you, I like to sing and dance. I even did disco dancing, with boys as well, most girls don't do that, but everybody dances, so why not? I like to listen to Middle Eastern music and I like Eyal Golan [a contemporary Israeli singer] ... I have his cassettes, I listen to Hebrew and Arabic all the time and it is easier to understand him when he sings. I know that his mother worked in an official capacity in Neveh Tirza [a women's prison]. The words are very pretty, and I think he sings about everything you feel."

It was not the first time that security prisoners told me that they were Eyal Golan fans because his songs spoke to them.

Huda spoke about her family again, discussing every topic only as it related to herself, as though the world revolved around her. "My brothers didn't interfere ... If they had problems they went to my father. I would do anything for my little brother. We went to the same university, he enrolled two years after me and didn't know anyone. I said, it's not like high school, you have to write down things [if you want to remember them] ... I would tell him what to do, how to look for work, how to talk to people. At first he wouldn't accept what I said but after he saw that I could help him he would say, 'I have a problem,' and ask me if I could talk to people for him.

"My sister was older than I but I was the one who helped her with everything. She worked, she was shy and she would begin crying any time there was a problem ... I don't cry when I have problems. She would talk to me about her job and tell me if someone looked at her ...

"I studied and worked. My sister and I didn't like the idea of getting married, we wanted to date someone special because we knew [there was nothing wrong with us,] we had everything [to offer]. I have everything, praise Allah, my studies, and I have money. So I don't have to get married for money, a house, clothing ... I have [them all], my father gave me everything.

"I don't need a man, I don't want troubles and then after a year, two years, he'll tell me to go home to my father ... I haven't thought about children yet."

In Muslim society it is very easy for a man to divorce his wife. By saying "You are divorced" [literally, "driven away"] three times, the divorce is valid, on condition it is said in all earnestness and with intent, not during an argument. The woman, humiliated, must return to her father's house. It is therefore no wonder that educated Arab woman want to spare themselves the trials of an unsuitable marriage and to choose a husband for themselves.

"People tell me I'm stubborn ... I don't know why. It's nothing new, they started when I was a small child. I don't like being told what to do, only if I ask. Even here, so a couple of times there were problems. My parents didn't tell me what to do. They said, 'If you do thus and such it will be better, you'll only profit from it.' Even here, in jail, there are girls who do what I tell them, but if I were in their shoes I wouldn't do whatever I was told."

Huda spoke convincingly and well, but what she said was at odds with ordering someone to mix boiling margarine and sugar to spill on prisoners who refused to accept her authority.

"Do you believe in paradise?"

"Sometimes I do, and sometimes I don't," she answered. "Our religion says that if someone behaves [well], prays and does everything [right], then in the end he goes to paradise. Not only *shaheeds* go to paradise. So does someone who prayed, read the Qur'an, didn't steal or kill, didn't do forbidden things. I read the Qur'an all the time, I always did. The Qur'an is like school for me, it teaches you a lot of things ... It's true it was written a long time ago, but you feel it's something new, like it's telling you what to do for everything. One mistake is to yell at your parents and say 'No' to them. The way they helped you when you were little, you have to help them when they can't do anything.

"The Qur'an says women have all the rights ... From what I see in jail, I've been in jail for three years, and from what I see, I think you [the Jews] give women more respect ... Maybe it isn't exactly like that and in private it's the same ... I didn't know any Jews before I came to jail ... I wanted them to feel the way we feel. Not revenge ..."

Once Huda started talking it was hard to get a word in edgewise. She seemed to feel she had to say everything, to tell her whole story. Every time she thought of something, even something unrelated to what she had been saying, she had to talk about it lest she forget. The atmosphere during our conversations was good, and the very fact they were held made it possible for the other prisoners to open up, because they obeyed her unthinkingly.

A few months after our first conversation I asked to speak to her again. She came in holding a plastic cup of coffee, and I offered her mineral water.

"No, thank you, I drink coffee. Do you want me to ask them to make you some?"

"Uh-uh, just pour some of yours into my cup," I said, and moved a Styrofoam cup lying on the table toward her.

She could not hide her surprise, and very carefully poured exactly half her coffee into my cup.

"I put a lot of sugar into what I drink ... I can't drink anything if it isn't sweet," she mumbled as she poured.

"Let's drink to peace," I said, and raised my cup. "*L'chaim*."

I told Huda I had met a Muslim sheikh and that he had received me very politely and answered all my questions.

"Did he tell you about paradise and the *shaheeds*?" she asked with a smile. "On [Israeli TV] Channel 1, there was a very interesting program. Soldiers [who were stationed] at Hebron talked about how they behave at the checkpoints and in the villages, and they said they 'made a game of killing.' Is that what they do? On the program there were two children who wanted to commit suicide [i.e., suicide bombing attacks]. One was 14, maybe 16, they don't understand anything. They don't understand that they're going to die, they wanted to be big shots in their village ...

"Maybe someone who commits suicide has the strength for it ... If a person wants to do something [like that] he's afraid ... They weren't afraid. From what I understand of the stories about the *shaheeds* and their families, they were well-liked, not just insignificant people. They were outgoing and liked to help people, and they would give away whatever they had. I think that's important, to give up everything you have, even your body, your soul, to help other people, to help your people ...

"I know people who said they wanted to do something. That was the reason I did what I did. OK, I didn't try to carry out a suicide bombing attack. They wanted people to pay attention to [the Palestinians], they wanted the Israelis to feel what we feel. That isn't revenge. Someone who wanted to be a *shaheed* did so because he said, enough bloodshed ...

"Do you know [the works of] Machiavelli? I don't remember the name of the book exactly. We studied it at the university."

"Do you mean *The Prince*?"

"Yes. That's where he teaches that the ends justify the means. It doesn't matter what you did, because you achieved your end. Some of the suicide bombers thought like that. Maybe the way they chose wasn't exactly the right one."

"Do you really think that the message of the suicide bombers' act is 'enough bloodshed?' Doesn't it seem strange to you that they do it by murdering innocent civilians Israelis, Americans and others?"

Huda squirmed in her chair. I usually tried to avoid arguments during the interviews, but being told that the way to stop bloodshed was by blowing up Israelis, Americans, and Europeans in general was something I had to respond to. "On the same program," I continued, "did you hear what the mother of Sabih said, the boy who was sent to blow himself up? She said that she wished she could have died instead of him. You know, even when a mother takes her children to the dentist, she wishes she could bear the pain instead of her child. No parent can stand the thought of his or her child in pain."

Huda nodded and said, "Eventually, it's all of society's loss, because they if they all blow themselves up at that [early] age, if they all die, who's left? They have to build the [Palestinian] state. If you tally up how many killed themselves, and the large number in jail, then who's left? Girls? Who are the girls supposed to marry? There are a lot of things that don't make themselves felt now, but people will feel them in a couple of years.

"Because of the security situation," she said, "I felt that no one thought about us as the Palestinian people, they all thought we were sub-human. They treated us like animals. We always came second, in spite of the peace process . . . The whole world saw what was going on and was silent. I wanted to do something. I did absolutely everything alone, almost . . .

"I wanted to do something special, [and if I did then] maybe [someone would] pay attention to my people . . . I also want to say that I didn't mean or want to kill anyone . . . I was sick after I made my decision, maybe I . . . I felt a little that I was doing something wrong, and I had a fever inside . . . My mother didn't know but she asked me if I was sick . . . I didn't eat and I was tired . . ."

Huda's statement that she didn't mean to kill anyone does not bear scrutiny. She acted in a very smart, cruel, callous way, and there is no doubt she knew her action would result in the death of an innocent boy. At a different meeting she announced that she had no regrets and was not sorry about anything. She was apparently either moody or had a desire to present a certain image.

"Yesterday," she said, "I saw on TV that there was a meeting between Yossi Beilin [a dovish Israeli politician] and Abu Ala [Palestinian Authority prime minister until the Hamas government was established in January 2006] I didn't know whether to laugh or cry. In Gaza and Rafah people get killed, and the other side sends suicide bombers, and these two hug each other and drink coffee. I thought, if the two of them can do that, why do they have to send children to their deaths? They sat there like two people who had known each other for 20 years, 'How are you?' and 'What's new?' . . . It's a heavy price, why do we have to pay it?

"By Allah, what are they doing? In the end everyone worries about his seat [in parliament]. I saw in the newspaper that they let Arafat leave the Muqataa [a Palestinian Authority building in Ramallah where Arafat stayed under siege for more than two years until he was permitted by the Israeli authorities to leave for medical treatment in France, where he died under mysterious circumstances] to sit in a corner and get some air. What is this, a game? They said he was OK, so they let him sit out in the open for a few hours . . .That's exactly what they do in prison.

"Maybe, when I was a little girl, I also thought that Jews were only soldiers, like you see on TV. Seeing a Jewish man or woman is something else for Palestinians . . . Israelis and Palestinians are more alike than different. I watch all the TV programs and I learn a lot. It's the same, you don't feel any difference.

"We need young people. I want to be like a Jewish person my age, not like people my grandfather's age who think the world never changes because they themselves can't do anything. I don't believe in leaders, they don't understand more than we do. I have the Qur'an, I know what's permissible and what's forbidden, so I don't believe a single word they say."

Suddenly Huda changed the subject and said, "You've talked to a lot of girls. Am I like the rest of them or is there something special about me? Do you think we are the same, or am I something different?"

It was a completely unexpected question. "You're a charismatic leader," I said, and explained to her what "charismatic" meant. "You look at the political situation from a different perspective . . ."

"So are you saying I have a chance . . . that I can play an important role? Could I succeed at something like that?"

"Yes, I think so," I answered.

"Do you think other people agree with me in my society, in Palestinian society?"

"You have to answer that," I said.

"I know the answer, but I'm asking you. Because if it is unacceptable, I can convince them."

Huda wanted positive personal reinforcement from me that in the future she could be a leader in Palestinian society. We had finished talking, and on our way out she said, "Do you think there is discrimination between men and women, never mind where?"

"Yes," I said, "even in the West. Men tend to forget women's ranks and titles, but they protect their own, and heaven help anyone who forgets . . . So I let women call me by my first name, but I make the men call me 'Doctor.'" Huda burst out laughing and we parted.

CHAPTER 9

The Book of Mug Shots: "Huda Can't Talk to You Now, She's Having Her Face Done"

The exterminators came to spray Wing 2 and the day turned into a holiday for the female prisoners. They all gathered in the exercise yard and their happiness knew no bounds. They walked around linked arm-in-arm, chatted, giggled, and generally expressed their joy at being able to enjoy themselves together. Some of them were dressed in traditional clothing while others wore shirts and jeans, even tight jeans. I noticed one young woman walking around and moving her head to the music coming from her Walkman. She was buttoned up to the neck in confining clothing, but the music liberated her and she swayed to the beat of whatever it was she was listening to. It was a real girls' party, both on a different planet and identical to every other noisy collection of teenage girls.

Huda walked toward me. It was March 23, 2004, the day after Ahmad Yassin had died in a targeted killing. The previous evening I wondered whether it might not be a good idea to call off the next day's meeting, lest the prisoners riot and make interviews impossible. In the end I decided not to cancel.

I asked Huda to take me to the four month-old baby in prison with his mother. We found him lying in a padded baby carrier while a young woman wearing traditional dress sat next to him mumbling prayers.

I approached with Huda as my escort. There was no way we could pass through the bars encircling the exercise yard. I knelt down and stretched out my hand to take the baby's chubby fingers. Like Walid, a baby in the other wing, he obviously received devoted care from the women around him.

I stroked his hand and he tried to grasp my finger, like any other baby anywhere else in the world. Suddenly I heard a woman's voice calling "*Hamsa, hamsa....*" She was joined by another woman or two, and it was easy to understand that they were trying to protect the child from the Jewish woman's evil eye. I stood up and said in Arabic, "*Hamsa* for all the children in the world."

Huda stood there watching silently. Side by side we walked up a flight of stairs. I suggested she eat with her friends. I would wait for her, I said. She really wanted to be with them, and it wasn't every day they had the opportunity to eat together. They arranged trays of food—rice and meat—on mattresses in the yard and sat around them, their legs folded under them. Huda sat in the center, obviously in complete control of the group.

During the entire meal, which lasted quite some time, the girls kept talking, laughing, pushing each other gently and even singing. They didn't seem to be discussing the death of Ahmad Yassin. One of them later told me, "We sent the meal back," that is, on the previous day they had foregone a meal to protest the killing. The same thing happened some three weeks later when Yassin's successor, 'Abd al-Rantisi, also died in a targeted killing. Their entire protest consisted of foregoing a meal.

Shafiqa, the suicide bomber who did not carry out her mission, did feel it necessary to talk about Yassin's death. "I don't feel right," she said, "because of what happened yesterday. How do you feel, what do you think? After all, you met him and talked to him."

At our previous meeting I had told Shafiqa about interviewing him a few years earlier. Now she looked at me and kept waiting for an answer. I decided not to say anything, because I knew nothing I said would satisfy her, and I saw no reason to be evasive.

"I want peace," said Shafiqa after a while. "[What happened] yesterday broke all the rules... Do people think there won't be explosions? There will be. How long will we be in this cycle of blood, this river of blood?" She spoke forcefully. When I didn't answer, she changed the subject and asked me what I thought about the Geneva Accord [a memorandum of understanding between the representatives of Israel's left wing and Palestinian representatives. It never received formal recognition.]

"I keep away from politics," I answered. During all the interviews I made a point of not talking politics, and, insofar as was possible, not even directly mentioning the Palestinian–Israeli conflict, but I did allow those I interviewed to talk about it if they chose.

Shafiqa said, "If I were Israeli, and I know how to think like an Israeli... I would think that Sharon should worry about his people more, because he needs security and we, the Palestinians, need more security... Who is Ahmad Yassin? Right, he is the Hamas leader. He's an old man. When he was younger he was a fighter... I don't think Jordan or the United States will help us if we Palestinians don't help ourselves. If we're talking about a group of our people who live here, maybe they'll say there should be peace here, Geneva is necessary and we have to go back to Oslo. There will be people for and against, but how can you prove it if yesterday they killed sheikh Yassin...If Sharon leaves the Gaza Strip, it will be a good point for whoever wants peace and their leaders. [This conversation took place after Israeli prime minister Sharon had announced the disengagement plan. In August 2005, he evacuated the Jewish settlements in the Gaza Strip and some in Samaria, a disengagement process that was difficult and painful for the settlers and many other Israelis, to the point of the fear of civil war. It is still difficult to evaluate its influence on Israeli society. However, as the result of a brain hemorrhage, he has been in a coma since January 2006.] I have to think about my people's economy. The way I think is more progressive. This is already the 21st century."

She kept speaking as if to herself, and suddenly turned to me and asked, "What do you want out of all of this? Do you want something?"

Almost without thinking I said, "I want to raise my children in security in the State of Israel." Then I smiled at her and waited to see what she would say.

"If you smile at people, it means you keep your promises and so do they," she said, smiling back. "We're here and you're here. Nothing can be taken by force. You can't convince people you exist, that the State of Israel exists."

"There is nothing to convince," I said, "the State of Israel exists."

"I'm very sorry about what happened yesterday," said Shafiqa, "because he was Ahmad Yassin, and I think about it and my imagination floats upward..."

She went on to speak of other things. "There are a lot of women here who want peace, and others want to remain at war. I want peace, and to convince the girls that peace is the only solution...We can live together, we can sit and talk, and maybe even live on the same street. You have to be able to respect other opinions..."

As opposed to what might be expected from someone who had intended to carry out a suicide bombing attack, Shafiqa expressed liberal opinions, and she seemed sincere in her desire for peace. Nevertheless, I wondered what she meant when she said, "We can live together on the same street." A street in Israel or a street in Islamic Palestine? Was it a way of hinting that Israel should not be a Jewish state?

She said, "Maybe Sharon and Arafat [who was still alive at the time] are the problem. Maybe they are too old." Clearly, she saw herself as part of the younger generation which desired a genuine change. Proof of that was that she did not want her body blown to bits and spread out in a 10-yard radius. She was among the more intelligent and well-educated prisoners, but most likely not representative of the group. As far as they were concerned, she was a coward who changed her mind at the last minute, who disappointed her dispatchers, who had lost her chance to become a *shaheeda*.

❖

One day I stood in the outer yard and watched the female security prisoners preparing themselves for visits and for a photographer. On my way in the guard at the gate told me that the prisoners wouldn't have time for me because "A 'book' is being done about them, they're getting their pictures taken for themselves and for their families." I had assumed they were being photographed for security reasons and walked over to Huda's wing. There was a great deal of hustle and bustle in the exercise yard, because the women prisoners were busy making themselves look nice for their families.

Saida, an Israeli Arab girl in jail for security offenses, gave me a big grin. Huda had appointed her to help me translate from Arabic to Hebrew. "I passed my matriculation exam in Hebrew," Saida said proudly, and in fact, her Hebrew was very good indeed, as might be expected from an Israeli Arab who lived in a city with both a Jewish and Arab population. Her translations were exact, because although I have difficulty expressing myself in Arabic, I understand it pretty well. In any case, Saida knew she couldn't fool me by mistranslating.

From the outset Saida was very friendly, and even more so when I told her I had an aunt with the same name as hers. She did not really seem to believe me. I asked her why it was hard for her to imagine a Jewish woman with an Arabic name—in Iraq Saida was quite common as a woman's name, and, I said, "I think it is quite a pretty name," which brought down the barriers between us.

There was something very Israeli about her appearance: she wore jeans and a cotton knit shirt; she also expressed herself forthrightly. On the other hand, she knew how to blend in with the other prisoners quite naturally.

Her first question, through the bars of the exercise yard, was, "How were the holidays? Did you and your family go somewhere?" [This was a few days after Passover and Independence Day, when almost every Israeli with a driver's license seems to feel the need to get into a car and either visit relatives or find a place for a picnic.] I looked at her. Her hair was smooth and well taken-care of. She used a minimal amount of makeup, just pink lipstick. "You look wonderful," I said, and she was very pleased. She pointed at Huda and said, "Huda is having a facial, she won't be able to talk to you now." I laughed and said, "Maybe I could have a facial here now, then I wouldn't have to go to the cosmetician."

The "cosmetician" was one of the prisoners, a woman wearing traditional dress. She was obviously pleased at being given a professional title. Yes, she said, she liked helping the women look better.

Shafiqa beckoned to me from a corner of the yard. "I'll be there in a second," she called, and she continued a lively conversation with a friend. A few minutes later she came over and thrust her hand through the bars. If it hadn't been for the bars and walls, it might have been a normal meeting between two old friends, not between a potential Palestinian suicide bomber and a Jewish woman who might easily have been one of her victims. In any case, after the many hours of conversation and interviews we had spent together, a certain closeness had developed between us, and she not only asked after my children, but we even spoke about the possibility of my coming to visit her once she was released.

"I hope to have children some day," she said, "although it's hard to imagine how that could happen when I'm in prison. But in any case I hope to be a mother."

"On the one hand," I said, "motherhood is difficult and demanding, but on the other, it is very satisfying. Women bring life into the world."

"Yes, I understand," she said, and repeated, "I hope to be a mother some day." My immediate thought was that only a short while ago this young woman, who wanted to desperately to have children, was ready to blow herself up and kill as many Jews as she could, among them children... But I remembered that she had changed her mind and that she was among the very few who regarded the Jews she was about to kill as innocent victims. She had a great need to express herself, to talk, never mind about what, and I fulfilled that need. She was intelligent and understood the damage she had done to herself.

Our conversation was cut short by the wail of an infant, the son of one of the prisoners. The noise and excitement around us continued. Prisoners waited in line to have their eyebrows plucked and blue eye-shadow applied to their lids. The giggles and beauty tips heard on all sides reminded me of a beauty parlor or spa where conversations unique to women take place.

The prisoners attached great importance to their appearances and expressions of femininity, especially when their families came to visit, for the visits meant contact with the outside world. Even those sentenced to life imprisonment wanted to preserve their feminine appeal. A woman's desire to make herself more beautiful does not disappear regardless of the circumstances. I was reminded of having interviewed a woman accused of committing murder, famous because she was married to a respected television commentator. She told me that being in prison had ruined her skin. Although she had been cut off from her family and previous life, and was aware that there was a good chance she would be convicted of murder and imprisoned for life, at that moment what bothered her was that she had wrinkles...

It turned out that the photographer did not belong to the security establishment, but was a private individual who would later give the pictures to the prisoners' families. A large piece of white cloth had been hung from the bars, since no one wanted to be photographed with prison bars in the background. The prisoners organized themselves and got ready. They made up their faces, smoothed down their clothing, and while the other prisoners advised them on how to pose, they had their pictures taken one after another. More than once a prisoner would approach the woman about to be photographed and pose her, move her leg a little or have her sit differently. The other prisoners sat nearby, giggling and chatting.

The photographer worked quickly and the women seemed to move on a conveyor belt, like mug shots being taken of potential murderers, one after another.

Suddenly Na'ima, the deputy spokeswoman, came over and spread on the ground an enormous woolen blanket decorated with a picture of two kittens. On the blanket she gently placed a seven month-old baby, and next to him a toy car. The baby was wearing a white summer overall and had a red bandana tied around his head. They explained that the baby's mother wanted a picture of the boy for herself and her family. It was a rare opportunity to photograph the baby in his early stages of development, because prisoners are not allowed to have cameras.

The baby looked sweet with the bandana tied around his head. The women cooed and made faces so that he would smile at the camera. After he had been photographed several times his mother changed his clothing and dressed him in a tiny pair of jeans and a striped shirt. The blanket was spread out again but this time the kittens were upside down. Na'ima was unhappy with the arrangement, so she picked up the blanket and turned it around, this time with the kittens right side up and the toy car facing the camera. For a minute it was possible to forget that we were in a prison yard and not a photographer's studio.

While the others were being photographed Huda was being attended to by four prisoners, all of whom were beautifying her at the same time: one combed her hair, another plucked her eyebrows, a third tied the red bandana, which had previously been on the baby's head, around her wrist, and the fourth held a colorful rubber hair band, ready to gather her hair into a pony tail when the time came. The woman described by the Israeli media as a monster held a small mirror, which was part of a makeup kit. She didn't stop looking into it for a minute, holding it at arm's length so that the other women could continue their cosmetic duties. She only put it down when it was her turn to be photographed. As soon as her picture had been taken she lit a cigarette, holding it as usual between two fingers, like a man.

Not long before, Tali Hatuel, a pregnant Israel woman, and her four little girls had been killed by terrorists as they drove in the family car on the Kissufim road, which serviced the Israeli settlements in the Gaza Strip. I asked Huda if she had heard about it. She said, "I heard about an attack where a woman was killed, I didn't hear she was pregnant. We [prisoners] didn't talk about it, but last night the army killed four boys in Nablus. Most of the girls here know them, so you can imagine how hard it was. They came from the same neighborhood and the same Tanzim [a Palestinian terrorist organization which grew out of Fatah]."

She expressed no emotion for the woman and her daughters, only comparing their murder to the killing of wanted terrorists in Nablus. I said nothing, but she must have known what I was thinking, because she said, "Don't take what I said as something extreme. You can't judge a person. Everyone has to put himself in the other's person's place, and only then to judge him."

CHAPTER 10

The Value of Women: "I'll Never Do Anyone Any Good, Anyway"

In the maximum security wing of the prison I suddenly saw a baby crawl toward the kitchen. Instinctively I looked around for the mother, because a kitchen is a dangerous place for a small child. "Whose baby is this?" I cried as the heavy door closed behind me. A pleasant-faced woman wearing glasses picked the baby up and held it.

I walked over to her. One of the staff had taken my bag so that my hands would be free for the infant. "How sweet he looks," I said, reaching out to take him. The woman looked at me searchingly, and as though it were perfectly natural, passed the baby over to me.

"What's his name?" I asked.

"Walid. Today's his birthday, he's one year old," she answered. I later found out that her name was Samira.

"He looks so sweet, and look at those big eyes," I said. I hugged him and stroked his face. He looked at me with his enormous green eyes. I could sense he felt secure in my arms, but no matter what I did, I couldn't get a smile. I rocked him in my arms. He was wearing clean brown clothing with matching brown leather shoes. He was very interested in what was going on around him, but he obviously knew that the woman holding him wasn't his mother.

A few years previously when I was doing research in women's prisons, I saw many babies. Even though it is customary for them to remain with their mothers for the first two years, I never got used to it.

A nice-looking, black-haired woman came over. "That's his mother," said Samira. The baby looked at his mother and stretched out his arms, turning his body and face toward her and propelling himself into her arms. "There's no one like a mother," I said, "he knows exactly whom he belongs to." She smiled at me. "May God grant him health," I said in Arabic, "and good luck, and a very happy birthday," I added.

"Yes," she answered, and said "Mazal tov" in clumsy Hebrew.

The prisoners watched me carefully as I walked to the staff room where I sat and interviewed prisoners. The short meeting with the baby had broken the ice somewhat. I could tell by the way they looked at me that I was more than a "Jewish enemy," I was also another woman. It was the same kind of empathy all women share when they talk about their children.

Near the staff room one of the guards introduced himself and told me what his job was. "Tell me," he said, looking at the baby, "doesn't he have the eyes of a suicide bomber?"

"Babies are babies everywhere," I answered. "He's a lovely baby. Do *you* think he has the eyes of a suicide bomber?"

"Yes," he answered immediately, "I do, I see a suicide bomber."

It was the deadly, inhuman suicide bombing attacks that had given birth to such a statement, to the claim that the desire to become a *shaheed* was something Muslims terrorists got along with their mother's milk. Was it really so?

Generally speaking, Palestinian mothers and fathers did not want their children to die, not even if it meant many Jews died as well. The London-based Arabic newspaper Al-Hayat printed an interview with the father of a suicide bomber,[1] who mourned the death of his son and the cynical exploitation of young Palestinian men by the suicide bombing death cult. "They [the dispatchers] convinced my eldest son to blow himself up in an Israeli city . . . and that's what he did. Now they are running after his brother to convince him to do the same thing . . . " wailed the father. He called the Palestinian leaders who had come after his remaining son "snakes."

The bereaved father complained that the terrorist organizations' ideologues and clerics never sent their own children on suicide bombing attack, and said that as far as he was concerned, it was the road to death, not martyrdom. "Who gave them religious justification to send our children to blow themselves up?" he cried.

Even those who are willing to carry out suicide bombing attacks themselves reject the idea that those they love follow in their footsteps.

Fatima was a suicide bomber who was apprehended on her way to the target. The night before, she slept in the dorms at a university in the Palestinian Authority. A female student agreed to let her stay over in her room, even though she knew what Fatima's plans were [a situation not unknown in the world of terrorism]. She even agreed to become a *shaheeda* herself should Fatima change her mind.

Fatima told me about her 3-year-old nephew. "He was the most important thing in my life. If a minute went by and I didn't see him, it made me crazy. He slept in my house. He was a sensitive, softhearted child. If he saw another child cry, he would wipe away his tears. He understood things, he was never disrespectful of people older than himself because that's the way I taught him to behave. He was clean, and if he got dirty at all he couldn't stand it, someone had to clean him off. He was very smart.

"He used to ask about the paradise of the *shaheeds* all the time. In the beginning I wasn't afraid he would want to be a *shaheed* [because] he was still a baby. I could make him want to be a *shaheed* and I could make him not want to be one . . .

"If something happens to him I'll collapse. My life won't be worth anything if he dies. When he used to ask me about paradise I didn't answer. I was afraid he would begin to think about it and grow up with those ideas."

Fatima, herself almost a suicide bomber, described a compulsive thought process characteristic of drug and gambling addicts. Among the addicts themselves, the thought process is called *duda* in Arabic, a worm. She didn't want those close to her to become infected by it, and understood that the child, who was so important to her, would need to be protected from the desire to become a *shaheed*, and if he weren't, he would think about it all the time and he wouldn't rest until he blew himself up. She thought she could control her infant nephew's thoughts and desires, as if she knew which button to press to turn a baby into a future *shaheed*, although she loved him too much for that and felt she had to save his life.

Fatima repeatedly stated that she was the one who had made him think about becoming a *shaheed*, but on the other hand, she didn't hide her fear lest he grow up wanting to do just that. She did not relate to a suicide bombing attack's massively destructive impact, and the subject apparently had no meaning for her.

"Fatima," I said, "you yourself were ready to die so that you could murder Jews, right?"

"It's not the same thing," she said belligerently. "He's still a baby and I want to keep him away from it.

❖

During one of my visits to the prison, Latifa, Walid's mother, asked if she could speak to me. She got straight to the point: "I only found out I was pregnant when I was in the *zinzana* [paddy wagon]."

Latifa came from one of the villages east of Jerusalem and had an Israeli identity card. She said that before her marriage she was involved with a boy who, according to her story, got her involved in security violations. "I'm 20, I've been married for two years, and my husband, he's 21 and comes from East Jerusalem. He's at home now and I don't know where he works.

"I was with my boyfriend... After he found out I had gotten married he was investigated and he told them I wanted to go with him to an attack... Before I was married, I talked to him. When I got married, I didn't talk to him any more. You can't even say hello to a man [once you're married]...

"I went to school for nine years. I got married when I was 18. All I did was stay at home until my wedding. My husband is one of my cousins, his mother is my mother's sister. We played together when we were children, and we had only been married for two months when they took me away. I told my husband I wanted to take care of the baby in prison, the child wants only me... I'm very tired because of him... I'm still nursing... I want to go home to my husband, I want it to be me and him and Walid. What do I care about Jews and Arabs, I don't want anything. I like to do things but I can't because of Walid. He sits with me all the time, he doesn't want to be with anyone else. He doesn't want to sit with the older women [prisoners 40 years and older]. They help me, but Walid doesn't want them.

"My husband isn't religious. He doesn't want me to wear a *hijab*. He tells me to wear pants and a shirt, he say's that's good. I always loved my husband, ever since we were little children. If I'm here in prison and Walid is outside, well, I want to take care of him there too. My mother cries all the time... My husband is going crazy, he loves me... There are no problems between Israelis and Arabs where I live.

"The boy who wanted me to carry out the attack with him is now in prison himself. He's from Nablus. I don't talk to him, he never said anything to me, not even during the trial.

"I'm tired but at night I can't fall asleep. The baby sees me and comes over. He can't be outside without me. His father wants to kiss him, to pick him up..."

Latifa was afraid of the day Walid had his second birthday because according to law he would then be given to his father and she would continue serving her sentence. She kept repeating that since her marriage she had not spoken to another man, but it was clear that before her marriage she had had a very close relationship with a man who had tried to use her to carry out an attack. In any event, because of Walid, her sentence was reduced and she and her son left prison together.

❖

"It's special if a woman carries out a suicide bombing attack," said Yusra, a suicide bomber who was arrested before she could reach the site of the planned attack. She sat at the corner of the table, close to me. We had shaken hands and introduced ourselves. She was wearing a tailored, olive-green *galabiya* with green buttons down the side and embroidered sleeves. She wore a black veil which came down to her bosom. There was no way of distinguishing her figure under her clothing, but when she crossed her legs a pair of tight fire-engine red pants could be seen beneath her dress. The color of her pants didn't seem to belong to her or to the place.

The suicide bomber who carried out the suicide bombing attack in the Maxim Restaurant in Haifa, killing 21 Israeli civilians, among them women and children and six members of a single family, came from Nablus. The Palestinian Islamic Jihad claimed responsibility for the attack, although it was never verified if she belonged to the organization or if she simply volunteered to get revenge because Israeli soldiers had caused the deaths of her brother and fiancé. The pictures of her in the newspapers showed her wrapped in a black *hijab*, which entirely covered her hair, but on her sensuous lips she wore bright red lipstick, very much like the opening shots of "The Rocky Horror Picture Show."

I asked Jemila, a Palestinian social worker, active in women's rights issues, if she could explain the orthodox Muslim women's penchant for heavy makeup. Wasn't it against their religion?

"Women make up their faces despite the *hijab*," she answered, wearing Western dress herself. "Not all of them wear the *hijab*, but those who do want to show that they are still women. It's like an other alternative: OK, *hijab*, but full makeup . . . "

Neither Jemila nor the director of the women's rights organization she worked for, could state with any certainty that the Maxim suicide bomber had belonged to the Palestinian Islamic Jihad. However, on occasion even male *shaheeds* are adopted by terrorist organizations after their deaths. "When a lot of people were killed at Al-Aqsa [when the intifada began in 2000], some of them didn't belong an organization, but when they died people came from the organizations and told the families that their dead relatives had been in the organization, so that it would become famous. If an organization has a large number of *shaheeds*, it is more active and it is regarded more highly." That is, a terrorist organization's status is in part determined by the number of its *shaheeds*. Even Al-Qaeda wants as many terrorist attacks and *shaheeds* as possible as part of bin Laden's global jihad, to increase the organization's reputation. There are terrorist attacks carried out by Al-Qaeda sympathizers, such as al-Zarqawi in Iraq and the Chechens who attack Russians, and often the media make no distinction between the organizations, so that Al-Qaeda has become the first name on the world terrorist map.

Ayisha was sentenced for smuggling terrorists into Israeli territory, who intended to carry out attacks. She was a big, 21 year-old girl who wore a black *galabiya* and a gray head-covering, socks, and slippers. A heavy smoker, the smell of cigarettes clung to her clothing and surrounded her. Like many of the female prisoners who regularly used makeup, despite her traditional dress and modest appearance, her face was heavily made up, especially her eyes. Her lids were covered in metallic green eye-shadow and her long lashes had been covered with blue mascara and carefully curled.

"You made yourself up very prettily today," I said, and she smiled, happy with the compliment. Her heavy, almost provocative makeup strongly contradicted her modest, enveloping clothing. One the one hand, she broadcast the message, "Don't look at me," while on the other, it was impossible not to.

Murad told me that sometimes makeup was a compromise. The man of the house, whether husband, father, or brother, compels the girl to wear traditional Muslim dress, but is willing to overlook eye makeup, so she can express her femininity. There are other ways. "I know some women," he said, "who wear short skirts or dresses under their *galabiya*, so that even if no one sees they still know it is there and it gives them a special feeling, contact, however tenuous, with the other world."

Receiving a compliment from me made it easier for Ayisha to open up and talk. "When I was four, during the first intifada, they destroyed our house because my brother was involved in security [i.e., terrorist] activity. They told us we had half an hour to gather our belongings and leave. They closed up the house and razed it to the ground with dynamite. There were pictures of the house blowing up in all the newspapers and I remember them very clearly. I remember my mother standing there with my eldest brother, and his wife standing next to him, nine months pregnant. We only got about half of our things out of the house. The rest was buried under the rubble. My brother was in an Israeli jail and got out when the Oslo Accord was signed. He got married and lives abroad, and hasn't committed any security crimes."

❖

I first met Fatima when she was put in prison. I saw before me a small, insecure woman with a strong need for emotional contact. She chain smoked, and that annoyed me, but I didn't say anything because I wanted her to be relaxed.

She was wearing traditional clothes, a gray dress too long for her and a *hijab* sloppily set in place, with tresses of hair peeking out from under. She was very short, perhaps less than five feet. At first she was hesitant and sounded unconfident, swinging between tears and laughter as she told me the story of her life.

Fatima was 25 years old, fourth of nine brothers and sisters. Her family was defined as traditional, not religious. She described her relationship with her 15-year-old brother, Muhammad, "her little brother," as very significant. She told him all her deepest secrets, including things she kept from her parents. "We even smoked [cigarettes] together and our parents didn't know. He's the brother I love best and the one I care about the most.

"I was 25 and unmarried. I didn't like my life at home. When I was 17 I tried to hurt myself [commit suicide] twice, but they stopped me . . . Until I was 20 I wore ordinary clothes and I even used to play outside with other children, and I didn't care if they were boys or girls. [She meant she was a tomboy.] One day one of my girlfriends said, 'The way you dress and act is shameful. Find religion, and then you will be able to find a husband.' So when I was 20 I became more religious, I started wearing traditional clothes and behaving like a girl. I really wanted to get married a lot."

She became less of a rebel and more outwardly religious, but not inwardly, only as a way of improving her status and making it possible to find a husband, despite her "advanced" age, by Palestinian standards.

She finished the tenth grade and dropped out of school. She worked arranging flowers, although not on a regular, permanent basis. She also had two nonmalignant growths removed, which probably frightened her a great deal. At home there were conflicts with her parents because of the limitations they placed on her, especially the fact that they forbid her to leave the house lest people gossip that she was looking for trouble. She described her mother as neglectful, ignorant, lacking even elementary education and as not caring about her because in the eyes of the family she was weak and problematical, a girl who had to be watched all the time and restrained lest she bring shame on the family. Her father, who had worked in construction in Israel many years before, was unemployed.

Fatima told me that she had met almost no Jews at all, except for when she was a very small child and they used to go to a sewing shop in the Tulkarm region, which was managed by a Jewish woman. She said that the woman had been very nice to her and was warm and open, and always gave her candy. She expressed no personal grudge or anger at Jews resulting from direct contact. She was not politically involved, and said that the news didn't interest her. On the other hand, she said, she had heard her father complain about Hamas and accuse them of "trading in the blood of *shaheeds*." He was against suicide bombing attacks, which he saw on television, and claimed that the [terrorist] organizations were exploiting unfortunate people and turning them into suicide bombers.

"One day I left the house. I went to the area around Jenin and I saw a boy with one shoulder lower than the other getting into a taxi. He was a cripple. He looked at me and I looked at him. At that moment I fell in love with him. And I know that he fell in love with me. I told my father to arrange something so we could get married. At first my father wouldn't agree because he was a cripple and he didn't look too good. His shoulder was crooked. But my father went to his family to try and see if a wedding could be arranged. There was an argument over the dowry. His parents weren't willing to pay what my father wanted, so everything was called off and there was no wedding. I loved him but my father couldn't arrange it so we could get married. So I said, 'I'll get my revenge against my father by becoming a *shaheeda*.'"

Fatima cried as she told her story. She kept saying that the boy was her only chance to marry and her father had ruined it. She was very angry with him, and even if her mother had an opinion she couldn't express it, it was the father who decided everything. She felt abandoned by her mother, and was angry that she hadn't even tried to convince him not to be so stubborn about the size of the dowry.

She decided to take revenge, especially against her father. One day she happened to meet a Fatah/Tanzim operative who was well known in the area for recruiting suicide bombers. She knew his name, as he knew hers. Fatima asked to carry out a suicide bombing attack. "From the moment I decided to kill myself I knew I had to do it. Maybe then my father would understand."

Events proceeded quickly and Fatima had no control over them. She left her parents' house and was sent in secret to an apartment she could hide in. An older woman stayed with her all the time. "She told me it was worth my while to become a *shaheeda* and that I would go to paradise. All the time she was with me and didn't leave me alone for a second. She really behaved like a mother."

It is interesting that when the suicide bombers are women, there is usually another woman involved in their recruitment, who then stays with the potential suicide bomber, reinforces her desire to kill herself, and prevents her from changing her mind. It can either be a good friend or an older, maternal figure.

The involvement of another woman is intended to ensure that the *shaheeda*'s reputation remains spotless despite her dealings with men. However, the potential female suicide bomber is nevertheless constantly exposed to the presence of men whom she would never have met otherwise.

The explosive belt was brought to the apartment to make sure it would fit Fatima's little body. "I couldn't wear the belt and it kept falling off. It was so heavy it made me feel I was nailed to the floor... After that I was caught and they took me to prison... They exploited me... I feel so much remorse... All I want is my mother."

Fatima's sobbing was heart-rending. She stood up and fell into my arms, her head on my bosom, her whole body shaking with sobs. I couldn't help thinking that she was exactly the same size as my daughter. I tried to soothe her, gently stroking her hair. Only yesterday this confused child-woman, holding on to me like a toddler, wanted to kill my children, and now I was comforting her and trying to calm her down, and even felt sorry for her. For a long time she refused to let go of me. Finally, she sat down and said she wanted to write me a letter:

Prisoner's letter to Anat Berko

The letter reads:

To dear, honored, charming and nice

Dr. [drawing of heart] Anat

Fatima Pokemon [the nickname the prison guards gave her]

[Signature]

With honest respect and love

We want peace

[Signature]

The meeting was held, as noted, shortly after her incarceration. Being imprisoned for the first time is traumatic for almost all the prisoners, and also for a girl like Fatima, who had serious difficulties at home. I met her again several months later. She was still open and happy to meet me, but the prison's influence and the indoctrination she had undergone had left their mark. She had gone through the prison mill and now belonged to the security prisoners' subculture. The previously childish woman who had looked for a mother figure and who had been cynically exploited by wanted Fatah Tanzim operatives, no longer spoke about her personal distress as the reason for her decision to become a *shaheeda*. She now spoke of jihad and the desire for revenge as her motives for wanting to carry out a suicide bombing attack, and regurgitated what had been dictated to her by the other prisoners.

"I regard every one who is killed as my brother, and every mother who was killed is my mother. I have become much stronger in prison. I now have a stronger personality. I have learned to suffer more. On TV I saw that a [Palestinian] woman was hurt and the arm and leg of the baby in her womb were cut off."

I don't know if there was actually such an event reported or whether she had simply taken a story the other prisoners told her as her own. In any case, it was one of the local myths, and it enabled her to do a better job of expressing herself and marketing herself and the *shuhada* while spicing up her statements by recounting stories, which had little or nothing to do with the truth. However, the combination of truth and imagination works well, and Palestinian children (who later become Palestinian adults) grow up hearing stories of doubtful veracity recounted as the absolute truth, filling them with national-religious fervor.

Fatima was very relaxed, sleepy, almost apathetic, during our second and later meetings. Her face still showed signs of the boiling margarine and sugar burns she had received. She told me her life was very hard and that she missed her mother. "The only thing that could have influenced me not to become a *shaheeda* was my mother's tears. It's hard for me to think about how she's crying, but the real reason I did it was because of the verses in the Qur'an that call for jihad, Jerusalem, the pictures of Palestinian children who were hurt . . . Just as the State of Israel wants its children to be happy, we want our children to live and be happy." She went on to say that before she left for the suicide bombing attack she tried to keep a low profile so as not to draw attention to herself. But she wanted to spend more time with her family, because "being a *shaheeda* means death, it's not like a trip you come back from, so you want to be with your family a little more . . . "

She stopped talking and played with the tissue she was holding, rolling the paper into little balls, focusing intently on her fingers. Then she said, "My decision to commit a suicide bombing attack was based on my love for my nation and for Allah and on the religious issue, jihad. You can't make a distinction between them. There is a verse in the Qur'an where the prophet Muhammad says that anyone who hears a Muslim calling for someone to help the Muslims and does not answer the call is not considered a Muslim. I heard the cries of the Palestinian children and I had to hold out a helping hand.

"I have no regrets. Quite the opposite, I have become stronger in prison. When I was arrested, I was homesick and that made me regret what I had done. Now I am stronger. A *shaheed* can help 70 of his relatives, Allah will forgive them their sins and they won't go to hell. I wrote a will. My family hasn't seen it. I gave it to the person in charge of the action I was supposed to carry out. The first thing I wrote was to my parents, that when they hear I'm a *shaheeda*, they should pray and thank Allah because one way or another everyone dies, and what I did makes all Palestine proud."

It was not the first time I had heard the claim that in the end everyone dies but that it was preferable to die a little earlier as a *shaheed*.

"In the past they didn't agree that women perform *istishhad*. In my opinion, now they will send more women, there was even a case not long ago of a woman who blew herself up [she meant Reem Riyashi, who blew herself up on January 14, 2004, at the Erez crossing point in the Gaza Strip]. In any case, my life won't do anyone any good, and there are a lot of people who want to do it [i.e., carry out suicide bombing attacks] to become *shaheeds*, and nothing can stop them. They don't care if their houses get destroyed. What is important is that the nation and the homeland are not destroyed."

Then she said, "All those newspapers and the interviews with us about *istishhad* . . . Do the interviewers want to analyze the suicide bomber or to make themselves famous at his expense?"

I answered directly, saying that "People don't understand how someone kills himself in order to kill other people."

"Why don't they understand our situation?" she asked. "As far as I'm concerned, the picture is very clear. As a people, we [Palestinians] have suffered a great deal. For 75 years we have been killed, our rights have been denied, and no one helps us or makes peace. Even the occupation doesn't leave our lands. They [the suicide bombers] defend the faith and the *rasoul* (Muhammad, Allah's messenger) and they fulfill the request of the people who lost children in the war.

"I wanted to kill myself but I failed, and I was imprisoned, but prison doesn't influence me at all. Being here has only strengthened me and made me more determined. I'm not a person without feelings, or who doesn't love life, as the saying goes. I wanted to sacrifice myself for the children who would live their lives in happiness, and that was all." She watched me, waiting for a response.

"I'm not a politician and I don't suppose I ever will be," I said, "and I wish there were peace among nations. Every individual has the right to a good life." Fatima smiled, raised her hands, and said, "*Inshallah.*" Then she stood up and hugged me. I extended my hand to shake hers in parting, and she grasped both of my hands in hers and held them for a long time, her way of saying goodbye. Finally she smiled, stroked my hand, released it, and went to her room, her emotions evident on her face and body language.

I have to admit that the encounter made me emotional. In my mind's eye I could see the miniature woman I had initially met, more frightened, more like a helpless child. In the end, even the rhetoric of jihad and *istishhad* couldn't hide the weak, desperate woman inside who needed warmth and love, no matter from whom. At that moment I couldn't picture her as a suicide bomber, she was nothing more than an unfortunate woman who had been cynically exploited and now, after two years in prison, no longer dared to express her true feelings.

In June 2005, a 21-year-old female Palestinian suicide bomber was apprehended at the Erez crossing point in the Gaza Strip on her way to receive medical care at the hospital in Beersheba. The young woman's body was covered with scars, the result of a fire caused by an exploding cooking gas balloon in her house. A pious Muslim woman, she was wearing explosive undergarments with which men had dressed her. When she was caught on her way through the crossing point, she said she wanted to kill a lot of Jews. One could only surmise that the unfortunate woman's scars made her unattractive, and that she had been told that if she became a *shaheeda* she would be pretty and find a husband in paradise.

Hers was an exceptional case because her parents not only knew about her plans, but they were even there when she put on the suicide bomb. Thus, beyond the scars on her body she had terrible emotional problems, some of them caused by her having been raped as a child. Her parents used to tease her and say she would never find a husband, and participated in her decision to choose to be a *shaheeda*. It was another example of the cynical exploitation of a young woman's distress and her rejection by Palestinian society. She did not dare raise her eyes and every little thing made her burst out in tears. Even in prison she couldn't find her place, and the other security prisoners told me they walked in tiptoe around her because "everything offends her and makes her cry." When I met her I saw that she had a pleasant enough face, but on her throat were scars caused by the burns, which covered her body and destroyed her self-image as a woman.

"She can't even dress herself," the other prisoners told me, "and she keeps to herself, she thinks people are laughing at her all the time." She had apparently had emotional problems even before the attempted attack, and being in prison made life more difficult for her.

❖

"Do you want coffee?" Yusra asked me at our second meeting, and offered me a steaming cup of strong, good-smelling coffee. It was early in the morning, and many of the prisoners were still asleep. She wore a *galabiya* and a *hijab*, both black, traditional Muslim dress that covered her from head to toe. When she offered me the coffee she looked at me with her defiant black eyes as waiting for me to refuse, perhaps because I feared she had put poison in the coffee, or perhaps out of a desire to avoid the intimacy of sharing the same cup of coffee.

I told her that I liked Arab coffee with cardamom very much, it was what we had drunk at home. I sipped and complimented her on it: "Apparently you have to come from the Middle East to know how to make coffee." In fact, the long years I spent in the army forced me to become accustomed to a weak morning drink, which I sometimes thought was coffee, sometimes tea.

Taking a sip of the coffee made me feel that I had passed some kind of bravery test, and that maybe we had come closer. Only then did I take a small china cup and pour some out of my cup, saying, "Drink with me. I don't want to drink alone. You know the saying, 'Eat and drink alone, die alone.' . . . " She smiled and nodded. But we both knew we weren't two friends enjoying our morning coffee in a café, but a Jewish woman and a Palestinian suicide bomber meeting in a prison.

I asked her to tell me about her life. "I'm 20 years old. I never had a boyfriend. There is no such thing in our society. I didn't have anything, no friends, nothing . . . First I want to tell you the story of the eviction in '48 [i.e., the Arab refugees who fled the State of Israel when it was established].

My father was married to his first wife and lived in Jaffa [the southern half of Tel Aviv]. They fled from Jaffa because they had two small children. They decided to split up, each one going a different way and taking one child so that if one of them died, it wouldn't mean the whole family died. My father's wife was killed along the way. The infant continued nursing at her breast even though she was dead.

"The next day the Jordanian army came and heard a baby crying. One of them took the child, someone from a family in Jordan, and adopted him. He raised him for eight years and then my father found out about it and went to take him. His adoptive father didn't want to let my father have him, saying the child was used to him. He told the child that when he was 20 he had adopted him and then introduced him to my father, the boy's real father.

"After he became a refugee, my father fled to Nablus and my aunt, my father's sister, lived with him and brought up the two children." Yusra didn't see the contradictions in her story: first she spoke of two children, one of whom was adopted by a Jordanian, and now she said that her aunt brought up two children. Her father married after the death of his first wife, and that may have mixed her up.

"We live on the main street in Nablus. Israeli tanks passed right under my window. At first it made us very afraid, but we got used to it.

"I'm the youngest girl in the family. We are seven brothers and three sisters. One brother died as a *shaheed* when I was five, and my father died the year after. My father always used to spoil me and take me on trips to Gaza and Jordan. My brother was killed on our front doorstep. Soldiers shot him...I remember very little of him.

"My mother suffered a great deal. I'm very attached to her and I tell her everything. After my brother was killed, my father died of heart trouble. Three of my brothers were put into prison in Israel because of security problems [i.e., terrorist activities]. My mother is a broken woman. The hardest thing for us was when my brother was suddenly killed. My father died too, but he was sick, he was in the hospital. After my brother died things were very hard and then three of my brothers were arrested. That was when things at home became terrible. We were a very close family and suddenly there was what happened to my brother, and my mother and brothers took it very hard and were very upset, because there had been a special relationship between all the boys. I don't exactly remember because I was only five years old."

She took a deep breath and said, "For the Palestinian people, everything is sad..." Then she looked at me and leaned toward me, as if trying to assess whether I understood the difficulties and traumas she had experienced.

"Do you know what was hardest for me? Seeing the birds, the pigeons my brother raised, die. My brother who died as a *shaheed* raised pigeons. He loved them and took care of them. He fed them and they used to fly around him. After he died they died as well, and as a small child that had a lot of influence on me.

"So right after that, after my brother and father died, one brother was badly wounded in the neck and was treated in Russia, and three brothers went to prison because of security problems.

"Thanks to Allah, now all my brothers are married. Only my sisters, one is 39, the other is 38 and I, we haven't gotten married yet. My sisters are studying the Qur'an. It isn't acceptable in our society for a girl to have a boyfriend. Our parents promise us to future bridegrooms when we're little. People came to ask for my sisters' hand, but they weren't interested. They studied the Qur'an and didn't want to get married, there was no reason, they just stayed at home with my mother . . . I'm very attached to my mother, too. When I came home from school I told her everything that happened during the day. My mother worries a lot, and gives warmth and love. She would do anything for us, make us tea or coffee or food . . . She always made sure to make the coffee for us herself.

"I'm studying accounting at the university and I also like to get girls to become more religious. I've been religious since I was a little girl. My parents were as well. I wanted to go to Saudi Arabia on a *hajj*, but I was arrested."

Yusra had a strong need to express herself, but she could also be deathly silent, a silence filled with rage and violence ready to explode at any moment. When we first started speaking she radiated great suspicion.

"I don't know anyone who went out on a suicide bombing mission, but I heard about some who had carried out suicide bombing attacks. I went to visit *shaheeds'* families even though I didn't know them. They came from my neighborhood, so I went to visit." She paused and then said, "I wanted to be a *shaheeda* to get revenge on the Jews, because of my religion and my love of paradise. There is no difference between a *shaheed* and a *shaheeda* in paradise, except for the 72 virgins the *shaheed* gets. Paradise is the most important thing. After that, revenge. Because of my brother, who was a *shaheed*, there are 72 [sic] people who will find a place in paradise, and I wanted a higher rank in paradise and I could only get it if I was a *shaheeda*. When I volunteered to be a *shaheeda*, the most important thing was killing as many Jews as possible, never mind how. The decision to commit suicide was mine alone. If I had told someone of my decision they would have tried to stop me, so I preferred not to tell anyone.

"During the month I was waiting to carry out the attack I prayed and came closer to Allah. I prayed at night and got up early in the morning to pray, to read the Qur'an Surahs called Al-Baqarah ["The Cow"] and Al-Anfal ["The Spoils of War"]. [Her knowledge of the Qur'an was imperfect, and she was only reciting what had been dictated to her.] Those are the two Surahs, which refer to the *shahadah* and say, 'Don't think those who died and became *shaheeds* are really dead; no, they are alive!' They have children

and they can have children and they don't die, and with Allah's help I too
will get married and have children."

She smiled when she said it, and I couldn't resist the temptation to ask,
"How is it that yesterday you wanted to blow yourself up, and today you're
talking about a wedding and children?"

"It's fate. I didn't succeed in becoming a *shaheeda*, so I have to think
about other things. I'm planning to have a family and children, but I haven't
changed my mind about carrying out a suicide bombing attack. I did what
I thought was right but it didn't turn out the way I planned . . . I didn't
succeed in blowing myself up . . . Everything is in the hands of Allah [an
attitude characteristic of Palestinian suicide bombers]. If I get married and
have children, I'll teach them things like religion and becoming *shaheeds*. If
the situation remains the same, that is certainly what I'll teach them. Because
as long as we feel that our lands were stolen our opinions won't change.
There are mothers who accompanied their children on the way to actions
[i.e., suicide bombing attacks] and even had their pictures taken with them
before the action."

I asked her what she thought about the dispatchers who never sent their
own children to commit suicide. It is worthwhile to note that in March
2006, Palestinian Authority Hamas prime minister Ismail Haniya stated he
would not send his own son to carry out a suicide bombing attack, although
in almost every speech he said he would, of course, continue to send the
sons of others and would glorify them as *shaheeds*. "The dispatchers are
the brains of the actions," she answered. "They can't carry out actions
because they are wanted, so they plan them instead. The brains and the
planners, those are the ones who dispatch the suicide bombers, they didn't
come looking for me, the opposite was true: other suicide bombers besides
me look for them. Until we get our rights there will be no end to it [suicide
bombing attacks]."

What she said was reminiscent of what a dispatcher once said: "Everyone
has his job to do." Generally, suicide bomber dispatchers look for subcon-
tractors to carry out the assignment and do not come into direct contact with
potential suicide bombers. But there are people who criticized the division
of roles.

"At least everyone has the same God," I said. "You know, my family
comes from Iraq. I bet my uncles look like your uncles, and we grew up
on the same food." Once I said something similar to a dispatcher and he
grew genuinely emotional. Yusra, however, answered sternly, "You just said
something very nice, that your family comes from Iraq. You have no place
here! You can go back to Iraq." It wasn't the first time a suicide bomber or
dispatcher had told me that all the Jews in Israel should go back to where
they came from.

The dispatchers also said that the Jews should return to the Arab countries
they were expelled from, or to Europe, where they were slaughtered, but no

one mentioned the Jews who lived for untold generations in the Land of Israel. Their comments were echoed by Iranian president Ahmadinejad at a press conference in Teheran on April 24, 2006, when he said that the Jews were a European problem and ought to go back there.

"No," I said, "I can't. My family was expelled, thrown out. They threw out all the Jews. My family fled Iraq as refugees, they had nothing, they were persecuted. In Iraq they had everything, a villa, an expensive car, and they arrived in Israel with nothing. It took them years to get on their feet. I know just what my parents thought about Iraq. From earliest childhood we heard stories about how Jews were persecuted and slaughtered. My mother told us that when her mother was 11, her grandfather was taken out of his house, as were other Jews, tied up in sacks and thrown into the Tigris River never to be seen again, not even the remains of their bodies were ever found. In addition, the Iraqi secret police raided Jewish homes in Baghdad on the Sabbath. They would come in vans with cannons mounted in front and look for Stars of David or other signs that the houses were inhabited by Jews. My mother told me that my grandmother buried a silver plate engraved with a Star of David under the parsley in the garden just in time. They could hear the screams of pain and cries of sorrow from the neighboring houses as innocent Jews were abducted, tortured and killed."

"What fault is it of mine?" asked Yusra. "If you meant there was some similarity between us, well, maybe . . . if circumstances permitted . . . But you put me in prison and close the door, and it's the same with all the Jews. You think you close us off in prison, but we are close to Allah and lead our own lives. We will get compensation from Allah for all the days in prison.

The same thing was said by many other women prisoners.

"All the Jews have to leave here. Definitely . . . Why did the Jews choose the land of Palestine, anyway?"

She, like other prisoners, was totally unwilling to accept the State of Israel, regardless of its borders. I usually did my best not to get dragged into political discussions, but this time I couldn't restrain myself. "Do you know that the Israelites are mentioned in the Old Testament and even in the Qur'an?"

Her eyes glittered vindictively and she said, "It says that the Jews killed all the prophets, so what will they do to us? Surah Al-Israa' ["The Night Journey"] tells us that you shouldn't be unjust twice, like Israel. It is forbidden for a people to be unjust twice. Once the Jews killed the prophets and once they killed the Palestinians. The Qur'an also says that the Israelites will rise up, and then they will fall again . . ." Again, her knowledge of the Qur'an was far from perfect.

"I hope that you, the Jews, show your children the real picture. Just the way we Palestinians show our children both sides and allow them to judge, I hope you do the same thing. We don't encourage our children to hate the

Jews. We just tell them the truth, that the Jews killed their families, and they reach the conclusion to hate the Jews on their own."

Indoctrinating hatred of the Jews is open and well known in Palestinian society. Incitement to hating the Jews and the Western world begins in infancy and continues in every educational, religious, and social framework imaginable.

I didn't want to continue arguing with her, and simply said, "I hope we can teach our children to love, which is harder than teaching them to hate. And without brainwashing them, just teaching them to love their fellow man."

"We think differently," she said smiling, and shook my hand firmly.

The yells and giggles rose up from the yard. Someone who didn't know would think they were a group of teenage girls romping in a swimming pool and splashing each other. The women in the prison yards moved around, hugged each other, held hands, some of them calling to each other from opposite ends of the yard, others standing in corners and giggling.

Yusra continued talking, but it was hard to hear her over the noise coming from the yard. "It's more impressive when a woman carries out a suicide bombing attack, because this is the Middle East and a woman is very limited, and that makes her action special. Not only that, the Qur'an allows it, because we are in a state of war and this is jihad."

I asked her about Western clothing, which most of the female suicide bombers wore on the way to the target. "Yes, it is permissible to remove the *hijab* and wear pants. And even to go with a man and even with several men is safe, because they're the ones driving her to the attack. The goal is clear: to carry out an attack. So there is nothing to worry about when it comes to the woman's honor. When it comes to driving a woman who wants to carry out an attack, it's well known that the man only escorts her to the site of the attack and then returns to where he came from, and it's not a love tryst, or marriage or anything like that."

It was a "legitimate adventure" within a society where women are forbidden many things and limited in others.

"I didn't want to become a *shaheeda* only because of my brother, because as far as I'm concerned, anyone who is wounded or killed is my brother. I thought about being a *shaheeda* for an entire month. It was the best month of my life . . . I felt I would do something very special and that life would be more beautiful and easier . . ."

CHAPTER 11

The Terrorist's Dream: "I've Wanted to Be a Shaheeda Ever Since I Was a Little Girl"

Women suicide bombers are relatively rare in Palestinian terrorism, but as it increases, the use of women and children as terrorists does also. There are, however, similar situations elsewhere. In Sri Lanka there is an organization called The Tamil Tigers, whose women members, known as "birds of freedom," carried out about 30 percent of the suicide bombing attacks between 1987 and 2000. On April 25, 2006, a female Tamil Tiger suicide bomber pretended she was pregnant to gain entry to a military base. She blew herself up, critically wounding Sarath Fonseka, the Sri Lankan army chief of staff, and killing eight others.

In 1991 a female suicide bomber assassinated Indian prime minister Rajiv Gandhi, and the Kurdish PKK (Kurdistan Workers' Party) used women between 1995 and 1999 in their struggle against the Turks. For the female suicide bombers it was a golden opportunity to improve their status, and often the only way to find a legitimate solution for personal problems. The woman was usually escorted by a man, perhaps as gesture of respect, perhaps as a way of making sure she would go through with the attack.

In the Muslim Chechens' struggle against Russia, about one third of the suicide bombers have been women. Some of them, called "black widows," blow themselves up to avenge injured or dead husbands. Women were involved in some of the deadliest attacks, the explosion in the Moscow subway, for example. Chechen women were apparently involved in two Russian plane crashes, the attacks on the theatre in Moscow in 2002, and at the school in Beslan in 2004. Such attacks often begin with taking hostages and end as suicide attacks resulting in hundreds of deaths. In Beslan, for example, half of the victims were children and parents who had come to the school on September 1, and whole families were wiped out. In a certain sense, the female suicide bombers, without being aware of it, were the expression of a unique wave of feminism, which allowed them to improve their social status and to prove that even in traditional societies, women could take part in military struggles.

As of the writing of this book, Palestinian women have carried out ten suicide bombing attacks. The first blew herself up on Jaffa Road in Jerusalem in January 2002. She was a woman in her 30s, who when she was 16 married a cousin. She was in love with him when they married but for nine years she could not conceive a child. Her husband divorced her, remarried and fathered children. It is more than likely that her inability to conceive and realize herself as a woman and mother led her to take the desperate step of blowing herself up.

More than 20 women have been caught and arrested on their way to carrying out suicide bombing attacks, or while preparing to do so. Most of them were in their 20s, single, and had high school educations. Most of them belonged to Fatah, but some of them were in the Popular Front for the Liberation of Palestine, and some others belonged to the Palestinian Islamic Jihad. Only two women who blew themselves up in Gaza belonged to Hamas.

When a woman decides or is pressured into carrying out a suicide bombing attack, she does not consult her family because she knows they will never agree. Not telling them violates a moral-social Arab norm, because in effect, the family is pushed aside. As soon as she becomes part of a plan to carry out a suicide bombing attack, the family no longer has any influence over her, she no longer belongs to them and there is no way for her to find her way back home.

"I didn't tell my family anything ... My father would have killed me if he had known I was training with *shabbab*," said Nazima, a girl who had been forced into becoming a *shaheeda*. They even made her sign a statement to the effect that she undertook every "military action" of her own free will. That was done to prevent her family from taking to task the men she had come into contact with.

Generally, older women or friends are involved in recruiting and escorting female suicide bombers, and they keep the secret. They play a dominant role in the preparations, and one of their functions is to prevent the potential suicide bomber from having second thoughts, by force if necessary.

"She [the older woman] was like a mother, she caressed me when I was upset and said that my whole family would be proud of me and that I was bringing them honor," Fatima said.

Even the woman who carried out the suicide bombing attack at the Maxim Restaurant was recruited by women who belonged to the Palestinian Islamic Jihad. They sensed she was becoming religious, because, among other things, she had taken to wearing traditional clothing. In fact, a Palestinian Islamic

Jihad operative once told me that "For us, a woman who becomes religious is like a ninja; she even dresses like one and looks like one ..."

The motivation to carry out a suicide bombing attack varies from woman to woman, and it can be romantic, personal, or in some way related to her family. When, for example in the case of Fatima, a family prevents or does not agree to a romantic relationship, regardless of what the two young people want, the matter ends there. Shafiqa, on the other hand, had no father and felt abandoned when her mother remarried when she was 10 years old. "I was very angry with my mother," she said. "She deserted me and remarried, even though she knew that my father's family would take me from her [if she did] ..."

There were also instances of female suicide bombers from refugee camps who were apparently unwed and pregnant, or had reputations for being wanton. They were in great danger, their lives threatened by family members who wanted to "protect the family's honor." A suicide bombing attack would be a respectable way out for her and her family: honor instead of shame and humiliation, and she would save herself from being murdered by relatives. Apparently the woman who blew herself up at the Gaza border crossing was such a person. According to certain newspaper accounts, her husband and another man, who was a Hamas member, sent her to carry out the attack because she was suspected of having had an extramarital affair, and in such cases, the merest whisper of a rumor is sufficient. Presumably, that was the reason Hamas, which generally opposes suicide bombing attacks carried out by women, gave its blessing.

Nevertheless, most of the women who remained alive said their main motives were religion and the desire to participate in the national struggle. Even Fatima, who cried and regretted her actions when she was incarcerated, had, within a few months, adopted a different outlook and was proud of what she had done, at least when other people were listening.

No psychopathological analysis of female suicide bombing terrorists can be performed here. But it should be mentioned that at least one young woman (from Bethlehem) arrested on her way to an attack said that she wanted to commit suicide because her husband was violent with her and raped her. Carrying out the attack would have wiped the slate clean for her and brought respect and money to her family, and she would not be considered as having committed suicide for reasons of personal distress, *intihar*, which is forbidden by Islam, but rather *istishhad*.

In some instances, the main motive is vengeance, but it is often accompanied by a personal or family problem. That was the motive for the attack carried out on February 27, 2002, by Darin 'Eisha, who blew herself up at the Maccabim checkpoint near Modi'in. Hiba Daraghmeh, who blew herself up at the entrance to the shopping mall in Afula, near Haifa, on May 19, 2003, apparently wanted revenge for the imprisonment of her brother and the wounds he received when he was resisting arrest. Before blowing herself up on October 4, 2003, Hanadi Jaradat said she wanted revenge for the deaths of her brother and fiancé.[1]

Yusra also spoke of revenge and the desire to kill Jewish children. "Yes," she said, "I would blow myself up in a kindergarten because of what you did to Muhammad al-Dura..." He was an 11-year-old boy killed at the beginning of the second intifada at the Nezarim checkpoint in the Gaza Strip, although it was never conclusively proved that the shots that killed him were fired by Israeli soldiers and not by Palestinian terrorists themselves.

Sometimes the nationalist motive is part of a family pattern. Abir decided to carry out a suicide bombing attack after her husband was wounded by IDF fire. Her brother carried out a suicide bombing attack in Tel Aviv and Darin 'Eisha was her cousin. A deep sense of identification with suicide bombing relatives and their glorification after the attacks lead others in the family to adopt the same behavior patterns.

The nationalist motive cannot always be distinguished from the religious. Some of the female suicide bombers were newly religious women who wanted to become *shaheedas* as part of the "return to Islam." They almost certainly received indoctrination in the mosques and study groups. That granted, the religious motive is not always dominant among female suicide bombers and not even among the males. Only in one case, that of Hiba Daraghmeh, did her father claim that religion was one of the factors influencing her decision to become a suicide bomber. For the other women there was almost always another factor, personal or familial.[2] Daragmeh began to turn to religion after she had been raped by an uncle, her mother's brother, when she was 14 years old. The secret was kept by the family so she could find a husband. That is, outside the family the secret was kept, but eventually her mother told a newspaper reporter that the girl's world had been completely destroyed. Since the rape she had enveloped herself in traditional clothing, covered her face with a veil and even wore long gloves. She hid herself to such a degree that she would look for an isolated spot to eat and only then remove her veil.

Teenage rebellion may also be a factor in suicide bombing attacks for both sexes. Sometimes it seems that the women pressured into becoming suicide bombers are actually adolescents looking for excitement and adventure. The dispatchers know how to channel rebellion into terrorist activity. There were echoes of that in the stories of Fatima and Nazima. One aspect of such a rebellion is overthrowing parental authority. A significant blow is given to the father's patriarchal standing when his daughter is recruited for terrorism. He is made contemptible, not only in his own eyes but also in those of society as well. He has been circumvented, he has not been respected, and his daughter has been taken from him. He has lost his power as a man to instill fear; he is seen as weak and unable to protect his family. His agreement has not been required or even allowed when usually he has the last say in everything his daughter does. If she does not die her worth will decrease because she evaded the supervision of her father and family before she was placed under her husband's authority ...

Suicide bombers do not require any military skill, complicated training, or prolonged instruction. Sometimes only a few hours are sufficient from the time the suicide bomber is chosen until he—or she—is sent to carry out the attack.

Shafiqa, the suicide bomber who changed her mind, said, "I was in the car with a 16-year old boy. The two of us were supposed to blow ourselves up in the same [general] area. When we got there, I asked him if he was certain he wanted to [do it] ... By then I didn't know what I wanted ... It pained me to think that such a young boy was going to die ... He was only 16 ... He didn't say anything all the time we were in the car. He didn't speak at all. He was shy, he didn't even look at me when I spoke to him ... We only met just before we were out to leave for the attack ..."

Shafiqa was only 20 years old but there was something maternal in the way she described her young partner. "Shafiqa," I said, "you yourself wanted to blow yourself up, why did you care about what someone else did?"

"I'm a special case," she said. "I felt sorry for him. He was only a boy, what had he seen of life? I could also see that he didn't know why he was going to do it. He didn't say anything, he was closed off within himself and sad ... I wanted ... I felt the need to rescue him ... He stopped talking and I couldn't get through to him. He was focused on what he was going to do ...

"They got the boy ready beforehand ... They prepared each of us separately. We met only two hours before the attack. I had never met him before ... He looked younger than he really was, like a child. I couldn't stop thinking about how young he was, and about how he hadn't lived at all and about how he really didn't know what he was doing to himself and his family." Possibly her last-ditch attempt to stop him from killing himself influenced her and made her change her mind before it was too late.

"I wrote a will, a letter to my relatives ... I gave them everything ... Not something specific. But my family didn't read the will because in the end I came home and took it so they wouldn't see it. I gave all my money to the man who recruited me ... What do I need money for if I'm going to die?"

She looked at me and we both started to laugh. "I don't believe it," I said, "are you saying that they not only recruited you to kill yourself, but you paid them to let you do it?" In addition, according to some of the indictments, sometimes potential female suicide bombers are exploited sexually as well, and sometimes they agree to it because in any case, they are going to die, so they have nothing to lose.

Shafiqa laughed to herself and said, "It's true, now it does sound funny. It's a good thing I'm smarter now than I was then. But it's the truth, the people who recruited me and dispatched me used and abused me. They said that in any case, after I became a *shaheeda* I wouldn't need money because

I would be dead, so it was best that I gave them my money. They talked to me about paradise and about the attack."

"How much time passed from when they recruited you until you were on your way to the attack?" I asked.

"I didn't even have time to think. Maybe two days...There was a boy who asked me, when we were alone once, if I could be a *shaheeda*. I didn't want to answer immediately. I told him I had to think about it. He told me to think about it and get back to him. I knew the boy who had sent me, we had met before, we were friendly. He, the one who recruited me, knew a boy, someone important to me, who had performed *istishhad*, and said that he knew me, I mean the one who recruited me, through him, the one who wanted to be my fiancé, and then the Israeli army killed him with a helicopter.

"Yes, he wanted us to be engaged, but I kept saying no. He asked my uncle. I was afraid that if I married him he would die because of his activity [i.e., terrorist activity]. I thought I would meet him in paradise, the man who was killed."

Shafiqa spoke of two men in her life in an intimate and relatively more open way than was usual for an Arab girl. The boy who wanted to be her fiancé was killed, and then there was the other, the one she met in the Internet chat room and with whom she had a virtual romance.

"Our parents don't understand anything about computers and they don't know who we're talking to," one of the prisoners said.

"It took me a long time to decide," said Shafiqa. "It was wonderful to say good-bye to life. I felt I was up in the clouds from the moment I knew I was going to become a *shaheeda*." A sensation of euphoria is described by suicide bombers, male and female, about the period between the decision to become a *shaheed* and the attack. It is an expression of their sense of liberation from an unhappy life and a "high" caused by the decision to carry out "the act."

"When I came home after I hadn't done anything I was depressed. They arrested me the next week..." she said. The fluctuations between ecstasy and the depths of despair recurred in the conversations of suicide bombers who remained alive for whatever reason, either because they were caught or because they had changed their minds.

"So why didn't you detonate the device? You were already at the site of the attack. The boy had already blown himself up, killed and wounded Israeli civilians, why didn't you do the same?"

She thought for a moment before answering. "I thought about a lot of things just then. I saw a woman with a little baby in a carriage. And I thought, why do I have to do this to that woman and her child? The baby was cute and reminded me of my nephews, just children. I looked at the sky and thought about Allah. And something inside me said 'No, I don't have to do this, I won't be doing something good for Allah.' I thought about the people who loved me and about the innocent people in the street . . . It was a very difficult moment for me and I had a very hard decision to make."

She spoke of the difficult times in her life: "I don't want to die . . .I called the people who had sent me [and asked them] to come and take me back . . . there was the attack [the suicide bombing attack carried out by her partner, the 16-year-old boy] and there was a big mess . . . They hung up on me, they told me that lots of people were waiting for me to blow myself up, so I had better do it . . . I cried and begged them to take me back to my village . . . I was in the middle of a big Israeli city and the boy had blown himself up. I didn't know what to do. So I called them, I called them three times until they finally came to get me, and then the one who had sent me out said, 'Maybe Allah chose this for you, chose life, maybe it's better than death . . .'"

"So in the end, what were you thinking about when you knew you were going to die?" I asked.

"I wasn't thinking about anything, not about blowing myself up and not about the Jews. Right before the attack all of a sudden I began to feel sorry . . . I thought about Allah, that if he thought it was good for me to die on that day he would take my soul. I thought about the innocent people in the street and about the mother and the baby in the carriage . . ."

Often those I interviewed, men and women alike, spoke about Allah as a real entity who had the prophet Muhammad, another entity, standing next to him. Shafiqa transferred the responsibility from herself to Allah with the feeling that any decision would be in his name and in accordance with his will.

"I started wearing a *hijab* before the man I knew died, and I continued doing so . . . I don't know, I think about taking it off, I don't know, a lot of things have changed . . . Two months before I met the man who sent me to carry out the attack, I became stronger in my religion . . ."

Shafiqa hinted that she was not entirely comfortable with her new interest in religion and that she was still thinking about it, but in prison she was afraid to change her appearance and had decided to retain traditional dress. "I could see that a lot of people had different opinions about the fact that I had become more religious. My uncle asked me why I was wearing a *hijab*, started wearing it a month before the action, [I mean] the attack I was supposed to carry out. He and his family lived on the second floor of our house. I told him I wanted to know more about religion . . . and the whole family was suspicious of me. I told them they had nothing to be suspicious about, that I wasn't thinking about a way to die, that people who commit suicide think only about themselves and about life and not about their families. When I told my family that they believed that I wasn't going to do anything . . ."

Very often the family of a potential suicide bomber senses changes in the offspring and can help prevent the attack and their deaths by contacting the authorities. That was also revealed by the investigation of the suicide bombing attacks in London on July 7, 2005: the parents of one of the terrorists appealed to the police and said they were afraid of what their son was going to do and feared for his life. Among the Palestinians as well there were cases of parents who reported the disappearance of a son or a daughter, fearing for their lives and not wanting them to become *shaheeds*. Parents want their children to live but are also afraid that the family will suffer, that the Israeli army will raze their house and they will not be able to receive permits to enter Israel to work, etc.

Suddenly she smiled and said, "I saw you talking to Huda, our spokeswoman. What did you think of her?"

"She's very nice," I answered, knowing that whatever I said would influence our conversation. Happiness flooded Shafiqa's face. "Yes, she's my friend," she said. Claiming friendship with Huda increased Shafiqa's status among the prisoners. She felt better when I had a good word for a significant figure in her life.

"I spoke to my aunt about Ayat al-Akhras [who carried out the suicide bombing attack in a supermarket in Jerusalem, March 29, 2002]. Why did she do it? I talked about it with my uncle as well, and even with my friend, Alfred. He said she was a nice girl, he said that she was young [she was 18] and shouldn't have done it. I went to her house to see her family. It was important for me to visit the families of *shaheeds* before I performed the act." Visiting the houses of *shaheeds* and spending time with their families was reported as common practice by potential suicide bombers who were arrested. She went back to talking about her own life. "My father was killed in a car accident the same year I was born. I was just a baby when he died and I never knew him. We used to live in Jordan. I was an only child. I lived with two aunts and a grandmother, I love them a lot, they brought me up. I miss my mother. I haven't seen her for four years. I left her when I was 10. She married someone else and I felt that although she did it to better her own life, it hurt me when she took another man to replace my father."

"But Shafiqa," I said, "you said your father died when you were a baby. Shouldn't your mother be allowed to remarry after 10 years?"

"But I never expected her to do it when I was 10. What makes me angry is that she chose a new husband and not me. Now I can say it was a good thing for her, but it meant that even though I was a child I was separated from her and went to live with my grandparents. I couldn't stay in the same house with a new husband, and my mother chose a new husband. She knew she was giving me up and she chose him anyway, and I couldn't forgive her. She made a decision about her life—her liberty—and, well, I took my liberty. She has no right to tell me what to do or not to do. I have a half-brother, he's 13 years old, I met him when I was in Jordan and he talks to me on the phone. I don't like him too much ... I don't know, I don't feel he's really my brother. Maybe when I get older I'll have feelings for him ... I view him as a child, he's nothing special as far as I'm concerned. He's the result of the relations my mother had with another man, not my father. My relationship with my mother is very superficial even though she loves me a lot and buys me clothes, but they don't mean anything to me ..."

Shafiqa's pain was evident when she spoke about separating from her mother. She only spoke about her after we had had many long conversations. Arab customs oblige a mother, divorced or widowed, to abandon the idea of remarriage if she wants to raise her children herself. Deciding to remarry is a fateful decision because it almost always involves ceding the right to raise children from a previous marriage, and the children will know that she prefers a "strange man" to them. They will always belong to their biological father or to his family.

Shafiqa never overcame the trauma of being separated from her mother, especially since shortly thereafter her mother gave birth to another child, fathered by the man who in Shafiqa's eyes had replaced her father. Her compensation was two unmarried aunts in their thirties who took care of her, and her grandparents. In fact, she said, "I love my unmarried aunts because they think only about me ..."

It was difficult for Shafiqa to talk about it, and she said, "What I miss is the university, my freedom and my boyfriend ..."

I laughed and said, "Finally there is someone here who talks about 'her boyfriend.' So far, every time I ask about a boyfriend, I'm told that there is no such thing in Arab society and that it's shameful to talk about such things. Everyone seems afraid to talk about relationships with boys."

Shafiqa was one of the few Palestinian women who ever spoke of having a male friend and regarded it as perfectly legitimate. She even used the English word "lover," although probably without the sexual connotation.

She smiled and said, "I know what you're talking about. [In our society] it's a problem. But today we all use the Internet to communicate. Sometimes it is easier to talk about intimate things with someone who knows you and sometimes with someone who doesn't know you. Maybe the person you write to can help you in some way ..."

For Shafiqa the Internet was not only a means of contacting the outside world and allowing herself a relationship considered forbidden by Palestinian society, such as a direct or even romantic relationship between a man and a woman. She could also use it to call for help, to contact someone who would listen to her without being subjected to inspection.

Of her "boyfriend" she said, "We've been together for four or five years. He talks to my aunt. One way or another, we're engaged ... He's 27 and lives in Kuwait, and we use the Internet to contact each other. I exchange emails with him every night. I've only seen him three times, and that was when I visited my mother. He can't come here. Only my aunt has spoken to him on the phone. She trusts me, she's like a friend. We have secrets we share with each other, and we tell each other everything. I told her everything about my boyfriend, you know what I feel, Doktora Anat."

She seemed to be waiting for an approval of her feelings, an expression of female solidarity. "Don't call me 'Doktora Anat,' just 'Anat.' It's only important that men don't forget the 'Dr.' You know why? Because they usually forget titles when they talk to women. They never forget their own, however . . ." It was the same thing I had said to Huda.

Shafiqa burst out laughing. "I never thought about it," she said. "OK, that's what I'll call you, Anat. You know, I don't think deeply about things. I don't know, I even thought I would go to hell . . . When I changed my mind it was because I thought I would never get out of hell if I killed innocent people, if I caused the deaths of people who were just walking in the street. I know that Allah forbids that."

❖

One of the reasons Shafiqa changed her mind was the thought that it was forbidden to kill the innocent. Suha had completely different reasons. She was 19 years old when I first met her. She had been arrested when she was 17¹/₂, when she and a classmate were on their way to an attack.

"I spoke to someone from the camp, a man who was about 30. I told him that I wanted to carry out a suicide bombing attack. At first he refused. He said I was underage and told me to go to school. Later he suggested I do other military work [i.e., engage in terrorist activities], but not a suicide bombing attack, but I wouldn't give up. I told him that I wanted to be a *shaheeda*."

Suha was a pretty girl with a slightly round figure wearing a *hijab* and very tight jeans; her face was innocent of makeup. I noticed that her nails were bitten to the quick.

"My mother was the only person I was afraid I would hurt if I became a *shaheeda*," she said. "My life outside was like anyone else's. I don't take things to heart. My mother is my best friend, but I'm friends with my father, too. My sisters are married. At home it was just my 15-year old brother and myself. It was nice at home, we like to laugh, there was a lot of warmth. They spoiled me more than any other child, especially my mother. I had a lovely childhood in spite of the first intifada. It interrupted my schooling, I went to school one day and then the next day I didn't, but the years in elementary school were very nice." She laughed and it was obvious she felt comfortable talking about her home and school.

"I went to an all-girls school and I didn't even have time to do matriculation exams because I was arrested after I wanted to be a *shaheeda*. My girlfriend also wanted to be a *shaheeda*. It was our secret and we talked about it a lot," she said through her giggles. I smiled and said, "Do you want to tell me that instead of doing homework you decided to blow yourselves up? Was school really so boring?"

She burst out laughing. Her lightheartedness was difficult to understand. Here was a girl who planned to blow herself up and to kill other people in the process, and now she was in prison and all she could do was laugh.

"It wasn't so terrible. What I didn't do then, my matriculation exams, I'll do now, in prison," she answered.

"Did you always laugh so much?" I asked in all seriousness.

"Yes," she said. "I was always happy and smiling, but during the days I knew I was going to die, I wanted to spend more time with my family. I didn't want them to know I had decided to commit suicide, but I became closer to Allah and I prayed more ..."

She spoke rapidly, tapping her foot a little nervously. She was restless and kept moving all the time. "Those were the last days of my life. That's what I felt. I tried to behave normally, to live a normal life so that no one at school would sense anything ... But I became closer to my mother. She was the only one who could have made me change my mind ... My mother has good feelings, she has a good heart, she loves me more than my brother and sisters. She loves me most of all. She always takes care of me and of the house ... There were just the four of us at home."

A year after our conversation her mother died of heart failure. The other prisoners told me that Suha collapsed and cried for days. Her mother had come to visit her only 2 days before her death. I went to her room to comfort her. I told her that I knew from personal experience how terrible it was to lose a parent. She became so emotional she almost cried, and nodded.

"Mother" was a word often repeated with an intensity impossible to describe. Not only the female suicide bombers, but also the males and even the dispatchers spoke with terrific yearning for the enchanted moments of life with their mothers. In 2005, even a PKK female suicide bomber whom I chanced to talk with told me that on her way to an attack deep inside Turkey, the only thing that could have changed her mind was thinking about her mother. "Not my father, only my mother ..." After she had been caught and was sentenced and there was no way for her to go home, she said emotionally that she longed for her mother.

In October 2005 the Israeli army asked the mother of a wanted terrorist who had barricaded himself in his house to surrender. She did so and he gave himself up without a shot being fired.

The mother's special status in Arab society is very interesting. She is more important than other women in a society in which women are inferior and often placed in humiliating situations. Even Ahmad Yassin stated that "the world is under the heel of mothers" who suffer and endure a daily battle for the sake of their families.

"I wanted to become a lawyer and even my father wanted me to become one ... He's a good father, because in our society a lot of fathers don't want their daughters to study anything ... As far as my father was concerned, studies were the only thing that could help a girl ... The whole family used to go on trips to Israel. I was in Haifa, Netanya and Jaffa. I love Jaffa because my grandfather and grandmother come from there ... How would you like to visit me in the Balata refugee camp near Nablus?" said Suha, and burst out laughing. "I wouldn't if I were you ... If you come visit me in Balata you might not get out alive ... You know, people in refugee camps think dangerous thoughts.

"I didn't know if my friends would be angry with me for becoming a *shaheeda* or if maybe they would follow in my footsteps. I've wanted to be a *shaheeda* ever since I was a little girl. I was convinced on the inside that I wanted to be a *shaheeda*. I love the idea of dying as a *shaheeda*, really, to die. Even before I was 15, during the first intifada, I thought about it." She spoke with great pathos and conviction, as if suddenly something had made her serious.

Suha continued speaking while biting the little that was left of her fingernails. "I wanted to be a *shaheeda*. It was because of the land. The *shaheeds* defend the land, they don't care about themselves, about their bodies, they only care about the land and their country."

"Why do you bite your fingernails so far down? It looks terrible. It isn't healthy. You have beautiful hands, you should do something about it." For some reason she was touched. Perhaps she was crying out for some kind of maternal care, never mind what kind. Suha the potential suicide bomber took both my hands in hers and looked at my nails. "Yours are long," she said without releasing my hands. After looking at them for a long time she turned them over and looked at my palms. She grasped my hands firmly, as though trying to draw strength from them. The mask of the girl who had wanted to be a *shaheeda* slipped and the bloodthirsty terrorist became a frightened adolescent who was trying to find herself.

She looked at me and I felt her soul crying out. She was looking for a mother figure, and what I said about biting her fingernails made her feel that someone cared: otherwise, why would I have said anything? "I thought I would reach paradise, that I would be Suha in paradise," she said in a spoiled little girl's voice.

"And what do you think now?" I asked. "If you had another chance, would you still want to carry out a suicide bombing attack?"

She shook her head as if waking up, trying to make sure she didn't say something forbidden. "No, I don't want to answer that ... I wanted to make a present for each of my relatives and I thought about buying teddy bears for my friends ... So they would remember me ...

"Will you come visit me again? When? I want you to come, I like you."

CHAPTER 12

Double Standard: "Sure, I'd Attack a Kindergarten! I Am Able to Look at Your Children—and Explode!"

My children were worried about my being exposed to danger during my visits to prisons, and they decided to write to the prisoners, especially the potential female suicide bombers, with whom I had the most contact. When I told Huda about it, she said, "Tell them that after Sheikh Yassin and Rantisi were killed [both belonged to Hamas and both died in targeted killings in the spring of 2004], the situation was very difficult, and even so, I watched Maccabi [the Israeli basketball team] on TV. I like the way they play, and when they won everyone cheered, and I was very pleased [with the victory]."

I told both Samira and Huda, the wing spokeswomen, that my children had questions for the women prisoners. By then I had visited the prison many times and the women were used to me. They even complained to me about things, like the lack of specific feminine hygiene products in the prison commissary. The prison staff took care of their requests in short order. Feminine hygiene products flooded the commissary, there were more brands of soap, shampoo, and cosmetics, for even in prison there was a demand for them.

After those problems had been solved I asked Samira to relay my daughters' questions to a number of the female prisoners, and to participate herself, to which she agreed.

I started by asking Fatima to answer the questions posed by my daughter Keshet, who was then nine years old. Young children are particularly affected by suicide bombing attacks, and she had erected a tent in the living room, a safe place at the center of the safest place in her life, and hung a sign on the opening which read "No suicide bombers allowed."

Her questions were the following:

How would you feel if the situation were reversed, that is, if you were a new generation of children living in Israel and there were attacks, for example, if I were a woman who wanted to attack you?

Do you have pity, even a little, for the children who almost died?

If they sent you to blow up a kindergarten, would you agree to do it?

Did someone force you to commit suicide?

Why did you want to do it?

Even after all this time in jail, do you still feel remorse?

What would you say to a Jewish child living in Israel today if he asked you why you wanted to be a suicide bomber?

What important thing was taken from you that made you want to be a suicide bomber?

Do you have any regrets?

"Ahh," said Fatima and smiled, "She's nine, she's just a little girl. Tell her that if I'm in Israel I love Israel, if I'm in Palestine I love Palestine." The translator left the room for a moment, and I asked Fatima to continue. I told her I spoke a little Arabic because my parents came from Iraq.

"Good for you," she said. "I love Iraq a lot, now and before. I don't believe what they said about Saddam ... Now I'm a Palestinian ... I love Palestine and your child loves Israel. If I were in her place I would be very angry about an attack, the same feeling she has now."

All of a sudden she realized what she had just said and changed her tone. "I'm speaking of myself as an Israeli, but it's really occupied Palestine. There is no such thing as Israel. As an Israeli, she should convince herself that the land of Palestine has been occupied, and there has to be an action [i.e., terrorist attack] against the occupation."

"Wait a second, Fatima" I said. "Try to give a logical answer. The question was what would happen if you were an Israeli child and she wanted to carry out an attack that would hurt you."

She softened and dropped the slogans. "If I were very little I would be afraid, I would have all kinds of fears ... I would be very surprised, and maybe I would go into shock. Or I would remember the day forever. It develops the way children think, hatred, revenge ..."

Again hatred overcame her. "No, we have no pity for children. You know what? They never pitied out children and I'm simply returning the favor, feel what we feel! ... Yes, I *would* attack a kindergarten, because a child the same age as yours died. Nihar was her name, and just as she wrote something on the blackboard a bullet hit her neck and she was killed. A lot of attacks happened in schools. In Jenin three children were killed and they weren't even four years old. It made me think, an eye for an eye, a tooth for a tooth ...

"No one forced me to go on a suicide bombing attack. I saw my country needed someone who would sacrifice himself, so I did it." Without a doubt, a year in prison had completely changed the girl who wept that she had been exploited by the Fatah/Tanzim because her father wouldn't let her marry the boy she wanted.

"I went to carry out a suicide bombing attack to defend Islam, to defend the nation ... I make a sacrifice so that others will live better lives, and to go to paradise ... There is a [Qur'an] verse that says that the pleasures of this life are worthless, and what remains is the end of days, and that is better ... [From here she waxed eloquent and described paradise in glowing terms.] I'm not sorry I wanted to carry out a suicide bombing attack, there is nothing for me to be sorry about ... Allah will reward me for every day I spend here in prison. I will be rewarded for every fraction of a second and every breath I take. Allah will take everything into account and reward me. Allah has taught me patience and I can withstand such blows, and I love my family and want to go back to them."

Many of the female terrorists spoke about Allah in a very personal way, and expected to meet him and Muhammad face of face in paradise.

I again asked why she wanted to commit suicide. Fatima answered, "For the same reason I said before. If it happens that I make a Muslim out of a Jewish child, so that he can see what Islam is and how good it is, I would do it." She raised her voice until she was practically screaming, placing her hands on her bosom and then turning them this way and that in the air for emphasis.

"Not every person is willing to be a *shaheed*, and that is the will of Allah. My answer is this: as the Jewish child loves Israel, which is his country, I love Palestine and its lands and I don't want anyone to take it away from me." She finished with a great sigh of relief.

I continued asking the prepared questions. "What important thing was taken from me? My nation was taken away. The smile was snatched right off the faces of the children of Palestine. Like a small child who likes to sit tranquilly in school, I want the same thing. During the first intifada they took away my childhood ... and didn't let me be happy."

Having to concentrate on the questions seemed to make Fatima excited and emotional. She recited all the answers she had learned in prison. Just as I got to the last question, whether she had any regrets, the silence was broken by the rising call of a female muezzin, "*Allahu Akbar*. ['Allah is great']."

Fatima was silent for a moment while she chose her words: "I feel no remorse. I feel disappointment. It was a *fashla* (screw-up), I failed, because I wanted to do something for the children whose fathers had been killed before their eyes and the sister [of the father] who died before him. The children were afraid of the planes, the tanks, the army."

❖

I asked Yusra the same questions. She only managed to answer in slogans. She answered the first question, about the situations being reversed, as follows: "Since we are a Muslim country, no one would ever consider the possibility that anyone would do something against us, because Allah is with us. The person in the front line, the Palestinian man, is always in the front line, but opposite him is an Israeli soldier, but he can't stand up against us because we have something stronger ... If it were the other way around, we would be very angry with those carrying out the attacks, the people who hurt us. We would be very sorry about the people who got hurt in attacks against us." After a pause she said, "Let's try to end it all by doing it our way, by finding new believers in Islam and then the attacks against us will stop, because it's Islam."

Trying to make Yusra feel sorry for the Israeli children killed by Palestinian terrorists was like waving a cape in front of a bull. "No, I have no pity at all! What really gets under my skin is that I see that your children are happy and ours aren't. Our children were killed, we lost children, and the other side has to lose them too."

The other side does. Between the beginning of the Al-Aqsa intifada (September 2000) and December 2005 there were 146 suicide bombing attack which killed 525 Israelis and wounded thousands. Of the 525, 140 were children.

Not only was it evident that Yusra found it hard to cope with the questions, they also seemed to increase her desire to vent her anger and hatred, especially at children. Perhaps part of her rage was caused by the fear that she would never be a mother. She was not the only female terrorist who reacted that way to children.

When asked if she was prepared to attack a kindergarten, she shifted in her chair as though trying to decide if it was a good idea to answer. Finally she said, "I don't want to answer. I see those who fell as *shaheeds*, your child sees a lot of people dead on your side, but she doesn't know anything of my side. The Palestinians see both sides."

As far as matters are reflected in the Palestinian media, there is no basis in fact for the claim that Palestinians see both sides. Palestinian television deliberately demonizes Jews and Israelis. Because of my work I watch a lot of Palestinian TV, and my youngest daughter once watched with me and was surprised to note that there were no children's programs, only scenes of attacking Israelis. "Don't they have lives?" she wanted to know.

Yusra continued, "As soon as the Israeli infant grows up he will take arms against us ... Of course I would attack a kindergarten ... I can watch your children eating and playing and blow myself up in the middle of them. Once in the Gaza Strip they shot at children in a school and threw [tear] gas at them." In the meantime, in August 2005, the Israeli settlements in the Gaza Strip were evacuated and the entire area was turned over to the

Palestinian Authority, yet the terrorist attacks continue. Since then, more than 560 rockets and mortar shells have been fired at Israeli population centers in the western Negev.

"Do you think," I asked, "that the Israeli security forces deliberately try to hurt civilians? Sometimes, at least, Palestinian civilians are harmed inadvertently, because gunfights take place with civilian neighborhoods where wanted terrorists are hiding."

"Yes, I think the Israeli army deliberately tries to hurt us," she answered. "They have only one goal, to harm every Palestinian, man, woman or child, it makes no difference." She really seemed to believe what she was saying.

She answered the questions on the list one by one, stressing the fact that no one had forced her into carrying out a suicide bombing attack. "We carry out those attacks because of paradise. We imagine it as a very beautiful place, pastoral, and hope to enter ... The situation [for us] is not easy ... Every day people are wounded, every day people are killed."

Talking about paradise stimulated her, and her words were accompanied by excited gestures. Her voice as well, which had previously been monotone, became more animated.

"I don't regret anything," she said. "On the contrary, prison should strengthen me. It strengthens me and all the girls."

As to what she would answer the Jewish child who asked why she wanted to commit suicide, she said, "In the first place, I would show him the pictures of the Palestinians who were killed, of the children who were hurt. This land is ours, this country is ours. I would tell him about how much we suffer ... Maybe I would conduct an experiment. If he held something in his hand, I would take it away by force and see how he reacted. I would show him that it's the same with us, we had something and it was taken away. It's only a natural reaction, when it happens you feel you want to explode ... Maybe I would let him sit down and talk to Palestinian children his age."

Her comments reminded me of what Sheikh Yassin had told me, that "justice is justice all over the world, that is, I take your watch and say let's reach a peaceful agreement, and you say good, but first give me back my watch," although by "watch" he meant the State of Israel. Anyone who has any doubts as to the Palestinian terrorist organizations' real aims should look at their insignia, where "Palestine" is depicted as the area covered by the West Bank, the Gaza Strip, and the entire State of Israel. However, the comparison between the Palestinian–Israeli conflict and a children's squabble is a recurring theme among Palestinians.

Yusra said, "There's no hope of peace. As far as we're concerned, it's in the hands of Allah. As long as things stay the way they are, there's no peace, there won't be peace. If I see someone living in my house, I won't be able to go on living. It's the same thing, the State of Israel won't be able to go on living." She had no remorse and no hope. As to the important thing taken

from her, because of which she decided to become a suicide bomber, she said, "the nation of Islam ... Maybe the *shaheeds*, the wounded ... I think about them a lot. Liberty and independence ... It's hard to live without independence." She spoke in slogans and if she had personal opinions, she kept them to herself.

❖

Shafiqa reacted completely differently. There was a closeness between us, even though at first she hadn't wanted to talk to me. She had a great need to express herself but also had no patience. Apparently she was afraid that spending a lot of time with me would inspire suspicion among her friends, even though Huda had given her approval.

When I read her the list of questions, she said it was exactly the kind of dialogue she had been looking for, something that would let her express herself.

"In the 12th grade I belonged to a peace organization, children for peace with children from Tel Aviv. We met once a week in Latrun [in Israel, near Jerusalem]. I have three Israeli girlfriends," she said, "their names are Leah, Lee and Lily."

"When you went to blow yourself up, did you think that Leah, Lee and Lily might be among the victims?" I asked.

"No," she cried, shocked. "I want to say that I like you a lot, I wouldn't have hurt you ..." She spoke to her friends in the second person plural, as though they were there with her. But she remembered where she was and said calmly, "If my friends from Tel Aviv put themselves in my shoes, they would do exactly the same thing."

"Yesterday," I said, "they sent a 14-year old boy to blow himself up at a checkpoint near Nablus, and the week before it was an 11-year old boy to whom they had given five shekels [about $1.25] ... Do you really think that's the path to take? Look at where it's led."

"That's why I say that to blow yourself up with civilians is not the solution," she answered. "Even if after that there's paradise, the people who plan for the suicide bombers to blow themselves up with civilians exploit others and also harm them."

I asked her if she was hinting that the dispatcher does not commit a suicide bombing attack or send his relatives. "Today they send children," I said, "and it's heartbreaking ... Maybe tomorrow they'll send the retarded, mentally ill and cripples ..."

"What happened exactly at the checkpoint with the little boy who wanted to blow himself up with the soldiers?" I was surprised, because the prisoners had radios and television sets in their rooms. It was interesting that they didn't discuss such topics among themselves all the time.

"The child," I said, "tried to pass through the checkpoint with an explosive belt and it was discovered. No one shot him. The soldiers asked him to raise his shirt and take off the belt. After the device had been taken apart

one of the soldiers covered him with a military-issue jacket. One thing I can tell you for sure is that Rantisi's wife told a journalist, who recorded her, that she would never send her son to be a *shaheed*, he didn't have the time, he was studying, but on the other hand, she blessed and congratulated all the *shaheeds* . . ."

Shafiqa looked me right in the eye and asked, "Do you think I should be in prison? I changed my mind at the most difficult moment and didn't carry out the attack, but the judge wanted to give me 100 years in prison . . . But I said I was sorry! While I was waiting at the courthouse I talked to one of the Israeli soldiers for three hours. He told me he thought Allah would give me life because I gave life to innocent people."

"Wait a minute, Shafiqa," I said, "you did not give life to innocent people. Only God can do that. Maybe it would be more accurate to say that you did not take away the lives of innocent people." She had had the sensation of omnipotence characteristic of suicide bombers, a sensation of being drunk with power and the ability to decide who would live and who would die. It gives them a feeling of power, and later, at their trials, they often try to use the sensation of power to negotiate their sentences, like vendors at the bazaar in the Kasbah. On the other hand, thought should be given to finding a way of punishing suicide bombers who changed their minds that would encourage others to make the same decision.

"That's right, I didn't take anyone's life, so Allah gave me life. That's what the soldier in the courthouse told me. My aunt said that yesterday, my lover [sic] phoned her and told her he loved me and was waiting for me . . ." Her face lit up with happiness.

"And if you love each other, then everything is OK, right?" I asked with a smile.

"Right, even in prison."

We went back to the questions. She concentrated and thought about each question for a long time before she answered. As to how she would feel if the situations were reversed, she said, "I don't know. That was why I changed my mind. I'm against the attack in Madrid [March 11, 2004, shortly before the conversation took place]. When I saw the pictures [on television] I thought I could have been there, and my nephews could have been there. It's wrong to lose your life in a second because somebody or some organization thought you should."

I remembered the research I had done, which showed that a moral spark was only lit when someone close to the suicide bomber might have been a victim. Shafiqa identified with terrorism victims, as had some of the others. When she spoke about her beloved nephews, who might have been killed in the Madrid attack (or the one in London or the Sinai or Russia or Turkey or the United States) she transferred her warmth and love from them to the terrorist victims in accordance with the modularity of her moral judgment. Beforehand, the victims had had no humanity at all.

"As soon as I put on the explosive device, I looked around me at the people in the street. I asked myself why I had to die or why I had to kill people just because they were walking in the street with their children or sitting in a cafeteria having coffee. I called the people who had sent me three times to ask them to come get me because I had changed my mind. They refused to come and told me that a lot of people were waiting for my attack. They only came to get me after I had been shaking with fear for three hours . . ."

Shafiqa often went back to describe her feelings at the moment she changed her mind, but her dispatchers would not accept the fact that the missile they had fired might return to the launching pad without blowing up.

"I was both angry and frightened. I didn't want anyone to catch me right then, I wanted to go back to my village. I wept straight through, from half past two in the afternoon until half past five in the evening. I felt lost . . . I took off the [explosive] belt. I came home at six in the evening and the boy who was with me blew himself up at nine at night."

She often got the times and order of the events muddled, sometimes saying that he blew himself up before her, sometimes after, and contradicted herself in other ways as well. However, one of the counts of the indictment against her was that she had done nothing to prevent him from carrying out his attack.

"I think about him all the time. I spoke to him and asked him why he had to do it, why he wanted to do it. He only looked at me, and he said, 'All I have to do is push the button and I'll be in paradise.' He was only 16. I told him to come with me, that we would go back . . . He said he wanted to go back, he wanted to and I convinced him to go back. [But] when the car came to take me back to my village he said, "I don't want to go back, I want to stay in Israel for two or three days, to be in a different atmosphere, to see other people.' So the people who sent me gave him the explosive belt and took me." Apparently that was what he said at the beginning of the ride, and as they approached the target he retreated into himself and no longer spoke to her.

In the end, Shafiqa couldn't convince him and they parted and he, under the complete control of the dispatchers, blew himself up.

"I feel sorry for Israeli children. Of course I couldn't carry out an attack in a kindergarten, because they are angels. All children are angels, they're pure. They haven't decided to be criminals or to be killed. No one obliged me to carry out a suicide bombing attack, I wanted to do it, but when I changed my mind, those who sent me out told me that I didn't have the right . . . The man who sent me is now in prison . . . Of course they send other people, it's obvious they wouldn't send their own relatives.

"I was supposed to get engaged on March 12, 2002, and my fiancé was killed [by Israeli army gunfire] on March 8. If you have love and you lose it, and you're left with nothing, you want revenge. Because he is your whole life, and you don't know where he went. I loved him, I felt secure with him, I dreamed about having children, rosy dreams, about living with him. Everything vanished on one second. We felt very romantic about each other but we had never had sexual relations ... If we hadn't felt romantic we couldn't have been able to get engaged ... But he was killed before we got engaged.

"I don't feel remorse because I didn't do anything to feel sorry about, only in my thoughts, because I thought about carrying out a suicide bombing attack. If I had done it I would feel remorse, but I changed my mind at the last minute.

As to how she would explain to a Jewish child her desire to commit suicide, she said, "I would take her hand and caress her head and say, 'My son cannot live the same kind of life you do' ... I did it because they took my life away, my dreams, my boyfriend, my intended fiancé. Like I told you, if I had done it I would feel remorse ..."

"If you had done it," I said, "you wouldn't feel anything, you wouldn't be here."

She said, "I could have sent the boy who was with me ... I'm only responsible for myself, I can't tell someone else what to do. You have democracy, you can do what you want to, but not something bad for me. I am very surprised that there are Israeli Jews who want to know what we're like. I'll need that kind of relationship when I get out of here. I wish I could get out of here and meet you somewhere. I really want peace, peace in my soul, in my life and in my society."

Many of the female prisoners mentioned Eyal Golan, a popular Israeli singer, saying that his songs were full of feeling, and although they were in Hebrew, were meaningful for them. Shafiqa said, "People who dream about tomorrow, that's Allah's song ..." She began singing in Hebrew, "My God, my God, I don't know where, I don't know why, you are my love ... I like it when he says, 'No, don't turn me down, accept me, because every day that comes and goes is eternity without you, treat me like a child in pain, embrace me, I'm falling apart' ..."

When she finished singing there were tears in her eyes, and she said, "The truth, falling apart, but what would I do without you ..." She got up, leaned over me and hugged me, her cheek next to mine, then she turned her head in the other direction and said, "Thank you." That was Shafiqa, who at our first meeting refused to talk to me.

❖

My daughter Tzlil, who was then 15 years old, wrote a letter to Samira and Huda. After they had read and answered the questions themselves they allowed the prisoners in their wings to answer them.

[Date]

Dear Samira and Huda, please ask the other prisoners:

Sometimes I see a terrorist attack [on television] or something about the settlements and I have a lot of questions. It seems to me we are living in two different worlds, and then I ask myself if we are all human beings, if we all have the same needs: a home, a family, love, security . . . Do we all have dreams? Do we all have feelings? Do we all want the same thing, to live in peace with our families and to know that we are safe? So why is all of this going on? Can't there be peace? Do you have to hate me?

Thank you,

Tzlil

Fatima smiled as I read her the letter, "Thank her," she said. "Very sensitive questions. It's like she's right here, talking to me and asking me. It makes me want to cry." Suddenly she began weeping bitterly. She hung her head, stared at the floor for a minute, clamped her lips together and swallowed. She blew her nose on a paper tissue, her whole body trembling.

"All of us, in the end, are human," she said in a shaky voice. "We all want to live in peace, and every person wants to live with his family, his mother and father, in security and tranquility. It's the right of every baby, never mind what, it's his right to live his life and childhood. And I'm telling you, *Naram*, with the help of Allah we will live in peace. Like you say in your letter, Tzlil-*Naram*, we all have feelings, and if it's a Jewish baby or a Palestinian baby, it's still a baby. But what made this happen was the war, not me and not you, *Naram*. I hope we'll live in peace. In the end, I'm a human being and you're a human being."

It was interesting that she gave my daughter an Arabic name and referred to her by it, making her feel closer. As soon as that happened, the other prisoners began sending Tzlil their regards as if they knew her, although they had never met. On the other hand, my son, Yechiam, refused to write to them. He said he wasn't going to correspond with murderers, although Huda did ask why he hadn't written as well.

"The letter also asks if you have to hate," I reminded her.

"It's impossible to love the enemy [who took] your land . . . I don't know you [speaking as though the writer of the letter were sitting opposite her], but here in prison I respect the guards because they treat me with respect. We treat each other like human beings. It's the nation and the land, that's what we can't agree on."

As previously noted, Fatima had been indoctrinated and toughened in prison. When I first met her, shortly after she had been incarcerated, she had wept. By our later meetings she had learned to spout the anti-Israeli propaganda slogans she had learned. But the letter had reached her on another level, it had penetrated her jihadist façade and revealed the child-woman, frightened to the depth of her soul.

"I want to tell *Naram* about something that happened to me," she said. "Water and margarine and sugar that were boiling for an hour were thrown at me by [Huda], even though I'm a Palestinian and she's a Palestinian ... I don't have to hate, not you and not her ... But I hate her more than you, even though she's a Palestinian, because you never did anything to me. What do you think?" she asked emotionally. "I really got into your letter. I feel choked up ... I'm choked up with tears ... There's a girl like me ... what do I tell her ... a person like me. Of course I don't hate her, especially after her letter. If only, with the help of Allah, there will be peace and we will all live in peace, I wish it could happen ... I don't know if there will be two states, but there are political forces ... Tell her, *shalom* from Fatima."

Before we parted she held both my hands and stood next to me, as though waiting for me to hug her. I embraced her gently and couldn't help thinking that yesterday she wanted to kill my children and today she wanted a hug ...

❖

After Fatima came Yusra. She sat across from me listening intently to the letter. The expression on her face showed that it touched her. She shifted uncomfortably in her chair. After a long silence she said, as though speaking directly to Tzlil my child, "My hope is to love you, but when I see your father and brothers killing my people, I can't love you."

My children's father has devoted his life to understanding Arab culture and at the time of our conversation my son was barely adolescent, but I knew Yusra meant fathers and brothers collectively.

"They kill our children. Every human being hopes to live in peace and security. I hope for the best, and that with the help of Allah we'll be able to do good things ... Of course all people have things in common, like loving life, but I'm sorry to say that there's no one who appreciates that. He can't appreciate the fact that a person loves life and wishes to live well."

Her speech was confused and unclear and it was difficult to understand what she was trying to say. Not only that, she had planned to carry out a suicide bombing attack, and here she was, speaking about her love of life. "We were expelled from our lands and separated from our nation, not because that was what we wanted, only because there was a force stronger than us which forced us to do it. I hope your children learn about the Palestinians and their history, that they see our killed and wounded, how an attack against us looks. And at the same time, they will see our strength and how [our] babies hold rocks when the tanks come. If they're holding rocks when the enemy comes, they are surely thinking about other things, like life, and tranquility, and games. They only hope they can go to school and come home safely, that nothing will happen to them."

After that amazing speech, of which she apparently believed every word, she stopped, looked at me and smiled. Then she continued, "It's nice that even though there is a war [going on] there are people who think the way your daughter does. I ask that she visit the home of a wounded or dead Palestinian, or a *shaheed*, to see what it's like, that she goes to see how we live."

At that moment all I could think of was the bereaved families in Israel, America, London, and other places where suicide bombing terrorist attacks had been carried out, families whose lives had been destroyed in an instant by a suicide bomber who pressed the button on a detonator and killed or maimed their loved ones. But I had no desire to argue politics or to try to change her mind, I wanted her—and all the others—to feel free and relaxed in my presence and not to be afraid of how I would react. So I just told her that my daughter had, in fact, been to Arab and Bedouin villages, and that we always told our children that there was something common to all people, even if their nationalities, religions and way of life were different.

❖

Shafiqa answered with a great deal of emotion. She dictated her answer as follows: "Thank you for your letter *Naram*-Tzlil. I have a lot of answers. My name is Shafiqa, I'm 22 years old, a Palestinian, and I love life a lot. I want to enjoy every minute I'm alive. I forgot to say, I'm a Muslim, but Muslim doesn't equal terrorist ... I have asked myself all the questions you ask. I'm looking for a comfortable life, security, love and being loved. Actually, everyone fights for that. Since I don't have my life, there are a lot of things I have to do, my future is open before me ... The last thing I think about is hurting you. Really, I don't think about it and I don't want to do it, and believe me, we are all human beings. For my part, I really want peace and I search for it. When I was your age I was in a peace organization, so believe me when I say I have a heart and intelligence and needs. Think about it from your side, as an Israeli, search for peace, talk to your friends about peace. I promise to do the same thing. Tomorrow we can live on the same street [A phrase that repeated itself often in our conversations.]

Yours sincerely,
Shafiqa

CHAPTER 13

Is the "Other" a Human Being?
"Do Israeli Mothers Feel Pain
Like We Do?"

"A man expects a woman to do everything in the home and to work outside as well, so she has two jobs . . . and in addition, he expects Marilyn Monroe in his bed . . ."

So said Jemila the social worker, who belonged to the Palestinian Women's Society in East Jerusalem. She was about 40 years old, married, and with three grown children who were currently studying at various universities. Abir, the organization's chairwoman, was also about 40, unmarried, and still living at home. Neither of them had any links to terrorist activity, but what they had to say about the way Palestinian women—fairly progressive Palestinian women, it should be noted—view their lives and society was very interesting.

We met in East Jerusalem. After each of us had introduced herself and given a brief biography, we found it easy to talk. We began with coffee, and after about an hour Abir took a cake covered with pistachio nuts out of the refrigerator, very sweet, in Arab fashion. Abir said she had gotten up at 5 in the morning to make two cakes for our meeting. Her face shone with happiness when Jemila and I complimented her on it.

Jemila, who exuded humor and love of life, was wearing a light blue tailored pants suit. Her hair was pulled back and she wore almost no makeup.

She was careful to show Abir a lot of respect as chairwoman, and if she wanted to add something to what Abir said, she did it very delicately and politely. Jemila wore Western clothing, while Abir wore a long black dress and her head was covered with a *hijab*. She wore no makeup, and although she noted that she was wearing traditional clothing, it was not traditional religious Muslim attire, just a long black dress. She said that while she wore traditional clothing, her nieces did not.

"It was my own idea. My mother wanted me to wear ordinary clothes. Today most [Muslim Palestinian] women do wear traditional clothing, because of the political situation. At the end of the 1970s with the revolution in Iran there was a wave of people who became more religious. Only two of my brothers are religious ..."

"When people are desperate and afraid they look for a safe harbor in religion," said Jemila. They went on to talk about the organization. Many women participated in its activities, which included courses in computers, sewing, cooking, cosmetics, and gymnastics.

"Some of the women come to us with their problems, most of the time it's complaints about their husbands," said Jemila. "Sometimes the husband doesn't want to let them participate in sports, and even though the gymnastics teacher is a woman, the husband still won't agree. The very fact that the woman leaves the house bothers him. The women feel closed in. They become introverted because they're afraid. And the men are afraid that if the women leave the house they'll be exposed to all kinds of things." Opposition to women taking part in sports, even when all the participants involved are women, is very common in Arab society.

Jemila continued, "There is a difference between women and mothers in Arab society. Mothers have so much to do, not only in the house, if they are teachers or work someplace else. If I'm a teacher and one of my pupils has a problem with her eye or ear, I'm the one who takes care of it. Mothers take care of all the children in our society, not only their own at home, but all children. That's the Arab mother ...

"I think that Jews are afraid for their children too. The mother spends more time with the children than the father. She sees everything they do and she teaches them. Sometimes she wants to be their friend, to know if they have problems or if something is hard for them. If she isn't their friend, she'll lose them."

Jemila rolled her eyes and said slowly, "A woman is more emotional than a man."

I told them about my interview with Sheikh Ahmad Yassin. I had no way of knowing that a month after my conversation with Jemila the Israeli army would kill him. I told them that Yassin had said the world was under the feet of the mothers, which he meant in a very positive way, and that they had a central place among the *sahaba*, the companions of the prophet Muhammad. I asked for their opinion.

Jemila said, "In our tradition and religion the mother has a central place. I want to add something to what Sheikh Yassin said: You mention your mother three times and only after that, your father."

I had heard that expression beforehand from Samir, a Palestinian Islamic Jihad activist who said, "Paradise is under the feet of women. The mother suffers pregnancy, raises the child and sits by its bedside at night it necessary. The mother is something especially holy. You say mother three times, and father only once."

People who are not familiar with Arab society and culture tend to think that the family is patriarchal and that the woman has an inferior position. That is not entirely true, and the situation is far more complex. There is no room to analyze it here, but suffice to say that the mother, who carried out her purpose in life by having children, has a special, particularly respected place in the family. A childless married woman is like a tree that cannot bear fruit, and her husband gets rid of her through divorce. Wafaa Idris, the first female suicide bomber, is a tragic example of what happens in such a situation.

Jemila then said, "Men have no time ... They're selfish and egotistical." We laughed; Jemila smiled.

I said, "Israeli women always say that our lives would be easier if we had wives, because our husbands always say, 'My wife will do it, my wife will prepare it, talk to my wife ...'" They both laughed and the atmosphere in the room became lighter and familiar: women talking—and complaining—about their husbands.

Jemilia, either because of the closeness that had developed or in spite of it, went on to talk politics. "I feel very sorry when people die," she said, "and I ask how it helps us find a solution for our problems. But when we hear about a Palestinian who died violently, we can't stand watching it on TV. I prefer to watch Al-Jazeera [an Arabic satellite channel broadcast from Doha, Qatar] because they broadcast everything immediately. In general, maybe suicide bombers, or maybe most of them, have problems they want to escape from. Religion helps people. If they didn't believe in paradise, it would be hard. If they didn't believe in paradise, would they choose that way?"

Abir added, "I hear a lot of women who talk about wanting to be *sha-heedas* because of the situation, because they see Palestinian blood [spilled] every day ... Why does this happen to our people every day? It's impossible to understand it. Maybe they say, something bad was done to us and they want to kill them. We aren't birds, we're human beings, not birds sitting in trees to get shot at. In Europe and the United States they treat dogs better than they treat people here at the checkpoints.

"To get through the Ramallah checkpoint ... It's like animals. We aren't animals. And to build that wall ... For what, so we can be free animals in a zoo? Someone who wants to be a *shaheed* will pass through all the checkpoints and get into Israel ... Not all of us are suicide bombers."

The conversation turned to Reem Riyashi, the seventh female suicide bomber, who had blown herself up at the Erez checkpoint in the Gaza Strip (2004). There were rumors, which even reached the newspapers, that she had had an extramarital affair and that the attack was the "honorable" way her husband found to erase the shame. Jemila agreed that only something very serious could make the mother of two small children choose to end her life as a suicide bomber. But the question is, did she choose to end it that way herself?

Abir, who until then had kept quiet, said, "I'm a teacher at a girls' school. I know about incest. The girls keep to themselves and don't play with the others. There is a social worker who takes care of children with problems. She calls the mother in for a meeting. Before she talks to anyone else in the family she checks to see if the mother knows. Sometimes they do, sometimes they don't ... There is a woman who comes to the sports activities held at the Palestinian Women's Society and she brings her 11 year-old daughter with her every time. I asked her why. She said that she was afraid of her sons, that they would do something to their sister. She worries about the child all the time. The father can do nothing with the boys beyond beating them."

I asked if they thought incest was common in Arab society. Jemila said, "There is a lot of incest in Arab families and it is covered up. A lot of people know. Women are weak, so they're victims. In our organization we locate the poorer women, the ones who have to work to be less dependent on their husbands. We know that if we can give such a woman strength she will feel better and more confident. We teach courses in cooking, cosmetics and sewing. The woman's first problem is her financial situation. If we can solve that problem we can solve the others. Because of the political situation, the intifada, many men lost their places of work. The women are weak and not well educated, they have to take money from their husbands, but even if the woman works and has an education, she still gives her money to her husband. It's a patriarchal society, a society run by men."

Jemilia decided the time had come to show her cards. "Abir lives with her parents," she said angrily. "She is 40 and unmarried, and she always has to be home by eight o'clock at night because that's what her father says, and her mother agrees. I can't ask her to stay over at my house because she isn't allowed to sleep anywhere except at home."

Abir said, "I went out of the country. My parents knew I was going to visit relatives so they didn't impose limitations on me, but when I'm here I have to be at home. It's because of the neighbors."

The idea of a pajama party, for example, was completely foreign to them. Children in their society, they said, could never spend the night away from home unless they were going to very close relatives and only if they were very young. Jemila said, "It's getting worse and worse ... Families are afraid. The children watch TV, and you can see everything on TV. Every family has cable TV so they can watch all the channels, even sex ... But at the same time, everything is forbidden in Arab society, especially for girls. You can't live they way they do on TV ... It isn't healthy, it isn't logical to let children and families see things on TV and to live a different life in reality. There is an enormous gap between what we see and the way we live. Western society enters every Arab home through television. We have the reality of TV in front of us all the time.

"There is a program called 'Star Academy' in which men and women live in the same apartment. They have separate rooms, but you can watch the show 24 hours a day. You can even watch them while they sleep. Last week on a talk show they invited actors and a psychologist and they talked about the show. Some were in favor of it and some were against. The psychologist was both, because people want to live open lives. Men and women can live together as friends, they don't have to sleep together.

"It's an Arab version of a French program. Our female pupils watch it every night instead of doing homework because they want to see what's going on between the boys and girls. If I ask them what they want to do with their lives, they will tell me that they want to live the way they do on 'Star Academy.' Even my sister, who has a husband, wants to live like that ... There's another show, it's called 'Big Brother,' and they stopped broadcasting it. The Saudi Arabians paid not to have the show broadcast because it was against Islam, it had a man and a woman living together and they weren't married."

Both Jemila and Abir had experienced a technological revolution in their lives. Television, the Internet, and cellular phones, which brought the outside, and in this case Western, world into the lives of Arabs had influenced them as well. I could sense their curiosity and envy, the strong desire for a different life, one in which a woman had self-worth and could behave freely (relative to the extreme restrictions placed on an Arab woman) without having it cost her life. It made me think about the women who had preferred to become suicide bombers instead of being murdered or ostracized because they had violated—or were suspected of having violated—the many taboos imposed on Arab women. In essence, the Arab-Muslim world objects to the West for three reasons: gender, sex, and family matters.[1] There is even a *hadith* (part of the Muslim oral tradition) which states that when a Muslim marries, only half of his religion is correct, because he becomes vulnerable, as a religious Muslim, to the possible violations his wife may commit, and that reflects on him. The various approaches of the Muslim and Western worlds to many issues are different, especially in matters concerning women: how women look, the interaction between men and women, the attitude toward virginity, out-of-wedlock pregnancy, choice of a future husband (in Islam the parents choose the husband and often the bride and groom are closely related; often there are double weddings, two brothers marrying two sisters, etc.), the age people get married (Muslims in their teens). In addition Islam permits polygamy, and when a woman is raped, in many instances she is not only blamed but occasionally murdered.

I said, "I have met with dispatchers of suicide bombers and with women who wanted to carry out suicide bombing attacks. Sometimes it seemed that their reasons were personal or related to their families or society. What do you think?"

There was a stunned silence. "That's not true," was Abir's blurted out, almost knee-jerk reaction. Then she regained control of herself and said, "Marwa, one of my cousins, was in prison in 1994 because she tried to kill an Israeli soldier near the Wailing Wall … She had a lot of problems with her mother … Her mother beat her and told her she was a bad daughter and prayed for Allah to take her. Marwa hated herself, so she took a knife and tried to kill a soldier … She came to our house and told my sister that she wanted to kill a soldier. My sister was only 14 years old then, and everyone gave her whatever she wanted and she didn't have any problems with my mother or our relatives. Marwa wanted to take my sister with her. She convinced her that someone had to do something because the Jews were killing our people. She said to my sister, 'If you don't come with me, I'll go alone.' And my sister was afraid for her, so she went to the Wailing Wall with her. The soldiers took one look at their faces and knew they were hiding something. They said, 'Stop, we want to search you,' and then they found two knives and took them to jail."

More than two years later and only after American intervention, both girls, minors, were released.

"Now my sister is married and has two children and she doesn't run after soldiers with knives any more," said Abir, and we all laughed.

"Marwa came home as well, and got married and had three children. She got a divorce and now she works with former prisoners … Some of the women do it [carry out suicide bombing attacks] as a way to solve their problems … They have a lot of problems. Returning to Allah is better than living here. There are women who believe in paradise and want to go there." Recently there had been a spate of young Palestinian women who approached Israeli soldiers, took out knives and threw them into the air. They preferred being arrested to forced marriages or other situations beyond their control.

❖

As noted above, mothers have a special status in Arab society. I wanted to meet a *shaheed*'s mother to try to find out whether they really did rejoice and were proud that their sons or daughters had been killed in suicide bombing attacks or other violent actions and were considered *shaheeds* after their deaths.

Um-Nabil—Arabic for "Nabil's mother," as Abu Mazen is Arabic for "Mazen's father"—was the mother of one of those killed on September 29, 2000, the day the second intifada broke out, and her status was raised to *Um-Shaheed*, mother of a *shaheed*. We met one evening in a Palestinian women's club in one of the villages near Jerusalem. She waited for me with other Palestinian women, Abir and Jemila among them. Abir invited me to have something to eat with them. We sat around the table in the kitchen, which was furnished simply but with every possible electrical appliance, and the women told me that they usually ate together at the club every day.

The atmosphere was pleasant and relaxed. Um-Nabil sat a short distance from me, her face half-hidden by a black *hijab*. Under it, a white kerchief hiding her hair was visible. Her skin was dark because, explained Murad, the Arab journalist who had accompanied me, she was of Nigerian extraction. "There is a neighborhood they call 'the slaves' quarter,'" he said. "During the nineteenth century Muslims came there from Africa, and they had black skin."

Um-Nabil was tired and said she wanted to hold our conversation and go home as soon as possible, so she, Murad (who acted as translator when necessary) and I left the other women and went to one of the club's offices. "We were a family of four," she said, "father, mother and two sons. They are Muhammad, who is 23, and Nabil, who was 29 when he died as a *shaheed* on the first day of the Al-Aqsa intifada. Our life was tranquil and good. We all worked, my husband, myself and the boys. Our life was normal. Previously we had lived with my husband's family because of financial difficulties, until finally the boys found work and supported us. We rented a house and our situation improved. We had three years of independence and happiness, and I even found fiancées for the boys. They both got engaged.

"We live in Jerusalem. We have blue [Israeli] identity cards. Before that we lived in Bir Naballah. My husband became ill and to keep his rights we moved to Shuafat, into the Jerusalem municipality. Our financial situation was very good, and our total income was about 14,000 shekels a month [about $3,500 in 2000, a very respectable sum].

"At around that time Muhammad got married and we were paying $600 a month rent in Shuafat, which is very high. We had only lived there for two years when the intifada broke out. Our lives took a turn for the worse. We lost our son, Nabil. My husband had a heart attack, he had open heart surgery and as a result one of his legs is paralyzed. We all lost our jobs. From 14,000 shekels a month we went to nothing. There were a lot of charity organizations that helped us at that time."

Abir came in with a tray of coffee for us and a pack of cigarettes, which she offered to Murad. He took one and lit Abir's. I asked him how women who smoked were regarded in Arab society. He laughed and said, "When you want to say a woman is bad, you say she has a cigarette in her mouth ..." Abir said, "Everyone smokes today. Women even smoke narghilehs."

Um-Nabil continued, "I lost my job, my husband lost his job, my son lost his job. I'm a seamstress, but because of the situation, and after my son Nabil died, my sight got worse."

I looked at her and I wondered how old she was. She seemed ageless. Her face was smooth and unlined, but the burdens of life had left their mark. Her eyes were sad and she seemed very serious about everything. I asked her how old she was. "Forty-nine," she answered. She continued, "When I realized I was going to collapse from despair and loneliness and depression, I thought about my life and told myself to be stronger. There is the Al-Aqsa Charity Foundation in Jerusalem and it gives scholarships to the children of *shaheeds*, to pay for their schooling. Nabil, my son the *shaheed*, didn't have children. I asked for a scholarship but they wouldn't give me one. I went to

Jordan and appealed to women's organizations, and one of them gave me a scholarship. Through my studies I overcame my thoughts and now I'm studying education at Al-Quds University. I'm in my third year."

Um-Nabil said that her son hadn't chosen to be a *shaheed*. "He became one by chance. He went to pray and there was a riot on the Temple Mount and someone was yelling for all the young men to come to the Mount of Olives to donate blood. The police stood there and taunted those who came ... He was on his way home after prayers. We live near the hospital on the Mount of Olives. A sniper shot him and he died instantly. He was killed at 5:30 in the afternoon. By 8 that night we had already buried him."

According to the official police report, the actual circumstances surrounding his death are somewhat different and more complex.

Nabil's death as a *shaheed* raised her status greatly in Palestinian society, and she is now known as *Um-Shaheed*. Among the mothers, at least, there is no difference between one whose son chose to blow himself up and one whose son was killed by chance. All the *Um-Shaheed*s are the same. She spoke of her special status, about the honor and respect she received. "I have special status with Allah. I get a lot of respect from people. I get money, not just for my studies, but for travel, for research, for everything I do. People help a lot when they hear I'm a *shaheed*'s mother.

"We *shaheed*s' mothers are invited to all kinds of social functions and we are always honored guests. Those functions are like ceremonies. For example, at school everyone tells me, 'You lost one son, but all of us here are your sons and daughters.' Even the lecturers tell me that. The women's societies call me and invite me to all their events and ceremonies."

I told her that I had often seen *shaheed*s' mothers on TV holding up pictures and expressing joy after a son or daughter had been killed in a suicide bombing attack, and that as a mother I could never understand it, because what was more important to a mother than her children's lives? Um-Nabil nodded. "Even a cat that loses its kittens feels pain. I'm a mother, and while it's true that it's an honor to die as a *shaheed*, I lost my father, mother and uncle [through natural causes] and there is nothing worse than losing a child ... It's like a knife in your heart. It's the worst thing that can happen. We lose [someone] every day, and when I see the pain, I feel it every day."

She said, "I ask myself if Israeli mothers feel the pain the way we do. Where is the Israeli mother in all this?"

I said that mothers were mothers everywhere, and that it really didn't make any difference where they lived or whether they were Muslim, Christian, Jewish, or Buddhist. I said that Palestinian and Israeli women apparently had the same emotions, but that Israeli women—and not only they—were very angry about the way Palestinians used suicide bombers to indiscriminately murder Israeli civilians—children, women, total innocents.

She said, "Israeli mothers have a country and institutions that take care of their families, while we, Arab women, have nothing. There is no one to help us. They don't even help me with the rent [she is an Israeli with a blue ID] because I'm the mother of a *shaheed* ..."

I was quite surprised, because this woman, whose son was involved in violent anti-Israeli activity when he was killed thought she deserved recognition by the State of Israel as a bereaved mother. Israel officially recognizes as bereaved the parents of soldiers killed in the line of duty and the parents of terrorist victims. I said nothing, and she continued.

"People see what is going on, like the building of the [antiterrorist security] fence, and it's hard for me to get to the university, and there are soldiers who keep you from crossing the fence. So people, including mothers, say, if my son doesn't make a sacrifice, and the sons of others don't make a sacrifice, so how can we go on?

"The young people see how hard economic conditions are, there are no jobs, they have no life, so they sacrifice themselves so that others can live. It all depends on the family, its individual. [But] I don't believe there is a mother who wants to send her son off to die. In spite of all the rights and privileges that are given to mothers of *shaheeds* in life and in paradise, in spite of everything, I don't believe they do. No mother can do such a thing of her own free will, be happy and cheer after her son has died and become a *shaheed*. Even mothers who say they want their sons to be *shaheeds* aren't speaking from their hearts, but because they are under some kind of pressure or in a moment of anger they say they are willing to send their sons and all kinds of other things.

"It's obvious that there are those who dispatch others to carry out [suicide bombing] attacks against Israelis, but not their own children. Their children are studying abroad, all expenses paid. We are very angry about that."

The Palestinian writer and journalist 'Adel Abu Hashem, who lives in Saudi Arabia, posted an article on the Internet about the mother of three *shaheeds*. "In the dead of night," he wrote, "Um-Nidal Farhat urged her son to turn his body into a torch to light the way to the liberation of Palestine. That's what it means to be a Palestinian mother. She has always accustomed us to the fact that she is a factory for [the production of] men." It is interesting that the paean was written to the Palestinian mother's being "a factory for [the production of] men ..."

In Palestinian villages stories are told about "the magic of the *shaheeds*," reminiscent of stories in all religions about the power of relics and the graves of saints. Palestinians living near cemeteries have reported the odor of perfume wafting from the graves, and when they approached, they discovered that it came from the grave of a *shaheed*. Another story is the one about the grave of a *shaheed* in the Hebron cemetery that was opened by mistake, and to the amazement of one and all, the *shaheed* buried within had not decayed: since the *shaheed* has a special status, no worm will eat his body. Such folk tales are popular and widespread, and encourage others to become *shaheeds*.

Murad, who works for the foreign media, said, "Often, when we went to photograph mothers of *shaheeds*, they would praise their sons' actions to the cameras and in the presence of their relatives and neighbors. As soon as the cameras were turned off, they burst into tears and collapsed ... There were even mothers who cursed the dispatchers. The mothers behave the way society demands. It's a show, and they play their parts."

I asked Um-Nabil what she thought of about *shaheeda*s, and whether it was true they had been forced into it to preserve the family honor. She thought about it and said, "I have heard that a lot of the girls did it because they had lost something or were in difficult straits. I don't believe that. Wafaa' Idris [the first female suicide bomber] was an ambulance worker and saw people losing those they loved."

"But according to the newspapers," I said, "she was sterile and her husband divorced her and remarried, and that was why she became a suicide bomber. She felt humiliated and rejected by Palestinian society, where as a woman unable to bear children she was considered worthless. That was her way of gaining recognition and also of being released from her suffering."

Um-Nabil did not look surprised. "There are a lot of rumors," she said. "I don't believe rumors until it's been proved they're facts." She waited for me to assure her I had understood. "It depends on the girl's personality," she said. "For example, even if they spread a hundred rumors about me, I wouldn't sacrifice myself. If things weren't going well for her [a Palestinian woman], she could have picked up and left ... She could have left her family and moved to the Jewish side. There are Palestinian girls who move to Israel, build new lives and no one knows anything about them. No one can find them. I know a Palestinian girl who has lived in Israel for 15 years, she works there and everything has turned out fine. She lives in a Jewish neighborhood."

That is factually correct. Israeli society is diversified and pluralistic, and it is not difficult to be assimilated into it. A Palestinian woman threatened with murder perhaps can find refuge there.

Murad, who until then had translated without entering the discussion, said, "If a Palestinian girl leaves the house, her parents' or her husband's, she will never be able to go back. She may be able to meet her sisters, but she will never meet the men in the family, because they would kill her. The mother usually [secretly] supports her daughter."

Um-Nabil was tired and wanted to go home. I asked her one last question: in her opinion, would there be peace?

"Only if there is justice between Jews and Arabs, only then can there be peace. If there is a Palestinian state it mustn't be under the umbrella of Israel, but there has to be equality. Israelis and Palestinians *can* live together."

CHAPTER 14

A Teenage Shaheed: "My Classmate Enlisted Me as a Shaheed. He Was Paid and Gave Me 100 Shekels"*

For a long time I couldn't get Adballah Qur'an out of my mind. He was an 11-year-old Palestinian boy, a sixth grader, who had arrived at a military checkpoint near Nablus in March 2004. Without his knowledge an explosive device had been put into his backpack, and the terrorists planned to detonate it by remote control; it would have blown him up along with the soldiers at the checkpoint. The child had been fooled, that is, he had no idea of what his real purpose was. His handler, a terrorist from Fatah's Al-Aqsa Martyrs' Brigades, had cynically sent him to a terrible death.

When he was captured he told his story, and few hours later he was released and sent home, to the Balata refugee camp near Nablus. His dispatchers immediately told him to claim that his backpack contained spare parts, not explosives, and that the Israelis had invented a lie to use as propaganda. That was done despite the picture of the child with the explosive device on his back, which was broadcast to the whole world.

Murad said, "It depends on where they grow up. [Children] are exposed to propaganda, they see the *shaheeds* glorified as holy. Every child wants to be a *shaheed* ... It's a spontaneous reaction to the way they live. An entire generation grew up under Arafat and *shaheeds*, and they all watched television, which exposed them to all kinds of horrors ... In my opinion, children have been exploited for a long time." He also claimed that the original intention might not have been for the child to be a suicide bomber, but merely to smuggle the explosive device into Israel. "When the dispatchers saw that the army had captured him," he said, "they tried to detonate the device, not specifically to harm the soldiers [because a large number of

---

*About $22.

Palestinians were at the checkpoint at the time], but primarily to keep the child from saying anything ... Maybe, maybe not ...

"In choosing children or women, they are actually saying the Israeli enemy is humanitarian, because Jews are more merciful toward women and children," continued Murad sorrowfully. "There was the case of the woman in Hamza [a village near Jerusalem], who hid an explosive belt under the bed of a 6-month old infant. There was a woman who put an explosive belt in a baby carriage. And there were explosives smuggled in under the bodies of sick people or under stretchers in ambulances ...

"We live under Arafat's reign of terror [this was said before Arafat died in 2004]. He is godfather to all the militias. There is no law, no order, no court, only masked gunmen in the streets. From the first day Arafat set foot here he instituted anarchy. The régime of the militias is linked to money, corruption, the theft of cars in Israel ... They have killed people, raped women, kidnapped women from their husbands. Palestinian society is not so strong. People are busy looking for food for their children."

Murad said that voices could be heard in Palestinian society demanding that children be excluded from military activity. But I heard a different tone of voice a number of months previously from Abu Hilal, a former Palestinian Islamic Jihad activist who said, "It's a shame to send a child to blow himself up, because he does so without killing Jews. A child doesn't understand what he has to do, so he just presses the button ..." His concern was not for the child but for practical matters, that is, the chances that a child's attack would be "successful" were slim, and he would kill only himself, there was no morality involved.

Actually, such an attitude comes as no surprise to anyone familiar with the way Palestinian children are brainwashed. In both the formal and alternative educational systems, as in the Palestinian media, the word *shaheed* always has positive connotations. It is endlessly drummed into children that the solution to the Palestinian-Israeli conflict is a jihad, which will return the refugees to all the territory of "Palestine," that is, Israel, which per se never appears on the maps the children see.

The movie "Children Who Love the Homeland Love the Martyr's Death," which has often been broadcast on Palestinian television, shows Israeli soldiers firing guns, and, not necessarily with factual or temporal connection, Palestinian children carried on stretchers, their bodies wrapped in the Palestinian flag. The film is edited in such a way as to suggest that the children have been killed by the soldier's gunfire. The voiceover, full of pathos, says,

> Children who loved their country and loved the *shuhada* [*shaheeds*].
> The hearts of the children of Palestine are full not only of fear and
>   horror,
> But also of love, unprecedented, unique love, for martyrdom, death
>   for the sake of Allah.

The violence of the occupation and the terrorism of the occupying
   army led to outbreaks
of rage because a martyr's death became an exalted goal, worthy of
   praise.
This generation is a flock of birds throwing stones of fire at the
   Israeli army,
And turned it into chaff and disintegrated [imagery from the
   Qur'an].
Death as a martyr, in its glory and prestige,
Became the heart's desire of every soul living on this holy soil,
And every soul is filled with a love of fighting.
[The picture changes to a dead Palestinian child in his coffin.]
Because of the status and spiritual reward the *shaheed* gains
The *shaheed* and his martyrdom have become the heart's desire of
   many children
For it is the path to a position of honor,
To immortality in the memory and conscience of the people.
The children of Palestine continue to love their homeland and
   martyrdom
[and will do so] until the liberation of Palestine!
Until the liberation of Palestine!

I met Jalal, a tenth grader from Nablus, in prison. He was one of the
children who had been sent to the IDF checkpoint in Nablus wearing an
explosive belt. I was let into the youth wing of the security prisoners' section
and went through an iron door. Through an opening in another door a
guard called to the boy to come out.

Jalal was wearing a black T-shirt, short and faded, blue sweat pants and
sneakers. I introduced myself and shook his hand as we mounted the stairs
to the second floor, where the youth wing was. He seemed surprised at my
having shaken his hand. Another iron door opened and we entered a long
corridor with narrowly spaced cells on either side, a small opening in the
door of each. There were several youths clearing the corridor and preparing
lunch. A guard accompanied us to a room with a small table and plastic
chairs, which for some reason was called "the club."

We sat down opposite one another and I looked at him. He looked younger
than his 15 years, perhaps because he was only about 4 feet 5 inches tall,
very short for a tenth grader. On his left wrist he wore a kind of macramé
bracelet made of strands of pink and grey wool, and on his arm the letters
TJ were written in ink, J for Jalal and T for the name of his girlfriend. His
top lip was decorated with the beginnings of a mustache, and his brown hair
was heavy with gel, the ends fashioned into spikes in a row in the center of
his head. He had obviously spent a lot of time on his hairdo, probably more
than many girls would.

I asked him to tell me about his life. He said he would prefer to answer direct questions. It was hard for him to tell a long, connected story and he needed focused questions to keep him talking. Speech did not come easily to him, and while he spoke his tongue often protruded from his mouth. Nevertheless, he did not wander from the topic and answered every question clearly.

"Don't worry," I said, "you can speak freely ... Even sheikh Ahmad Yassin spoke to me, and for five hours."

Jalal was satisfied, and began telling me the story of his life. "I'm from Nablus, all my family, many generations, is from there. My mother finished high school and wanted to go to university, [but] in our society, when a woman is married she doesn't study at a university. My father went as far as the sixth grade, but when he was in school that was as far as you could go, it was like being in the 12th grade today. He knows how to read and write and he has an accounting certificate. We are two boys and two girls, and I'm the youngest. My father has a supermarket and I also have a store of my own, for perfumes and CDs and cassettes and gifts. I used some of the money [I earned] to buy more stock for the store and the rest I gave to my father. I would give it all to him and not take anything for myself, because he was building me a house. Three days after I was caught they poured the concrete [foundation]."

I asked him to tell me about his school and his friends. He shifted in his chair and put a hand on the backrest. His brown eyes were wide open as he spoke, as though he were trying to open them more than was possible.

"My school was OK, but sometimes I didn't like going. I was in the tenth grade and I wanted to study, but I stopped. It was *akbar* [the best] at school when all of us were together. I would drive all the teachers and the whole school crazy. There was a teacher who used to hit me, so I torched his car. He had a stick, the teacher had a stick, and he would hit our hands with it, and sometimes he would send me and my friends home from school. First we broke the windows in his car, then we poured gasoline all over it, me and my friends. I was the first one, I lit a match and then the others did the same. I was in jail, in an Arab jail, for two days ... Everything I did was because I didn't like the teacher, that's why I did it. I wasn't afraid."

Professor Ariel Merari of Tel Aviv University told me that in 1979, terrorists who had been arrested were interviewed and one of them recounted that he had gotten into trouble with an uncle and hurt him. How had he hurt him? He had hit the old man's head again and again until he went blind ... At that time, before they were recruited by the terrorist organizations, about half of the terrorists had criminal records.

Jalal said, "I used to not go home. I was with my friends all the time, hanging out and walking around, and I also sold perfume and gifts, and things my father gave me to sell. Sometimes things at home weren't so good, because I was away all the time so my father would hit me [when I came home]. He didn't hit the others, just me. I would come home at night to sleep, but sometimes I would get in around midnight. My father would say, 'Sit in the store with me,' and I would say, 'No,' so he would hit me.

"My father would lock me in the house, lock the door and beat me up. He would hit my body, my arms and my face. He only had one wife, that was OK, but because I'm a little disturbed he would hit me. He started hitting me when I was 12 ... I started smoking when I was 12, so he would hit me. My mother would say, 'Enough, leave him alone, I'll make him be good.' She told him she would explain [things] to me, help me understand.

"At school I would come into the class, stay for around three lessons, maximum, and then cut out, either alone or with friends. I didn't like sitting in class for a lot of lessons. I cared a lot about my sisters and brother. I would go to the village to visit my married sister, walk, not ride. There was a roadblock and I used to go around it. My sister has children and I played with them."

Jalal seemed excited to be talking, and he missed his family. I asked him what was hardest about his life. "My whole life is hard," he answered. "When I go to court, I don't want my mother to meet me because I'm not allowed to talk to her in the courthouse, so that's why I don't want to meet her there. What I love most of all in my whole life is my mother and father and my sisters and my brother, that's all."

As in discussions with dispatchers and other potential suicide bombers, the mother was held in great regard. She was usually the most significant figure in their lives. "As much as you may love them, you caused your mother and father great sorrow," I said.

He nodded his head helplessly and said, "My mother went to the hospital ... My parents were very angry with me ... How could I do such a thing ... But I'm not sorry."

"But I bet your friends respect you more. How did they react? And now that you're in jail, has that raised your status?" I asked.

"Until now," he said, "I haven't seen any of them and I don't know anything about them. You want to know if I have status in prison? I'm not the only one who did it. All my friends did it. They all hold their heads high and aren't sorry for what they did, it's the usual thing with them."

Obviously not all his friends, and not all the prisoners, wore explosive belts and planned to blow themselves up, but Jalal seemed to want to emphasize that he was just a regular guy and that they were all the same.

"Were you ever in love?" I asked.

His eyes lit up. "Yes. I am in love with my neighbor. She's 15 $\frac{1}{2}$. I didn't speak to my mother about it, but she knows anyway. And [the girl] loves me, because she used to go out with me and we would go to coffee houses and restaurants and no one knew about it. My mother would ask me where I had been and I would tell her I was out with one of my [male] friends. The girl would say she had been with my mother."

He showed me her initial, written in pen on his arm. His hands were those of a ten-year-old child, out of proportion with his long, well-developed arms.

He sounded as though he were thoroughly in love. "When I eat and when I drink I remember her, how I met her, the beautiful days we had together. We used to go out every Thursday."

I was surprised by the ease and freedom with which he spoke about his girlfriend, and by the fact they would go out together in secret, an act unacceptable in Palestinian society and which endangered both their lives.

"If you loved her so much, why did you plan on giving her up?" I asked.

"Because it's better in paradise," he answered directly. "I would sell my parents and the whole world for paradise." He raised his chin and said, "I thought about being a *shaheed* from the day the intifada began, because they started razing houses, destroying families, killing children, so I decided that would be my path. I didn't work any more, I didn't go on trips during the summer any more, not with my family or friends or school, the way I did in the beginning. That wasn't the only reason I thought about dying, but also because of the *shaheeds* and Allah. Allah wrote in the Qur'an that *shaheeds* are for Allah. I wanted to kill a lot of Jews and get revenge. I wanted revenge because of the women who had to leave the buildings they razed, that was why I wanted to do it. It says in the Qur'an, 'Kill them!' They gave me 100 shekels [about $22] so that on the way to the target I would have money to buy something to eat, but I used it to buy my mother a pot . . ."

I asked him if he had thought about the people he would kill along with himself.

"When I put on the explosive belt all I thought about was dying and going to paradise, [and] I wasn't afraid . . . I didn't care, Allah said that was the way it would be with me."

"Who recruited you for the suicide bombing attack?" I asked.

"Hassan, a kid in my class. He's in jail now, I don't know anyone else, just Hassan. I was at the house of a friend named Mustafa, and I saw Hassan there. He shook my hand and asked me what I was doing there . . . He sat with me and Mustafa went to bring tea. Then he told me to be a *shaheed* . . . Hassan asked me what I thought about *istishhad*, that is, to be a *shaheed*, and I told him I agreed."

"Are you angry with him?" I asked.

Without hesitation he said, "Hassan is still my friend, and it's normal for him to recruit *shaheeds*. No, I'm not angry with him."

"Why didn't you ask him why he doesn't blow himself up?"

"I did ask him, and he said he was afraid to do things like that," he answered, squirming in his chair.

"So does that mean you were braver than Hassan?"

His sense of self-importance seemed to grow. "It's not a question of brave or afraid . . . I thought about becoming a *shaheed* from the beginning of the intifada, to go to paradise. Of course I thought I was more of a man than Hassan. He was afraid, I wasn't."

Jalal did not understand Hassan's sophistication and his manipulation in recruiting him. Hassan, the most successful child in class, a good student, much admired, "was afraid," while little, socially unsuccessful Jalal, who was often made fun of, was "more of a man," and volunteered to be a *shaheed*.

"Hassan and I were in the same class, but I'm older because I was left back. I got run over in the third grade and lost a year of school. I have 25 stitches in my scalp, and I got left back a year. One of my neighbors ran me over by accident. He didn't do it on purpose. My arms and legs were broken as well. They pulled me out from under the car and took me to the hospital in Nablus, and now I'm fine, *al-hamdullihah* ["May Allah be praised"]. Hassan is strong, he was OK in class and always answered the teacher's questions. We don't live near each other. His family is OK when it comes to money, they have enough, he's a good student and his mother has an education and helps him with his studies. His parents are divorced. Sometimes he lives with his mother and sometimes he lives with his father. He was young when his parents divorced, maybe eight years old. He lives with his mother's family. His father didn't get married again, his father works so his mother takes care of him because she's at home, and she didn't get married again either."(Remarrying would have meant giving up her son, who would have gone to live with his father or his father's family.) Jalal obviously admired Hassan a great deal.

"Then is your life worth less than Hassan's?" I asked.

"Once when some of the other guys were around Hassan asked me if I wanted to be a *shaheed* He said I would get money. He sent me to his *shabbab* and they gave me 100 shekels. They gave him more money, for another *shaheed*. He got money for recruiting *shaheeds*, he recruited me and got money and gave me 100 shekels of it."

A profitable business: a tenth-grade pupil found a way to make easy money by recruiting his fellow pupils for suicide bombing attacks. Hassan apparently did not suffer from an obvious emotional disturbance and was not a serial killer by proxy. According to everything Jalal said, in Palestinian terms, he was a normative child. The suicide bomber dispatchers as well were completely normative, in terms of Palestinian society. Recruiting an acquaintance to kill himself and others is apparently quite common.

"Jalal, do you feel Hassan sold you out?"

"That's the way things are done. He didn't sell me out. When I reached the roadblock I thought about my mother and the rest of the family, what would happen after I killed myself, and then I turned myself in. Most of all I thought about my mother, because she was sick and I was afraid she would have a heart attack. I wished I could go home, and I decided to go back to my parents and my family and I thought I would turn myself in ... [When I left to carry out the attack] I held my mother's hand tight and I told her I had already said my morning prayers, and I kissed her hand and she asked me where I was going, and I said, to school. And she said, may Allah watch over you. I saw all of them before I left, my brother and sister. None of them noticed anything. Only my sister could tell I was going to do it, because in the morning I disappeared ...

"[After I got the belt and wrote the letter] I went straight to the roadblock. On the day he recruited me, Hassan went to the *shabbab* [here, dispatchers]. The next day Hassan sent my friend 100 shekels for me and I went to pick up the belt, and they explained what I had to do, how to kill myself. I left at seven in the morning and that's how it began, and it ended at one in the afternoon, when I got caught. I left the house in the morning and I didn't come back.

"At the house where I was supposed to get the belt the sheikh talked to me. He said, 'You press the button. When you reach paradise, pray for us.' He said, 'You will be like the *shaheeds*, you will go to paradise.' He was a religious sheikh ... I didn't even fast during the last Ramadan, because I was hanging out with my friends the whole day. I didn't always say the prayers all the time, sometimes I did and sometimes I didn't ... But I did pray at the house [where I got the explosive belt] and I wrote a letter so that my parents and friends wouldn't be angry with me. I had my picture taken in Nablus ..."

He got up to demonstrate how he posed to the picture. He took two steps back and showed me how he held an M-16 rifle in one hand, a copy of the Qur'an in the other. Then he struck a macho pose and said, "They hung a gun on either side of me," balled his hands into fists and said, "and there were two hand grenades on the table," and pointed at the table next to him.

"I had a green headband with a Qur'an verse tied around my forehead. There was a picture of a *shaheed* in the background and a prayer rug was hanging on the wall. I came to take the belt. It took an hour ... There was someone in the room and then two more ... That day was like a present compared to all other days. The world was open for me ... I don't know why ... Maybe because I wanted to die."

"Were there other days in the past when you wanted to die?" I asked.

"I didn't want to die before then. Because I wanted to get revenge, because I thought about my mother and father."

Jalal looked at me. Not once during the entire conversation did he smile. He looked sad and a little distant. He said, "One of the soldiers at the roadblock said, 'Come here, kid,' so I went over to him, and he told me to lift up my shirt, and he saw the belt so they arrested me. I could have pressed the button and blown up the explosives, but I didn't want to."

I asked him if he felt anything toward his potential victims.

"The soldiers were very nice to me and I didn't want to hurt them. They didn't use handcuffs or tie me up. They brought me cigarettes and food, and I preferred not to hurt them. Beforehand I wanted to get revenge, but when I thought about my parents, I gave up the idea and turned myself in ... I wanted my friends to remember me for good things, for helping them, for helping them with money, and I used to let them have cassettes for free and they used to pay me later ... And then I thought that my friends would pray I go to paradise and see the prophet Muhammad and the *sahaba* [companions of the prophet], and I would get married in paradise and have children ..."

"What do you think about most of all now?" I asked.

"Most of all I think about my mother, about my girlfriend and my sisters."

"How do you think your mother feels?"

"She's not the only mother who has to be angry and sad ... There are a lot of people who did it, a lot of people died, and my mother accepts it as something normal. She feels they exploited me, but she says that it was written by Allah that I do what I did, and she accepts what Allah decided."

❖

Jahalia is what the Muslim tradition calls the pre-Islamic era, roughly the thousand years before the Christian era. According to the tradition, it was a time of polytheistic paganism, of primitiveness and barbaric cults. Some of the stories recount the burial of live girls. Can similarities be found between burying girls alive during the *jahalia* and the burial of *shaheeds* today?

That was what I asked sheikh Najah Baqarat, an Islamic scholar. I went to his home in Sur Bahir, an Arab village just southeast of Jerusalem, with my husband and Murad. When we entered, the men kissed and the sheikh shook my hand and invited us to sit down, saying *Ahalan wa-sahalan* ("Welcome") at least ten times. He left us for a moment and we could hear him ordering refreshments for the guests. We expected his wife, but instead, his son entered the room. The young man, who was studying for his MA at Bir Zeit University, placed a small table in front of each of us and served us cold drinks.

At the center of a wooden sideboard was a large picture of the two late Hamas leaders, Ahmad Yassin and 'Abd al-'Aziz Rantisi, neither of whom was alive at the time.

The sheikh said that according to Muslim tradition, during the *jahalia* many girls were buried alive, or thrown alive into pits to die. The usual reason was "to preserve the family's honor," or since girls could not fight and weren't considered workers, they were a financial burden.

"Do you view the *shaheeds* who blow themselves up as victims of Palestinian society, similar to what happened during the *jahalia*?" I asked.

The question must have hit a nerve, because he became emotional as he answered. "There is a difference between them, between the *shaheeds* and the *jahalia*. During the *jahalia* it was a question of minors who were killed or gotten rid of regardless of what they wanted. But the *shaheeds* are adults [sic] who have made their own decision. They are influenced by their environment, but the decision is theirs to make."

"The decision isn't always theirs," I said, and gave him examples of children who were sent to blow themselves up or cases in which peer pressure was used for manipulation.

He said, "You can't talk about *shaheeds* without mentioning the reasons they became *shaheeds*. Why did the Japanese act of kamikaze, which was relatively limited, spread to the Arab world, Iraq, Saudi Arabia, etc?"

The sheikh was apparently unaware of historical facts. The kamikazes were Japanese suicide pilots who "limited" their attacks to American warships towards the end of the Second World War. They did not attack civilians in supermarkets and restaurants and they did not attack buses. The phenomenon did not "spread" anywhere. As a tool to demoralize Israel, gain political ends and incidentally kill as many Jews as possible, suicide bombing was used by the Palestinians terrorist organizations and it is now employed by all such Arabic/Muslim organizations.

"If we keep putting our heads in the sand, things will only get worse. We have to know what causes such things. Not only the security of Israel, Jordan and Saudi Arabia is in danger, because it is an international phenomenon ...

"One of the primary reasons is that there are no institutions for youth. In Saudi Arabia there are only religious institutions. Come and pray ... They have no social life. A radical fundamentalist society is suffocating."

It was strange to hear such things from a sheikh who had pictures of Yassin and Rantisi in his living room.

"The young people have no clubs, no comfort, no sports, no education, and certainly no field trips. The absence of all those things makes them want to become *shaheeds*.

"The second thing is the lack of understanding of the essence of the Islamic way of thought. It fosters vengeance and is constantly simmering. People distanced themselves from Islam and that caused the desire for revenge. The atmosphere of lawlessness and constant simmering anger made people more extreme. People with a blood lust don't care whom they kill, Muslims in Jordan, Saudi Arabia, Iraq, the main thing is to kill. The means justify the end ...

"The Arab states have repressed the younger generation. The régimes have retained their own status, their centrality, and abandoned the younger generation. The new generation has grown up poor and without goals in life. It has no purpose and doesn't care if it lives or dies, is murdered or imprisoned. The young people have no interest in life because they're going to die anyway. And if someone does something extreme, like attempting a suicide bombing attack, and winds up alive, then he is disappointed."

"Do you believe that someone really chooses to be a *shaheed*, or are there other things influencing him?" I asked.

"It is only human nature to be influenced by society, one's education and the environment. My experience has shown me that *istishhad* will stop, and for several reasons: For more than 50 years, the Palestinians have tried all kinds of struggle; revolt, rockets, the intifada and *istishhad* and it hasn't gotten them anywhere. They'll look for something else. The Islamic sages disagree [with suicide bombing]. Many of them say it is forbidden to kill yourself to bring about change ..."

"You're only relating to the suicide of the *shaheed*, not the deaths of innocent victims," I said.

He answered, "People don't examine the various aspects of being *shaheeds*. 'Shaheed' doesn't mean being a terrorist and killing others. The *shuhada* [dying for the sake of Allah] is a status, not murder, and it is Allah who grants the status. The *shuhada* is not the automatic product of killing others, but a virtue given by Allah as a reward. Thirteen thousand people died of natural causes and were granted the status of *shaheeds*. That's right, natural causes. When someone dies because he blew himself up and killed other people there is no promise he will be considered a *shaheed* by Allah. What is important is what motivated him to do it. If he wanted to be thought of as very masculine or if there were financial considerations, then what he did will not make him a *shaheed*!"

The sheikh's son, who until then had sat quietly—although his discomfort was obvious—decided to enter the discussion. "People don't just blow themselves up for no reason. I see how it is on the way to Bir Zeit, when I go to the university, how they humiliate people at the roadblocks ... how other people get killed when they kill a wanted person ... The motivation isn't religious, because otherwise atheistic parties wouldn't send *shaheeds* ... The motivation for a suicide bombing attack comes from the Israeli war machine ..."

The sheikh stopped his son and said authoritatively, "As far as I know, Anat wanted to speak to *me* ..." and the young man, mortified, shrank down into his chair as far as possible.

And as if nothing untoward had happened, he continued, "The Islamic world should issue a *fatwa* against suicide bombing attacks. The real voice of Islam, which is moderate, should be heard."

"That's the problem," I said, "the moderates are not heard, and there are people who think that every Muslim is bin Laden."

The sheikh nodded. "In the coming days there should be agreements among the Arab states and between the Arab states and the West against radical Islam. Moderate Muslims who support dialogue should be in allegiance ... [But] if the West fights Islam then the moderate Muslims will join the extremists, and everyone will be an extremist ... When I was in Manhattan, in America, they said, 'Don't get out of the car, they'll kill you.' In America they'll kill you for a dollar ...

"There's rape and crime ... Someone killed his mother, his son and his wife for a fix. When you see America from the outside it's like a nice big watermelon, but when you cut into it you see it's full of worms. With us, in Muslim society, the watermelon is already open, so you can see the good part and the rotten part."

The son, who had slunk out of the room, now returned carrying a copper tray with little cups of Arab coffee. He leaned over in front of each guest and served each of us individually, in the traditional fashion of the Arab host.

"Do you think *shaheeds* and *shaheedas* have some special characteristics?" I asked.

"All the factions in Islam forbid women to participate in military actions. Before 1996 there were no Islamic women in prison, but the nonreligious factions managed to attract the Islamic factions and seduce them into letting women participate."

"And what is characteristic of the suicide bomber, the one who blows himself and others up?"

"The most important thing is that *shaheeds* are introverted, fixed on doing things in a certain way, and they think that paradise is just on the other side of the street ... Very simplistic. Usually they are people who don't talk a lot and their ability to express their needs and distress is limited. They can only express themselves by being dramatic and shouting. Most of them are usually quiet, the kind of people who sit in corners, in shadows, who don't put themselves forward and who are always in a dilemma over what they should do. Usually they have some kind of emotional problem because of some complex or other or because they are abused at home, or they're depressed or have financial problems, or problems related to morality.

"In my opinion, people who become suicide bombers have aggressive personalities, they have to be violent, and they have criminal personalities as well. I think it is easy to influence a potential suicide bomber, that he finds it hard to say no. He projects all his problems onto other people and justifies everything he does by blaming someone else. He thinks all his problems will be solved in 'the other world,' in paradise. They do it camouflaged as religion ... It's like coming up with a drug for the suicide bomber's pain, and on the bottle it says 'Qur'an, religion, masculinity, the way to liberation.' A little bottle for pain: 'The bottle for liberation from the occupation, the bottle that will release your masculinity ...'

"I think we are nearing the end of suicide bombing attacks, I don't think they will go on much longer, because more and more people aren't encouraging suicide bombing attacks. Everything I have said is a recommendation for how to prevent and stop suicide bombing attacks."

Unfortunately, as opposed to what the sheikh said in 2004, suicide bombing attacks did not stop, they continue in Israel and parts of the world, especially Iraq.

"What do you think about the use of children as suicide bombers?" I asked.

"It only reinforces what I just said. They've gone bankrupt so they use the small change. If I have 2,000 dollars, I spend dollars, not pennies. It's a sign of bankruptcy, because they use small children, not true believers. The prophet forbade 15- and 16-year old children to go to war because they were children. In the end he let them join the army but without weapons, and he didn't permit them to fight. Younger than 18, he's still a child, and it's forbidden to use him."

He said in a determined voice, "The use of children in suicide bombing attacks is a sign that the Palestinian organizations have gone bankrupt."

CHAPTER 15

Paradise: "All That Is Forbidden in This World Is Allowed in Paradise"

"Everything is allowed in paradise. Everything that is forbidden in this world is allowed in paradise," said Um-Nabil, mother of a *shaheed*, and she was not the only one to say it. She continued, "In this life we live and grow old and die. In paradise we all go back in time. We become younger. Allah puts us into this world to test us. When Allah sends us catastrophes, they are really signs of his mercy. He pities us.

"Allah put us on earth to build it, to carry out his commandments. Every religion has its own laws and principles, and its believers. In the end Allah sent us the Qur'an, which is true at all times in every place."

Fatima as well, the female suicide bomber, had her own description of paradise. "Paradise doesn't belong only to *shaheeds*. People who fast during Ramadan and others can get there as well: those who perform the *hajj* and who aren't unfaithful, don't lie and live with faith. In the Qur'an, a woman's mosque is her home. During Ramadan she can go to the mosque. I studied religion so I went to the mosque three times a week.

"There is a verse in the Qur'an which describes paradise. It's about the 70 virgins, actually, the 72 virgins, who wait for a man, a *shaheed*. The *shaheeda* is one of those 72 virgins. Paradise is more than real life. We don't live a real life. Now we're just passing through. Real life is in paradise. There is everything there. Everything you can think of is in paradise, food, really tasty food ... Allah is pleased with men. That's what it says in the *Surah Al-Baqarah* [and here she quoted by heart] 'Don't call those who died for the sake of Allah dead, for they are alive ...'"

She spoke with great force, and added, "*Shaheeds* can have children, because they aren't considered dead. When people see a *shaheed* they think that he's dead, [but] in fact he isn't dead, he's in paradise and he's still alive."

I asked her if *shaheedas* could have children in paradise or whether the privilege was reserved only for men. The question embarrassed her and she hesitated before answering. It turned out she was much better informed about what waited for male *shaheeds* than what waited for a *shaheeda* like herself. I could sense that she wanted to say that both sexes enjoyed the same rewards but that she couldn't bring herself to do it.

"Allah knows if a *shaheeda* can give birth in paradise," she said uncertainly. "There is a description of the beauty of paradise but nothing about women, whether they can give birth there or not ... The *Surah* called Al-Rahman describes paradise."

This is the description of paradise, *al-jannah*, as previously mentioned by Fatima:

> But for such as fear the time when they will stand before their
>   Lord there will be two gardens
> Then which of the favors of your Lord will you choose? [The
>   refrain repeats after every verse.]
> Containing all kinds of trees and delights
> In them will be two flowing springs;
> In them will be two kinds of every fruit.
> They will recline on carpets whose inner linings will be of rich
>   brocade: the fruit of the gardens will be near.
> In them will be chaste maidens restraining their glances
>   whom no man or jinn before them has touched
> Like unto rubies and coral ...
> And besides these two there are two other gardens
> Dark green in color.
> In them will be two springs pouring forth water in continuous
>   abundance:
> In them will be fruits and dates and pomegranates:
> In them will be fair, good, beautiful
> Companions restrained in pavilions
> Whom no man or jinn before them has touched
> Reclining on green cushions and rich carpets of beauty.

And if there is someone who is not enthusiastic about the idea of 72 virgins, the Qur'an promises 72 "eternally young boys" (*waldan muhaldoun*) who serve the residents of paradise and help them pass the time.

Shafiqa, the suicide bomber who changed her mind, did not have much to say about paradise. "I thought I would meet the man who was killed who wanted to be my fiancé. I would be able to rest in paradise and be near all the people I loved: the man who died, my grandfather, who raised me until I was 16. But I was afraid that if I hurt innocent people I might go to hell. I'm in prison and a lot of things have changed. From what I see and hear about what is going on now, I'm against suicide bombing attacks, because it's against my faith ... I don't know why ... If Allah wants me to die a Muslim, he took my soul somehow, because in suicide bombing attacks people blow themselves up with civilians ... Maybe something will change. I think I have a different idea of what paradise is, so I don't want to blow myself up and kill people.

"I want peace, to be able to go where I want, to do what I want. The Palestinians aren't allowed to do anything, everything is forbidden ... It's sad. When I go to the university, I don't want to wait at a roadblock for three hours. No one should have to do that. I don't want money, I'm not looking for money, all I want is peace and quiet."

For Shafiqa in prison, paradise was something different altogether, it was a place where she would not have to wait at a roadblock for three hours ...

"My mother was on the radio once, and she asked why I did it. My aunts also asked. I ruined my life and hurt the people who love me the most. People say I did it because I had problems. That's true, I did have problems. I don't know what I did ... Every time I get a letter from my mother I start crying ... may Allah help my mother."

Suddenly she stood up. She was half a head taller than I was, and she bent down to hug me. "I'm really happy I met you. Please come back and visit me again. With you I can talk about things I've never talked about before."

Suha, who was captured before she could blow herself up, asked me if I believed in paradise.

"I believe that wherever you are, you have to do the best you can," I said, not exactly a direct answer.

Her feet tapped the floor rhythmically and she continued talking about paradise, a topic which apparently interested her a great deal. "Life in paradise isn't like life here. It's different. Obviously paradise is mentioned in the Qur'an, and that's where I know about it from. There is everything in paradise, things that I don't have now ... Life is easier there, there is more greenery, no one gets sick and no one gets tired. People there are different from people here."

"The men get 72 virgins, one isn't enough ... What do women get?"

Suha burst out laughing. She bit her nails nervously, her eyes darting around the room, and she thought for a long time before answering. "The female *shaheeda* is one of the 72 virgins. I think I will be one of the virgins in paradise. Isn't that enough for the *shaheeds*?" she asked in perfect seriousness. "With the help of Allah, I hope to have children here [in this world], and if not, then in paradise."

Again, dreams of a home and children, the opposite of ending your life in suicide. Suha knew that in paradise the *shaheeds* were promised they could have children. When it came to women, the situation was fuzzy. It is hard to reconcile their having children with their being eternal virgins, black of eye, transparent of skin, with no menses, and no other "discharges," which is how they are described.

Fifteen-year-old Jalal said, "I would even sell my parents, the whole world, for paradise. Everything is there, Allah, freedom, the prophet Muhammad and his companions, and my friends the *shaheeds*. What can I say? No matter how much I add, it's still only the tiniest bit of paradise ..."

"There are 72 virgins, and Allah lets me marry 72 virgins. There are a lot of things I can't describe ... I'll find everything in paradise, a river of honey, a river of beer and alcohol, and anyway there are a lot of rivers in paradise ..." Alcoholic beverages figure prominently in descriptions of paradise because in this world Muslims are forbidden to drink them, even wine.

Huda as well told me what she expected in paradise. "I believe in paradise. I'm a Muslim and it's written in the Qur'an that everything we want is this world is ready for us in paradise. Everything I want, everything, even things I don't know about and don't dream about, everything I want is there. All the good things like the sea and rivers, not just water, a river of honey, everything I want, all the food you could want. Everything I can think of is there. And you don't feel tired, you don't want to sleep, you have clothes and a bed, everything you want. And you don't have to pray there, either, you did that in this world so you don't have to do it again. So people say, if life is hard in this world, in the end we will be able to rest forever in paradise."

Huda spoke excitedly, looking at me and not seeing me, as though in her imagination she could see her dreams coming true. I asked her what women would get in paradise instead of the 72 virgins the *shaheeds* got. As opposed to Fatima, she was clear on the subject: "Paradise is the same for men and women. Women aren't promised 72 virgins, because women are respected, and they don't want women to feel that they're being looked at as just wanting sex. But women have men for sex! If you fell in love with someone in this world and didn't marry him, even if it happened at a different time, 20 or 40 years, or even 200 years earlier, he will be in paradise and you will marry him there. If you don't marry him, you can have him for 'that' [sex]. But you can't talk about 'that' because you don't really know what paradise is ... The men talk about it, but for women it's something different, as far as I know 'that' remains respectable. I don't think that people only think about 'that.' ... If they do, it makes us less respectable."

Although Huda was a relatively modern and educated woman, she still could not bring herself to utter the words "sexual relations." When I asked her specifically if that was what she was referring to, she nodded. It was the only time in my experience that a Palestinian woman related directly to the subject of sexual relations in paradise. I asked her if she had heard about the suicide bomber who wrapped his penis in clean toilet paper before he blew himself up to keep it in pristine condition for the 72 virgins waiting for him in paradise. She smiled and said she hadn't heard the story but that she did not believe it. "People tell it," she said, "because they want to humiliate those who carry out the attacks, and maybe it's a way of preventing others from doing it.

"All of us think about 'that,' but it's not the only explanation of what is waiting for women in paradise. Today women in Palestinian society walk around alone, they go to the university and to work, so they are able to think differently. Some of the things that were forbidden or considered *ayib* [a shame], like talking to a boy, well, now girls talk to boys. There are girls who have a friend who is male, or a boyfriend ... I don't know what their families say to them, but I know such girls exist.

"When I was 'outside' not every home had Internet, but now everyone does. It lets boys and girls talk. Their parents don't understand about computers."

In fact, the Internet allows for communication between the sexes in a way that is beyond the controls and limitations of Palestinian parents. Shafiqa formed a romantic link with a boy in Kuwait via the Internet and eventually they conducted intimate, openly loving telephone conversations. Huda agreed with me when I said that it was a real revolution in the relations between men and women, and that electronic communications overcame inhibitions and broke down time-honored religious and cultural barriers.

I asked Huda if she believed two peoples could exist together, could live next to one another, with fairness and dignity. She nodded, but said, "It's hard for me to say what I feel, because ever since I was little I was taught that this is our country ... It's not Israel, it's Palestine. So it's hard for me to think the opposite." She also said that the Palestinians had seen Israeli democracy and adopted quite a few of the Israelis' behavior and ways of thinking, and that in Palestinian society there was more free expression than what was customary in most of the Arab states.

"My dream is to get out of prison and to be a leader in our army," she said. "Once I wanted to be the foreign minister of my country. I feel that I can speak for the [Palestinian] people and explain what the nation feels ... I think that's what it means to be foreign minister. I want peace, but with the way things are, I don't know ... Every day it gets harder. Every day it gets further away. *Inshallah* ... [May Allah grant it ...]"

Yusra, when asked what she expected from paradise, said, "There is no difference between a *shaheed* and *shaheeda* except for the 72 virgins the *shaheed* gets. They will be his wives. That's what we learned from the Qur'an and from the prophet."

I asked what women got in paradise. She thought for a minute and said, "There's something called 'the tortures of the grave.' According to our religion, a *shaheed* does not suffer them. If ordinary people are confused on Judgment Day, the *shaheed* and the *shaheeda* know everything about themselves."

I persisted, "What do women get in paradise?"

Yusra looked at me for a long time before answering, and then looked away and said, "We have a saying, that no eye has ever seen what is in paradise and no ear has ever heard. What is promised to the living in paradise— a-sahaba [the companions of Muhammad] and the revelation of Allah . . . Everything is there."

"And what else?"

"There is wine in paradise. You can drink wine and not get drunk. There is honey and yoghurt . . . What is important is being there, not the menu . . . Paradise is a place for a better life. I haven't thought about 72 men I want to save from the tortures of the grave. [She was referring to the Muslim tradition according to which a shaheed can provide 70 members of his family with a Get-Into-Paradise-Free card.] Our family is small and my brother is a shaheed, so there is no problem, and with the help of Allah, the whole family, all of us, will enter paradise."

"If your brother is a shaheed, and in any case your whole family will enter paradise, then wasn't it a pity that you wanted to die and be a shaheeda?" I asked. I could tell from the expression on her face that it wasn't the first time the thought had crossed her mind.

"It wasn't enough for me to enter paradise just because my brother was a shaheed," she answered. "I wanted a higher status when I entered, I didn't want to enter jannah [paradise] only because of my brother . . ." She thought for a minute and continued, "Becoming a shaheed or a shaheeda has a purpose, it's to please Allah . . . That's the most important thing. There are a lot of verses in the Qur'an [about it]. If an enemy comes to your door, you have to fight him and defend yourself, and I see [being a shaheeda] as self-defense."

She once told me that she was prepared to blow herself up in a kindergarten, saying, "I could be one of the 72 virgins in paradise, or the sayyida of the virgins, responsible for them."

Other would-be female suicide bombers expressed their desire to serve in paradise as a kind of on-demand factotum, responsible for the virgins. For some reason, they preferred it to serving the sexual needs of the indefatigable shaheeds . . . It is interesting to note that they have to serve the men, sexually and in general, both in paradise and on earth.

❖

Sheikh Yussuf, a devout Islamic activist who is a born-again Muslim, said of paradise, "Every man who lives in this world is committed to the da'wah [spreading Islam], to teaching [Jews and Christians] to enter paradise, to partake of Allah's mercy, that is the most important part of da'wah. It's the most important asset . . . What good will it do me to be prime minister or the richest man in the world or even to rule the whole world if in the end I wind up in jehanam [hell]? Which is better, to kill a Jew or to go to paradise? . . .

You can kill a hundred, a thousand, thousands, Hitler killed millions and didn't wipe them out ..."

I smiled and asked, "Why is it so important for you to get Jews and Christians into paradise? You can't even get along with the Jews in this world ..." He smiled back and said, "That is the *da'wah*, and that is what I believe in ..."

Abu Hilal, a former Palestinian Islamic Jihad activist, stated categorically that "It is forbidden to send a Muslim girl to war. I know. I have a BA from Al-Azhar [a Muslim university in Cairo] ... The *shaheed* believes he is not dead and that he receives [the services of] 72 virgins ... Throw a stone and you will hit 20 suicide bombers. People have nothing to lose. A young man grows up, doesn't see work, doesn't see food. If someone gives him 100 shekels [about $22] he'll kiss his hands." Like Jalal, who received the same amount and used it to buy a pot for his mother.

I met Abu Hilal at the home of a Palestinian on the outskirts of a refugee camp in East Jerusalem. Murad came with me.

Abu Hilal wore traditional Arab clothes. He was stocky and seemed more like a former prizefighter than an activist in an extremist religious terrorist organization. His Hebrew was fluent, apparently the result of many years in Israeli prisons. Only indirectly did he refer to the ideological change of heart, which led him to leave the Palestinian Islamic Jihad.

"The economic situation is bad and people pass the time in the mosques, because coffee houses and sports clubs cost money. Every day in the mosques they hear about what the Jews are doing, and that Al-Aqsa is in the hands of the Jews, and that Mecca and the Mosque of the Prophet in Madinah have to be liberated from the 'non-Muslims' [i.e., the America army presence in Saudi Arabia] ..."

I asked him to tell me what Muslim tradition said about paradise, and what *shaheeds* of both sexes could expect to find there. He squinted through his thick glasses, and said, "According to the Qur'an, if a person is good, Allah grants him a larger grave. If he is bad, Allah makes his grave smaller and angels beat him. There are two poles, what is desirable and what is undesirable, what is good and what is evil. There is a war between good and evil, and what is good is explained: paradise is fruit, virgins and palaces. If you go to hell you will have running sores and trees with bitter thorns will tear up your insides."

"So what do female suicide bombers receive in paradise? As far as I have been able to find out, no one has offered them 72 pretty-eyed virgin men."

He stuck his fork into the salad in front of him and tried to spear a fleeing olive. "It is forbidden by Muslim law for a woman to go to war," he said decisively. "A woman who wants to be a *shaheeda* has to look Western, she needs makeup, and that is forbidden because it will make men look at her. And after she has blown herself up she will be naked and sensitive parts of her body will be visible, things only other women are allowed to see."

"Abu Hilal, do you mean that her private parts will be strewn around and her modesty will be compromised because everyone will be able to see her nakedness?

"Yes," he nodded. "When the Chechens took over the theatre in Moscow, the women wore veils. The Chechens took women with them to deal with the women in the theatre because it is forbidden for men to touch women. There were *mujahidat* [female fighters], 10 women at the time of the prophet, who cared for the wounded, but they did not fight and were not killed ... Paradise is under the feet of the mothers [A familiar Arabic saying, used even by Ahmad Yassin] ... A mother suffers pregnancy, raises the children, sits with them at night and takes care of them. The mother is most holy. You say mother three times, and father only once ... You asked me what waits for the *shaheeda* in paradise. She will be one of the *houris* [Technically, "virgins" or "pure beings," but generally thought to be related etymologically to *hawira*, "black-eyed."] and will receive everything the *shaheed* receives. She will be beautiful for all eternity, *hour al-'ein* ... All the females are virgins in paradise. There are no sexual relations there. The houris will belong to the *shaheeds*. And if Adam and Eve had stayed in paradise, they wouldn't have had children. Wine is permitted in paradise, but natural wine, not man-made. There are rivers of wine, yoghurt and honey. The *shaheeda* receives sanctity. Even if she is ugly here, she will be beautiful in paradise, her skin will be white, her eyes will be black, her veins will be visible through her white skin. There is no menstruation in paradise, no need to go to the bathroom ... the *shaheed* lives with his soul and not his body."

Abu Hilal's description, which is entirely spiritual, is completely the opposite of Muslim traditions, which emphasize the quite physical, sensual pleasures waiting for the faithful in paradise. However, his description of the liberation from certain physical limitations, such as menstruation and the need to urinate and defecate, is consistent with another folktale, according to which the virgins in paradise are "eternally virgins." After each sexual encounter with a *shaheed* their hymens miraculously grow back and they are "pure" again.

Abu Hilal continued, "If a man goes to war and his arms and legs are cut off, they become trees in paradise. The trees wait for the person to whom they belong to arrive. If someone is a *shaheed*, Allah will forgive him everything ... A Sunni Muslim won't do that, he won't send women [to commit suicide] ... It's forbidden. A woman can help in many ways. If a woman goes to blow herself up, it is a disgrace for men, because there is no lack of men who will do it.

"The woman who blew herself up at the Maxim in Haifa in October 2003 saw her brother killed by [Israeli] soldiers. Then her boyfriend was killed, he was her fiancé and had promised to marry her, he wasn't on the wanted list but they killed him. If he slept with her, if she was no longer a virgin, that was the end of her. It would shame her, it would be a problem for her, people would say, to go him . . . She was a lawyer, not a goatherd, she didn't have a choice . . . Most people do it because of personal distress. There are women who were on their way to suicide bombing attacks and in the end they turned themselves in.

"Someone who is a suicide bomber with an explosive belt, that's someone who changed his mind, maybe people said he was a collaborator, or he was going to die one way or another, so it would be preferable for him to be a *shaheed*. The woman who blew herself up at Maxim's was not religious, because in her picture in the paper she was wearing makeup, even though she was wearing traditional clothes. She wore makeup when she walked into the restaurant, that means she didn't belong to the Palestinian Islamic Jihad. If she were not religious she wouldn't have any problems with dressing like a Western woman. With us, the Arabs, you can wear a ninja suit, it's the traditional dress of women with no connection to religion, and without a veil. There is a religious argument between the sheikhs, whether the woman should wrap a scarf around her head or wear a veil . . . There are a lot of disagreements when it comes to women. The Sunnis follow the four sheikhs.

"I don't know if you know this, but as a Sunni Muslim, I'm forbidden to marry a Shi'ite woman. I can marry a Jewish woman and I can eat and drink with a Jew or a Christian because they are 'the people of the Book.' The Shi'ites are infidels, because they had the truth and they abandoned it. A Sunni is greater than a Shi'ite. We aren't even allowed to participate in Shi'ite funerals or to pray in their mosques." The Sunni–Shi'ite rivalry in Iraq today has led to much bloodshed, the burning of mosques, and suicide bombing attacks.

"In view of what you have just said, how do you explain the collaboration between Sunni Palestinians and Hezbollah Shi'ites?" I asked.

The question seemed to embarrass him. He took a sip of coffee, spoke to our host for a moment, and then said, "There is collaboration with the Hezbollah because of Israel. Hassan Nasrallah [the Hezbollah leader] speaks about Sunnis and Shi'ites, and says that this is not the time to settle old scores."

The second time I met Abu Hilal was after Reem Riyashi blew herself up at the Erez crossing between the Gaza Strip and Israel in January 2004. It was the first time Hamas took responsibility for a suicide bombing attack carried out by a woman, and this one had two small children at home. He said, "This is the first time it has happened but in my opinion not the last. From the religious point of view, a woman who is a mother and has been sentenced to death must wait until she gives birth if she is pregnant, and her child must be two years old, and a sheikh must sign a paper saying who will bring up the baby. The prophet Muhammad said that. The suicide bomber, Reem Riyashi, had a child younger than two. How could she do it?

"Ahmad Yassin said to do it, to send women, but he didn't mean her personally. Sheikh Ahmad Yassin was the last to know about it, he is the cannon's sighting device ... Hamas is a global organization. The Muslim Brotherhood [founded in Egypt in 1924] and Hamas did not authorize women suicide bombers, and their leaders were chastised because of it. Hamas has only one *amir* [ruler] and he is Yussuf Qardawi [a very influential fundamentalist Muslim sheikh who lives in Qatar]. They rely on his *fatwas* [religious edicts] and read all his books, but quietly ... Qardawi is against it [allowing women to be suicide bombers]."

Abu Hilal's information was inaccurate. Qardawi did, in fact, issue a religious edict permitting—even encouraging—women to carry out suicide bombing attacks, and allowing them to wear Western dress if it would increase their chances of getting the job done.

"It turned out that Riyashi was involved with an other man and her husband caught her [according to the media]. Instead of all the shame and embarrassment, the husband sent her to blow herself up. Her brother did not authorize it and was not happy about what she did. Perhaps the lover also committed suicide, but there is a problem because the Gaza Strip is closed, there is a fence that closes it off. Because of the fence people can't get out of Tulkarm and Jenin. Just a couple of days ago they found five explosive belts.

"... In the past they sent 15-year olds, 16-year olds to be suicide bombers, and their families were against it. A child doesn't do anything, he just blows himself up alone. People don't have money, they go to the mosque to pray and Allah belongs to everyone, the rich and the poor. At the mosque they meet people who are waiting for someone like them. In the evening they turn on the TV and see the [Israeli] army shooting, they watch Al-Manar [the Hezbollah TV station which broadcasts from Lebanon], Al-Jazeera [Qatar], Al-Arabiya [Abu Dhabi] and Palestinian TV.

"... A secular régime should be instituted in the Palestinian Authority, they should get Dahlan or Abu 'Ala to head it [both of whom did in fact join the Palestinian régime after the death of Arafat]. A religious régime is a danger to the Jews and to the Arabs in the State of Israel."

In the January elections to the Palestinian Legislative Council, Hamas won a sweeping victory and in March 2006 its fundamentalist Islamic government was sworn in.

"In Israel the Islamic movement should be prevented [from existing]. If it continues it will be like the Gaza Strip here. They built an Islamic college in Baqa al-Gharbiya [a large Arab-Israeli town]. In Umm el-Fahm [a large Arab-Israeli town] there is an Islamic college that grants BA degrees, and for advanced studies there is Al-Najah University in Nablus, that's where Israel Arabs meet Palestinians wanted by the Israeli security forces and they become even more extreme ... They are building mosques in every Arab village, whereas personally I prefer community centers for sports and cultural activities for children and adults, with instructors. The Islamic movement raises children in its own kindergartens ... Kindergartens should be built and kindergarten teachers should be hired. Today no one sees it like that, but that's how to stop the attacks. You have to take people who care about more than money and a job, people who will build sports clubs so that people will spend their time there instead of in the mosques."

❖

During a visit to his house in the Arab village of Sur Bahir, I asked the Islamic scholar sheikh Najah Baqarat what he thought about paradise. I said, "Many of the people I have spoken to said they wanted to go to paradise and even described it in detail."

"According to my Islamic education, and I have read the Qur'an and the Sunnah, Allah created us to live happy lives in this world. He didn't create us so that we would start off miserable and unhappy, so that we should die. If Allah had wanted us to die he wouldn't have created us in the first place. Because of that Allah gave us a purpose in this world, to live and to feel that we were doing something and building the world. Our purpose here is to interact with other peoples and groups, generation after generation, including non-Muslims.

"Paradise is a repetition of what we do in this world. No one enters paradise to say if it is corporal or spiritual, no one goes to hell to tell us what it means to scorch or burn, or if it's lava or simple fire or the sun. Just as we believe in Allah without seeing him, and we believe in gravity and magnetism and we don't see them with our own eyes, we believe that there is paradise for those who take the straight path, and there is hell for criminals and murderers. So I'm against those who describe paradise in physical terms."

"But there are descriptions of paradise in the Qur'an. People who planned to carry out suicide bombing attacks told me about it. How is that compatible with what you say?"

His answer was ready: "That's done to make people do good things. If you keep walking you will reach the top of the *jebel* [mountain], and at the top of the mountain you will receive everything, trees and nice places, all the light can be given to create hope in a person. I can describe it like the Bahai gardens [beautifully landscaped gardens on Mt. Carmel in Israel] and make it seem beautiful or like Gaza, as something bad . . .

"According to the *hadith*, no eye has seen [paradise], no ear has heard and no one's heart has imagined it. No one can imagine or describe paradise in terms of human understanding. Everyone in the world thinks paradise belongs to him . . . Everyone describes paradise to himself as he understands it, everyone fashions his clothing according to his own measurements. That's why there is a difference of opinion between religions. Each religion says, I'm on the right path and all the others are going astray. The truth is that whoever believes in Allah and doesn't hurt other people will reach paradise. After all, paradise is big enough for everyone. It's bigger than the people who think it is intended for this *shaheed* or another think it is, or one religion or another . . ."

He took a sip of his coffee and continued, "There is a paradise, it was created and exists. Just as this world was created, so were paradise and hell. They are institutions which were created by Allah. Unfortunately, no one has reached them and [come back to] talk about them, whether they are physical or spiritual. The Qur'an has a detailed description, there are pomegranates, rivers, trees ... There is one tree under whose canopy you can ride a horse for 60 years in any direction ... That is a divine description which encourages us to carry out positive actions, so that we don't stray from the path.

"There are different statuses in paradise, there is the highest status and there is the middle status ... You can let your imagine run wild without limitation. Your imagination is allowed to exaggerate, it can draw a picture of what people who did good things in their lives will receive in paradise. It is permissible to exaggerate such descriptions to encourage people to do good things.

"... They say there is alcohol there, not the kind we know, not the kind that makes you drunk. There are a lot of similes and metaphors. If there is wine which doesn't make you drunk and act like a fool ... If there is alcohol here, there is also alcohol there. The point of all the description is to make people take the good path. Paradise can be seen the way you make promises to a schoolchild, you say, 'If you study hard and get good marks, I'll send you to Turkey on vacation, to Istanbul.' It's to encourage him to study hard ... but he's never seen Istanbul."

The Last Word

I finished writing this book in 2004 and prepared it for translation in 2006, after the mass-murder suicide bombing attacks in London, Jordan, Iraq and Egypt. In April 2006 there was a suicide bombing attack, the second in three months at the same fast-food restaurant near the old Central Bus Station in Tel Aviv. As these lines are being written, dozens more suicide bombing attacks are being planned. Posters of *shaheeds* are hung on the walls in Palestinian cities and villages, and each has his very brief moment in the sun. But beyond their families, who will remember them when their posters are taken down to make room for new *shaheeds*? The *shaheeds* and *shaheedas* are not the heroes they are made out to be. As far as their personalities go, they are the antitheses of the classic hero and heroine, marginal individuals or those whose families could not protect them from the "local heroes"— usually terrorists wanted by Israel—who recruited them or dispatched them to carry out a suicide bombing attack.

The global village seems to have an endless column of suicide bombers treading their way to a much-desired paradise, a place of virgins, wine, and the camaraderie of Muhammad and his companions; there are even those who expect Allah to reveal himself in person. For the suicide bombers, male and female, such dreams are a concrete reality, reinforced daily through in-doctrination and hate propaganda disseminated in the mosques, the streets, the schools, the media, and popular music. Thus suicide bombing, which is a very private act, has become common Palestinian property and has led to a cult of death and killing. The cult is not reserved only for Palestinian society, which created the wave of suicide bombers, but is also part of bin Laden's global jihad, which produces coordinated showcase attacks, the most conspicuous of which was on September 11, 2001 in the United States.

The mass religious ecstasy surrounding the *shaheeds* has created a sensation of enormous power. The *shaheed*'s act can be viewed as a kind of expressive suicide. It is his way, and of those who support him and those he represents, to express rage, envy, and hatred for the Jews, Israel, and the rest of the Western world, and to release deep, violent impulses, which are difficult to control. In the process of neutralization and rationalization, the suicide bombers take the roles of both victim and God. The suicide bomber feels drunk with power and a sense of omnipotence in that he can take the lives of others. The neutralizing technique engendering the denying of responsibility of this sort spread quickly. The sensation of moral outrage with the self and others is likely to be neutralized by the insistence that the attack is not a crime and that carrying it out is not a terrorist act, but rather something positive, as far as they are concerned, in view of the circumstances. For the terrorists, the attack is not really an attack, merely a reprisal or a just punishment, and the criminal, in this case the terrorist, turns himself into the avenger, and the victims of terrorism become those who are guilty of having done wrong.[1]

The suicide bomber is a link in the terrorism chain, and the dispatcher is the hub. Before the suicide bomber is sent on his mission, and sometimes only a short time before, he must undergo emotional processes that will neutralize his (or her) moral judgment and guilt at committing murder. As a result, the Israelis (or Americans, Brits, Turks, Iraqis, Egyptians, or Jordanian, or all of them together) become guilty in the process that leads the suicide bomber to commit the act.

As far as the suicide bombers and their dispatchers are concerned, the Israeli victims are not civilians, "because all of Israeli society has been mobilized." After one of the many suicide bombing attacks carried out at the shopping mall in Netanya, Hamas's Muhammad al-Zahar, who as of this writing is the foreign minister of the new Hamas government, said, "There are no children in Israel, because when they reach 18, every Israeli child becomes a soldier."

The monotheistic religions, Islam among them, firmly oppose suicide among their believers. However, even a superficial examination shows that the situation is neither clear nor simple.

In effect, it can be said that Samson was the first recorded suicide, and his last wish was "to [let me] die with the Philistines." Jewish law forbids suicide and the person who commits it is denied burial in a Jewish cemetery as a way of expressing the profound rejection of his act. But on the other hand, there are cases in which it is a matter of principle for the observant Jew to die a martyr's death. For example Hannah and her sons, who preferred to die rather than worship an idol, or the ten scholars who according to legend were put to death to expiate the sins of their ancestors, or the Jews in the Arabian peninsula who refused Muhammad's demand to convert to Islam and the German Jews who refused to convert to Christianity during the Crusades. They are only some of the examples of Jews whose deaths were praised and not condemned.

The same is true for Christianity. Jesus could have saved himself from crucifixion if he had told the Romans what they wanted to hear. Other Christians went to the lions willingly, rather than forsake their beliefs. Hundreds of early Christians became saints because of their refusal to renounce Christianity.

However, during the modern age at least, suicide for religious reasons is the province of Islam. The common denominator of the attacks on the United States on September 11, the Chechen suicide terrorists in Russia, and those in Egypt, Turkey, Iraq, Britain, Spain, Argentina, etc., was that they were all Muslims, and most if not all of them were fundamentalists who had declared a jihad on the infidel enemy. It is instrumental suicide terrorism, in which the act of blowing oneself up serves a tool for achieving a political or ideological goal.

The suicide bombers are radical Islam's strategic weapons against the West. As a weapon suicide bombing is cruel, effective, and frightening. However, it is a potential boomerang, as was seen in Saudi Arabia, for example. Suicide bombing attacks are one of the main, if not *the* main reason for the West's current Islamophobia. The continuation of such attacks will reinforce that fear and harm not only Muslims living in Western countries, but also Muslim countries interested in ties with the West.

Sending killers to blow themselves up, or what Prof. Rafael Israeli in 1997 called "Islamikazis,"[2] is horrifying, particularly in the context of the attacks on the World Trade Center and Pentagon on September 11, 2001. It threatens to set Muslim society back to the time of the *jahalia*, the period of ignorance before Islam. The suicide bombers are murderers, but even before that they are victims and scapegoats of Palestinian society. However, often both junior and senior dispatchers, such as Ahmad Yassin and bin Laden, had been in custody when they were merely whistling teakettles and had not yet turned into the steam engines that pushed suicide bombers in various places into carrying out the wholesale murder of innocent civilians. It was my doctoral thesis, which dealt with the dispatchers of suicide bombers, that clarified the question of whether dispatchers and master dispatchers had their own sense of moral judgment, and the answer was yes. The dispatchers judge issues according to two polarized criteria: one is normative and humane, and is used with regard to their own people, and the other is to delegitimize and dehumanize the victims of their terrorism. George Khoury, for example, scion of a prominent Arab family and a student at the Hebrew University, was killed by Fatah in a drive-by shooting as while he was jogging in Jerusalem in 2004; these terrorists were sure only Jews went jogging, and they felt justified in killing him. The organization offered to make him a *shaheed*. The family refused.

Various circles of opinion, such as those represented by Samuel Hunting-
ton in *Clash of Civilizations,* claim that there is a profound, insoluble conflict
between the Western world and the Arab/Muslim world, and use the practice of suicide bombing attacks to prove the claim. Moderate Arabs deplore
the fact that "today the West views every Muslim as a suicide bomber ..."

Some Muslim religious leaders claim they are opposed to suicide bombing
attacks, but are afraid to say so unambiguously and publicly. However, the
opposition of the overwhelming majority of such leaders stems not from the
fact that innocent civilians are killed, but rather from the fact that suicide
is forbidden by Islam. The religious leadership, like most of the Palestinian
population, thinks it is legitimate to use terrorism as a weapon against the
State of Israel. The same is true for bin Laden's terrorism, which wages a
jihad against the West, which he defines as Islam's war against the Jewish–
Crusader alliance.

Those who deal with the murderous industry of suicide bombing attacks
have no moral sense or moral dilemmas, they kill civilians in civilian envi-
ronments, and they have no compunction about sending their own people
to certain death. They dehumanize their victims (usually random civilians
who happen to be in the wrong place at the wrong time) even if they are
children. Not only is their violence indiscriminate, it is also justified by religious slogans and knows neither pity nor remorse. The dispatchers' motto,
which they do not bother to euphemize, is "It's my job to send the suicide
bomber and his job to blow himself up, to kill and be killed." They do not
feel the need for the families of the suicide bombers to share the burden.
In most cases, the dispatcher does not send one of his own close family.
There are exceptions, however, and they are the individuals known to have
collaborated with Israel or women who have posed "problems to the family honor." Such people, rather than be murdered or bring shame to their
families, take the "honorable" way out, what Ahmad Yassin described as
"an exceptional solution for the problem." After their deaths no one dares
to speak of the real reason the *shaheed* or *shaheeda* blew themselves up.

Responsibility for resolving the political Palestinian–Israeli conflict rests
with the leaders of both peoples. On the other hand, the key to stopping
suicide bombing attacks globally is in the hands of the Muslim religious
leadership, whose faint voices have so far done little or no good. They have
the moral responsibility to forcefully condemn suicide bombing attacks and
to issue unequivocal *fatwas* against them. The most effective way would
be to clearly state that those who carry out suicide bombing attacks not
only do not automatically go to paradise, but that they automatically go
to hell. Secular Jews and Christians view such things as slightly ridiculous,
but religious Muslims relate to them with the utmost seriousness. For them,
paradise and its pleasures seem completely realistic and, for many of those
whom I interviewed, were a determining factor in their decision to carry out
a suicide bombing attack.

In February 2005, after a suicide bombing attack in Tel Aviv, Abu Mazen, head of the Palestinian Authority, called it *intihar*, that is, unlawful suicide for personal reasons, as opposed to *istishhad*, self-sacrifice for the sake of Allah. The statement was important in itself, but Abu Mazen has no religious authority and thus all he could do was express an opinion. Therefore, it can be hoped that if the Muslim religious leadership publicly rejects suicide bombing attacks and removes its patronage from them, they will stop, or at least their incidence will decrease.

Ali Salem, the well-known liberal Egyptian journalist, clearly described the necessary change in Palestinian society in the London daily Arabic newspaper *Al-Hayat* in an article addressed to the participants of the Arab League Summit. He said, "What the Palestinian people need now is political leaders, men and women who are more eager for life than death. Political leaders who do not send children to blow themselves up for the sake of Allah but who send them, for the sake of life, for the sake of the life of their people, to school, hoping that in a few years they will turn into people beneficial to their families and nation. The time has come to live for our country and family, not to die for them ..."[3]

Muslim parents should also become more aware of the behavior of their children, and if they sense something that indicates that their children might be treading that particular path, they should appeal to the authorities. The parents of one of the suicide bombers in London reported that their son had disappeared and they were afraid something had happened to him. It is possible that if more attention had been paid to their complaint, the attack might have been prevented.

In writing this book I deliberately avoided academic descriptions of cultural conflicts, the religious aspects of jihad and *istishhad*, and dealing with psychological and sociological theories. My intention was to open a window for the reader onto the inner world of the men and women who blow themselves up and of the Palestinians who dispatch them on their missions, and to shed light, if possible, on the similarities between them and suicide bombers in other parts of the world. It forced me to divorce myself from the pain and anger I felt toward them, because in speaking with them, research methodology committed me to show empathy to individuals whose greatest desire was to slaughter as many Israelis as possible, to listen patiently to their stories and explanations, and to adopt an attitude which would enable them to express their feelings fully and freely. It was difficult and I often felt myself torn in two. Whether I succeeded or not is for the reader to decide.

NOTES

FOREWORD

1. The 114 chapters of the Qur'an are called Surahs, each with a different name. Al-Nisaa means "The Women," and is the third Surah.

CHAPTER 1

1. E. Durkheim, *Suicide* (Hebrew), Nimrod Press, Tel Aviv, 2002, p. 71.
2. Ibid., p. 121.

CHAPTER 3

1. Y. Schweitzer and S. Ferber, *Al-Qaeda and Globalization of Suicide Terrorism*. Tel Aviv University Press, 2005.

CHAPTER 4

1. D. Pizarro, "Nothing More Than Feeling? The Role of Emotions in Moral Judgment." *Journal for the Theory of Social Behavior*, 2000; 30: 355–375.

CHAPTER 10

1. Translated by MEMRI, the Middle East Media Research Institute, www. memri.org.

CHAPTER 11

1. *Haaretz*, October 17, 2003.

2. B. Victor, *Army of Roses: Inside the World of Palestinian Women Suicide Bombers.* Rodale Press, Emmaus, PA, 2003.

CHAPTER 13

1. According to a forthcoming article by Dr. Mordechai Kedar, Bar Ilan University.

THE LAST WORD

1. G. Sykes and D. Matza. "Techniques of Neutralization: A Theory of Delinquency." *American Sociological Review*, 1957; 22: 664–670.

2. R. Israeli. "Islamikazi—Suicide Bombing Terrorism," *Nativ* (Hebrew), 1997; 1–2: 54–55, 69–76.

3. MEMRI, Al-Hayat, London, May 4, 2004.

GLOSSARY

Allahu Akbar. "Allah is great": what the suicide bomber shouts as he detonates his explosive, what the terrorist shouts as he begins firing or stabbing

Akbar. Great, the best

Al-hamdullihah. Praise be to Allah

Ashdod. A city in the south of Israel

Ayib. Shame on you, that's shameful

Bat Yam. A city in the center of Israel, not far from Tel Aviv

Beersheba. A city in the south of Israel

Beit Naballah. A village in the West Bank

Beit Sahour. A village in the West Bank

Da'wah. The spread of the Islamic religion, teaching, indoctrination and the civilian infrastructure of the terrorist organizations

Fatah. The PLO

Fatwa. A religious Islamic edict

Galabiya. A traditional Muslim garment

Hadith. A saying from the Muslim oral tradition

Hajj. A pilgrimage to Mecca, one of the religious duties of Islam, to be performed at least once during a Muslim's life

Hamsa. An incantation to ward off the evil eye

Hijab. Traditional Islamic woman's head covering

Inshallah. "May Allah will it"

Intifada. Uprising

Al-Aqsa Intifada. The uprising which began in September 2000

Intihar. Suicide committed for personal reasons

Istishhad. Becoming a *shaheed* by carrying out a suicide bombing attack for the sake of Allah

Jahiliyyah. The state of ignorance of divine guidance, the pre-Muslim period

Jebel. Mountain

Jenin. A city in the northern West Bank

Jilbab. A kind of cloak that envelops the entire body

Kaddish. The Jewish prayer for the dead

Kafiyeh. Traditional Arab men's head covering

L'chaim. The traditional Jewish toast, "to life"

Mujahidat. Female jihad warriors

Mujahideen. Male jihad warrior

Naram. The Arabic translation of Tzlil, which means "a pleasant musical tone"

Netivot. A city in the south of Israel

Oslo. The Oslo Accords, signed by Yitzhak Rabin and Yasser Arafat in 1993

Petah Tikva. A city in the center of Israel, not far from Tel Aviv

Rasoul. Allah's messenger Muhammad

Sabra and Shatilla. Palestinian refugee camps in Lebanon

Shabbab. Boys, "the guys"

Shahadah. The tenets of the Muslim faith

Shaheed. A Muslim man who died as a martyr for the sake of Allah

Shaheeda. A Muslim woman who died as a martyr for the sake of Allah

Sharmouta. Whore

Shuhadaa. Martyrs who have died for the sake of Allah

Shuhadah. Dying for the sake of Allah

Yavneh. A city in the center of Israel, not far from Tel Aviv

Zinzana. The paddy wagon, a van used for transporting prisoners

SELECTED BIBLIOGRAPHY

Adelman, Madelaine, Edna Erez, and Nadera Shalhoub-Kevorkian (2003). Policing Violence Against Minority Women in Multicultural Societies: "Community" and the Politics of Exclusion. *Police and Society*, 7: 105–133. Available online at http://www.ojp.usdoj.gov/nij/publications/specialissue/6AdelmanErez.pdf

Adler, Freda (1975). *Sisters in Crime*. New York: McGraw-Hill.

Ahmed, Leila (1992). *Women and Gender in Islam: Historical Roots of a Modern Debate*. New Haven, CT: Yale University Press.

Al-Khayyat, S. (1990). *Honour & Shame: Women in Modern Iraq*. London: Saqi Books.

Atran, Scott (2003). Genesis of Suicide Terrorism. *Science*, 299: 1534–1539.

Barakat, Halim (1985). The Arab Family and the Challenge of Social Transformation. In E. W. Fernea, ed., *Women and the Family in the Middle East: New Voices of Change*, pp. 27–48. Austin, TX: University of Texas Press.

Berko, Anat and Edna Erez (2005). 'Ordinary People' and 'Death Work': Palestinian Suicide Bombers as Victimizers and Victims. *Violence and Victims*, 20(6): 603–623.

———— (forthcoming). Gender, Palestinian Women and Terrorism: Women's Liberation or Oppression? *Studies in Conflict and Terrorism*.

Berko, Anat, Yuval Wolf, and Moshe Addad (2005). The Moral Infrastructure of Chief Perpetrators of Suicidal Terrorism: An Analysis in Terms of Moral Judgment. *Israel Studies in Criminology*, 9: 10–47.

Bloom, Mia M. (2005). *Dying to Kill: The Allure of Suicide Terror*. New York: Columbia University Press.

Brunner, Claudia (2005). Female Suicide Bombers-Male suicide bombers? Looking for gender in reporting the Suicide Bombing of the Israeli-Palestinian Conflict. *Global Society*, 19(1): 29–48.

Crenshaw, Martha *(2002)*. *"Suicide" Terrorism in Comparative Perspective. In Boaz Ganor, ed., Countering Suicide Terrorism,* pp. 19–21. Herzliya, Israel: The International Policy Institute for Counter-Terrorism.

El Sarraj, Eyad (2002). *Wounds and Madness: Why We've Become Suicide Bombers.* PeaceWork. Available online at http://www.afsc.org/pwork/0205/020506a.htm

Ehrenfeld, Rachel. (2005). *Funding Evil.* Chicago and Los Angles: Bonus Books.

Erez, E. (2006). Protracted War, Terrorism and Mass Victimization: Exploring Victimological/Criminological Theories and Concepts in Addressing Terrorism in Israel. In U. Ewald and K. Turković, eds., *Large-Scale Victimisation as a Potential Source of Terrorist Activities—Importance of Regaining Security in Post-Conflict Societies,* pp. 89–102. NATO Security through Science Series, E: Human and Societal Dynamics, Vol. 13. The Netherlands: ISO Press.

Fernea, E. W. (1985). *Women and the Family in the Middle East: New Voices of Change.* Austin, TX: University of Texas Press.

Fighel, Yoni (2003). *Palestinian Islamic Jihad and Female Suicide Bombers.* International Policy Institute for Counter-Terrorism. Available online at http://www.ict.org.il/articles/articledet.cfm?articleid=499

Ganor, B. (2002). "Suicide Attacks in Israel." In *Countering Suicide Terrorism,* pp. 140–252. Herzliya, Israel: The International Policy Institute for Counter-Terrorism.

Ganor B. (2005) *The counter terrorism puzzle—A guide for decision makers,* Piscataway, New Jersey: Transaction.

Glaser, Barney G. (1992). *Basics of Grounded Theory Analysis.* Mill Valley, CA: Sociology Press.

Goldstein, Joshua S. (2001). *War and Gender: How Gender Shapes the War System and Vice Versa.* London: Cambridge University Press.

Hafez, Mohammed M. (2004). Manufacturing Human Bombs: Strategy, Culture, and Conflict in the Making of Palestinian Suicide Terrorism. Paper presented at the National Institute of Justice conference, Washington, DC, October 25–26, 2004.

Hasan, Manar (1999). The Politics of Honor: Patriarchy, the State and Family Honor Killing. In D. Izraeli et al., eds., *Sex, Gender and Politics,* pp. 267–305. Tel Aviv, Israel: Hakibutz Hameochad (in Hebrew).

Hassan, Riaz (2003). Suicide Bombing Driven More by Politics than Religious Zeal. *YaleGlobal Online.* Available online at: http://yaleglobal.yale.edu/article.print?id=3749

Hasso, Frances H. (2005). Discursive and Political Deployments of the 2002 Palestinian Women Suicide Bombers/Martyrs. *Feminist Review,* 81: 23–51.

Hoffman, Bruce. (2006). *Inside Terrorism.* New York: Columbia University Press.

Israeli, Raphael (2004). Palestinian Women: The Quest for a Voice in the Public Square Through "Islamikaze Martyrdom." *Terrorism and Political Violence,* 16(1): 66–96.

Juergensmeyer, Mark (2000). *Terror in the Mind of God: The Global Rise of Religious Violence.* Berkeley: University of California Press.

Katz, Jack (1983). A Theory of Qualitative Methodology. In R. Emerson, ed., *Contemporary Field Research,* pp. 127–148. Boston: Little, Brown and Co.

Kedar, Mordechai (2007). *Gap of Values: Gender and Family Issues as Source of Tension between Islam and the West*. Institute for Policy and Strategy, Inter-Disciplinary Center, Herzliya, Israel.

Korbin, Nancy (2005). Countering Terrorists' Motivations. Paper presented at the Annual Conference of the International Policy Center for Counter-Terrorism, The Interdisciplinary Center, Herzliya, Israel.

Merari, Ariel (2004). Suicide Terrorism in the Context of the Israeli Palestinian Conflict. Paper presented at the Suicide Terrorism Research Conference, National Institute of Justice, Washington, DC, October 25–26, 2004.

Moghadam A. (2003). Palestinian suicide terrorism in the second Intifada: Motivations and organizational aspects. *Studies in Conflict and Terrorism*, 26(2): 65–92.

Pape, Robert A. (2005). *Dying to Win: The Strategic Logic of Suicide Terrorism*. New York: Random House.

Patkin, Terri T. (2004). Explosive Baggage: Female Palestinian Suicide Bombers and the Rhetoric of Emotion. *Women and Language*, 27(2): 79–88.

Rubenberg, Cheryl A. (2001). *Palestinian Women: Patriarchy and Resistance in the West Bank*. Boulder, CO: Lynne Rienner.

Rubin, Irene and Herbert J Rubin (2004). *Qualitative Interviewing: The Art of Hearing Data*. Thousand Oaks, CA: Sage.

Sageman, M. (2004). *Understanding Terror Networks*. Philadelphia: University of Pennsylvania Press.

Schweitzer, Yoram (2006). Palestinian Female Suicide Bombers: Reality vs. Myth. In Y. Schweitzer, ed., *Female Suicide Bombers: Dying for Equality?* pp. 24–40. Memorandum No. 84 (August). Tel Aviv, Israel: Jaffee Center for Strategic Studies, Tel Aviv University.

Shalhoub-Kevorkian, Nadera (1999). The Politics of Disclosing Female Sexual Abuse: A Case Study of Palestinian Society. *Child Abuse and Neglect*, 23(12): 1275–1293.

——— (2003). Liberating Voices: The Political Implications of Palestinian Mothers Narrating Their Loss. *Women's Studies International Forum*, 26(5): 391–407.

——— (2005). Disclosure of Child Abuse in Conflict Areas. *Violence Against Women*, 11: 1263–1291.

Sharabi, Hishan (1975). *Mukadimat li-dirasat al-mujtam'a al-Arabi* (Introduction to Studies of Arab Society). Beirut: Dar Altali'a Liltiba'a Wa Al-nashr (in Arabic).

Stern, Jessica (2003). *Terror in the Name of God: Why Religious Militants Kill*. New York: Harper Collins.

Tzoreff, Mira (2006). The Palestinian Shahida: National Patriotism, Islamic Feminism,or Social Crisis. In Y. Schweitzer, ed., *Female Suicide Bombers: Dying for Equality?* pp. 12–23. Memorandum No. 84 (August). Tel Aviv, Israel: Jaffee Center for Strategic Studies, Tel Aviv University.

Victor, Barbara (2003). *Army of Roses: Inside the World of Palestinian Women Suicide Bombers*. Emmaus, PA: Rodale.

Weimann, Gabriel (2006). *Terror on the Internet: The New Arena, The New Challenges*. Washington, DC: The United States Institute of Peace.

INDEX

Abu Ala (Ahmed Qurei), 88
Afghanistan, 43
Ahmadinejad, Mahmoud, 33, 111
al-Akhras, Ayat, 1, 120
Al-Aqsa Charity Foundation, 143
Al-Aqsa intifada (second intifada), xv,
    8, 9, 17, 41, 84, 100, 116, 128,
    142, 143, 152
Al-Aqsa Martyrs' Brigades, 4,
    147
Alcohol, in paradise, 162, 164, 166,
    170
Al-Hayat (London-based Arabic
    newspaper), 97
Al-Jazeera, 139
Al-Qaeda, 11, 29, 43, 100
Anniversary, sanctifying, 73
Arafat, Musa, murder of, 8
Arafat, Yasser, 8, 65, 68, 84, 89, 92,
    148
Ashdod, 3, 31
Ashkenazi Jews, 15, 40
Atta, Muhammad, 9
Ayyash, Yehia ("the engineer"), 36, 38,
    39

Balata refugee camp, 36, 38, 123–24,
    147

Baqarat, Najah, 155, 169–70
Bat Yam, 30
Beersheba, 3, 30, 106
Beilin, Yossi, 88
Beit Sahour, 77, 78
bin Laden, Osama, xiv, 50; global jihad
    of, 12, 43, 100, 171, 174; influence
    of, 68; as son of rejected wife,
    25–26
Bir Naballah, 143
"Birds of freedom", 113
"Black widows", 113
Border searches: 33, 157; modesty
    considerations, 166
Born-again Muslim, 164

Café Apropo, bombings at,
    34–35
Cellular phones, 141
Charity organization, 143
Chechens, 100, 113–14, 168
Children: in Arab *vs.* Western society,
    15–16; aspirations for martyrdom,
    87, 149; as bombing victims,
    34–35, 38–39, 57, 83–84, 88, 116,
    172; of first *vs.* second wife,
    treatment of, 19, 25–26, 48;
    indoctrination of, 112, 148–49;

Child: (*Cont.*)
    recruitment of, 2, 147–48, 152–54;
    as suicide bombers, 2–3, 55,
    130–31, 132, 147–48, 158, 168;
    willingness to attack, 126, 127,
    128; of women in prison, 90–91,
    94, 95, 96–97, 98–99, 167. *See
    also* Jalal
Christianity, opposition to suicide, 173
Christians: paradise and, 165
Cigarette smoking, 82, 95, 101, 102,
    151; gender and, 76, 143
Clothing, female: traditional, 3, 70, 72,
    100, 101, 102, 107, 114, 119,
    137–38, 167; Western, 3, 70, 72,
    90, 93, 112, 137, 167, 168
Clothing, male traditional, 165
Collaboration issues, 1, 59–60, 167,
    174
Collective ego, 43
Colonialism, 63
Cosmetics, 3, 85, 93, 100, 101, 167
Criminal record, of terrorist, 150
Cult of death and killing, 171–72
Current intifada [Al-Aqsa intifada], xv,
    8, 9, 17, 41, 84, 100, 116, 128,
    142, 143, 152

Daraghmeh, Hiba, 9, 115–16
Da'wah (spread of Islamic religion), 16,
    43, 164–65
Death cult, 171–72
Deportation, from Israel, 20
Depression, 118, 143, 158
Deprivation, as motivating factor, 43
Dispatcher, suicide bomber: decision to
    join terrorist organization, 30–34;
    forces female to become *shaheeda*,
    5–8; lack of direct contact with
    suicide bomber, 110; motivating
    factors for, 33, 37–38, 41–42, 44;
    own relatives, not dispatching, 27,
    41, 110, 130, 132, 145, 174;
    psychological manipulation of
    bomber, 46, 172; relationship with
    family, 16–17, 23–24, 27–28, 30,
    31, 35, 38; as role model, 9, 10;

seen as morally normative, 42–43;
    sense of own moral judgment, 173;
    status of, 14, 15, 27; on suicide
    bomber *vs.* IDF military actions,
    28–29
Divorce: ease of husband to divorce
    wife, 86; male prisoner and, 21,
    22, 45–46, 77–78; wife infertility
    as reason for, 146. *See also*
    Remarriage
Domestic violence, 151
Dowry, 25, 103
Drugs, 53, 61–62
al-Dura, Muhammad, 116

Economic factors: dependency of
    women, 140; funding terrorist
    organization, 62; as motivation for
    bombing, 145, 165; as not
    motivation for bombing, 9, 15, 19,
    23, 30; Palestinians employed by
    Israelis, 143, 146; stipends for
    bomber family, 9, 23, 115
Education: aspirations of women, 74,
    75, 123; Palestinian females and, 5,
    30, 36, 41, 64, 72, 74, 75, 76, 81,
    82, 102, 143–44, 150; Palestinian
    males and, 15, 19–20, 26, 27, 29,
    30, 36, 40, 41, 45, 81, 82, 150,
    155, 165
Educational system, indoctrination by,
    148, 168–69, 171
'Eisha, Darin, 115, 116
"Ends justify the means", 87
Erez checkpoint, Palestinian taking Jews
    through, 31–32
Erez checkpoint bombing, 2, 105–6,
    139, 167
Explosive belt, 3, 5, 10, 11, 103, 132,
    148, 149, 152, 154, 168
Explosive device, 46; remote control,
    147–48
Explosive undergarments, 106
Extramarital sex, 168

Family: of collaborator, 1, 59–60;
    disintegration of Palestinian, 10,

15–16; religious, 20, 30; traditional, 101–2. *See also* Family, of *shaheed*; Father; Mother; Parents

Family, of *shaheed*: financial reward for, 9, 23, 115; reward after death, 105, 164; status of, 4, 10, 23–24, 31

Family honor, 8, 35, 60, 139, 155, 166–67, 174

Fast-food restaurant bombing, Tel Aviv, 171

Fasting, 154, 159; in prison, xiii, 72, 78

Fatah (PLO): displaced as ruling party, xiii–xiv; female suicide bomber in, 114; mistaken identity, in drive-by shooting by, 173

Fatah/Tanzim, 95, 103, 127

Father: daughter relationship with, 81–82, 108; family honor and, 6; lack of father figure, 7, 19, 26; loss of standing when daughter recruited, 116–17; physical abuse against son by, 150–51; revenge against as motivating factor, 102–3; as role model, 37. *See also* Family; Mother; Parents

Fatwa (religious Islamic edit), 9, 55, 157, 168, 174

Female suicide bomber. *See* Suicide bomber, female

Femininity, 48, 49, 94; cosmetic use, 3, 85, 93, 100, 101, 167; hair as symbol of, 47

Feminism, among Palestinian women, 114

First intifada, 17, 19, 23, 32, 37, 40, 101, 124, 127

First Lebanon War, 39, 56

Fonseka, Sarath, 113

Friendship, between Israelis and Palestinians, 15, 31–32, 47, 102

Fundamentalism, xiii, 16, 63, 70, 156, 168, 173

Funding terrorism, 62

Gandhi, Rajiv, 113

Gaza Strip: attack on school in, 128; border crossing bombing, 115; Erez checkpoint bombing, 2, 105–6, 139, 167; general anarchy in, 8; Israeli withdrawal from occupied territory, 92, 128–29; Nezarim checkpoint, 116; occupation in, 17

Gender factors: cigarette smoking, 76, 143; discrimination, 89; economic dependency of women, 140; family honor, 8, 35, 60, 139, 141, 155, 166–67, 174; language and, 47; as motivating factor, 1–2, 115, 116, 142, 146, 174; recruitment and training of bomber, 2–7, 5, 116–17; religious views, 141; rewards for martyrdom, 159–60, 161–64, 165; roles, 48–49

Geneva Accord, 91

Green headband, 11, 154

Hadith (saying from Muslim oral tradition): on male responsibility for wife behavior, 141; on paradise, 169

Haifa bombing, 9, 83–84, 100, 166–67

Hair covering, for woman, 46, 47, 50–51, 62, 67

Hamas: attacks claimed by, 167; conflict with Al-Fatah, 71; creation of, 39, 43; educational programs of, 16; social and charitable programs of, 16; takeover of Palestinian régime, xiii–xiv, 8, 168; universities and, 39–40, 168; use of women by, 114, 115, 168. *See also* Yassin, Ahmad

Hand grenades, 2, 7, 154

Haniya, Ismail, 71, 110

Hashem, Adel Abu, 145

Hatred, of Jews, xiii, 9, 11, 13, 23, 42–43, 72, 112, 126, 134, 171, 172

Hatuel, Tali, 95

Hawarah checkpoint, child suicide bomber at, 55

Hell, 122, 160, 164, 165, 169, 170, 174

Hezbollah, 8, 167; drug dealing by, 62

Hilal, Abu, 165–66
Historical relationship, between Arabs and Jews, 23
Hitler, Adolph, 165
Holocaust denial, 33
Home, destruction of, 23, 101, 106, 120, 152
Houris, 166
Humiliation, of occupation, 33, 157
Hunger strike, prison, 20

Identity card, 32, 81, 98, 143
IDF (Israeli Defense Forces), 8, 27, 29, 36, 116, 149
Idris, Wafaa, 139, 146
Incest, 140
India, female suicide bomber in, 113
Indoctrination: of children, 112, 148–49; by educational system, 52, 148, 168–69, 171; by media, 171; by mosques, 52, 116; by religious institutions, 43, 171; by television, 148–49; of women in prison, 104, 134
Inferiority, 43
Infertility, 114, 139, 146
Internet, 121, 141, 145, 163; chat rooms, 74–75, 118; exploitation of women on, 74–75
Interrogation, of Palestinian, 19, 40
Intifada: current, xv, 8, 9, 17, 41, 84, 100, 116, 128, 142, 143, 152; first, 17, 19, 23, 32, 37, 40, 101, 124, 127
Iran, xiv, 8, 16, 33, 111, 138
Iraq, 100, 110, 156, 158, 167, 171, 173; treatment of Jews in, 33, 111
Islam: opposition to suicide, 172, 174; religious suicide and, 172. *See also* Qur'an; Yassin, Ahmad
Islamikazis, 173
Israel: diversity/pluralism in, 146; questioning human fabric/moral structure of, 18, 40; settlements and, 2–3, 73, 95, 134; withdrawal from occupied territory, 92, 128–29

Israeli, Rafael, 173
Israeli Defense Forces (IDF), 8, 27, 29, 36, 116, 149
Israel Security Agency, 17
Istishhad (becoming *shaheed* by self-sacrifice for sake of Allah), 2, 5, 10, 43, 105–6, 115, 152, 156, 175
Izzedine al-Qassam Battalions, 34, 35

Jaffa Road bombing (Jerusalem), 114
Jahalia (pre-Islamic era), 173; burying girls alive during, 155
Jaradat, Hanadi, 9, 116 (it's a real name)
Jealousy, 43
Jenin, 1, 126
Jerusalem, bombings in, xiv, 1, 114, 120
Jewish society, Palestinian view on, 18, 40
Jews: Ashkenazi, 15, 40; call for return to country of origin, 33, 110–11; friendship with Palestinians, 15, 31–32, 47, 102; hatred toward, xiii, 9, 11, 13, 23, 42–43, 72, 112, 126, 134, 171, 172; Khaybar, 23; paradise and, 165; personal relationships, 31–32, 102; Sephardic, 15, 18, 40
Joint terrorist attacks, 11
Jordan, 3, 91
Judaism, opposition to suicide, 172–73

Kaddish (Jewish prayer for the dead), xv
Kafr Kana, 39
Kamikaze (divine wind) pilot, 13, 155–56
Khaybar Jews, 23
Khoury, George, 173
Kna'an, Fahed, 59
Kol Israel (Voice of Israel), 40
Ku Klux Klan, 42
Kuridsh PKK (Kurdistan Workers' Party), female suicide bombers in, 113, 123

Lebanon: civilians killed in, 56; Israeli army pulls out of, 40–41; Sabra–Shatilla massacre in, 82–83; terrorist organization in, 8, 62, 167; war in, 8, 39, 56
London, terrorist attacks in, 11, 119–20, 175
LTTE, cf. Tamil Tigers

Maccabim checkpoint suicide bombing, 115
Machiavelli, Niccolo, 87
Machismo, 22
Madrid, terrorist attacks in, 131
Magnetic identity card, 32
Makeup (cosmetics), 3, 85, 93, 100, 101, 167
Marriage, 38, 86, 102–3, 109, 141; arranged, 6; as end of life, 75; in paradise, 154, 162. *See also* Divorce; Remarriage
Marriage pressures, 21, 86, 109, 142
Martyrdom: denial of death, 54, 109–10, 159, 165; media portrayal of, 82, 100, 106; rewards in heaven for (*See* Paradise); teaching child about, 148–49
Marxism, 36, 59
Masculinity, 48, 49
Mashal, Khaled, xiv, 67
Maternal deprivation, 25–26
Maxim Restaurant bombing (Haifa), 9, 83–84, 100, 166–67
Mazen, Abu, 8, 71, 175
Media: coverage of female suicide bomber, 82, 100, 106; demonization of Jews and Israelis, 128; indoctrination by, 171; television, 89, 128
Memories, prisoner problem in facing, 22
Merari, Ariel, 150
Message of the People (television program), 12–13
Mishal, Shaul, 68
Modesty, during border searches, 166

Moscow movie theater bombings, 113–14, 166
Mosques, indoctrination by, 52, 116
Mossad, 67
Mother: desire to please, 21; of dispatcher, relationship with, 27, 28, 37, 38, 44; multiple roles of, 138; place in Arab society, 7–8, 138–39. *See also* Family; Father; Parents
Mother, of suicide bomber: assessment of daughter motivations, 146; encouragement of bombings, 145; grief and mourning, 108, 146; Palestinian son relationship with, 48; pride in martyrdom of child, 146; relationship with child, 7, 21, 23, 77, 102, 109, 122, 123; separation from, 25–26, 77, 78, 115, 120–21; special status of, 123, 144, 151; Um-Nabil, 142–45, 146, 159; willingness to sacrifice child, 145
Motivating factor, female suicide bomber: domestic violence, 115, 151; financial reward for family, 115; glorification, 116; honor, 1–2, 115, 116, 174; identification with suicide bombing relatives, 116; infertility, 146; lost childhood, 127; marriage pressures, 86, 142; nationalism, 115, 116, 124, 127; paradise, 124, 127, 129, 142; personal distress, 103, 104, 141–42; pregnancy, unwed, 115; religion, 115, 116, 127; respect for family, 115; revenge, 102–3, 109, 115–16, 127, 128, 133; romantic relationship, thwarted, 102–3, 115; self-hatred, 142; treatment at checkpoints, 33, 139; willingness to die, 124
Motivating factor, for bombing: among children, 152, 156; avenge death of child, 83; collaboration, 1, 174; depression, 118, 143, 158; divorce, 146; domestic violence, 115, 151;

Motivating factor (*Cont.*)
  economic factors, 145; education,
  desire for, 74, 75, 123; father
  figure, lack of, 7, 19, 26; female
  bomber (*See* Motivating factor,
  female suicide bomber); financial
  reward to family, 9, 115;
  glorification, 116; hatred for Jews,
  9, 11; heroization, 9–10; honor,
  1–2, 115, 116, 174; perceived
  humiliation at roadblock, 33, 139,
  157, 166; identification with
  suicide bomber relative, 116;
  infertility, 146; loathing of Western
  world, 9, 11; lost childhood, 127;
  male bomber (*See* Motivating
  factor, male suicide bomber);
  marriage pressures, 86, 142;
  martyrdom, desire for, 2, 63,
  148–49; nationalism, 9, 105, 115,
  116, 124, 127; oppression of
  occupation, 37–38, 41–42, 44;
  paradise, direct passage to, 9, 124,
  127, 129, 132, 142, 152; parent
  remarriage, 115; personal distress,
  103, 104, 141–42, 167; pregnancy,
  unwed, 115; religion, 9, 105, 115,
  116, 127; repression of youth, 156;
  respect for family, 115; revenge, 9,
  87, 102–3, 109, 115–16, 127, 128,
  133, 154, 156; romantic
  relationship, thwarted, 102–3, 115;
  self-hatred, 142; of suicide bomber
  dispatcher, 33, 37–38, 41–42, 44;
  willingness to die, 124
Motivating factor, male suicide bomber:
  collaboration, 1; oppression of
  occupations, 37–38, 41–42, 44;
  paradise, 132, 152; revenge, 154,
  156
Mubarak, Hosni, 68
Murad (Arab journalist accompanying
  author), 143, 155, 165; on child
  suicide bombers, 147–48; on
  effects of suicide bombings, 9; on
  femininity, 101; on honor, 2; on
  Huda, 80, 85; on Palestinian girls
  leaving home, 146; on Palestinian
  mothers, 146; on psychological
  effect of bombings, 9; on Yassin,
  67–68
Muslim Brotherhood, 168
Muslim religious leadership, as key to
  end suicide bombings, 175
Muslim religious parents, potential role
  in preventing suicide bombings,
  175
Mutual aid, in Palestinian society, 3,
  23–24

Nablus, 58, 59, 95, 99, 100, 108, 150,
  168
Nablus checkpoint, 55, 130, 147, 149
Nasrallah, Hassan, 27, 39, 167
Nationalism, 9, 105, 115, 116, 124,
  127
Negev, attacks in, 129
Netanyahu, Benjamin, 16
New York City, terrorist attacks on, 9,
  171
Nezarim checkpoint child murder, 116

Occupation, oppression of, 17, 37–38,
  41–42, 44
Oslo Accords, 8, 17, 91, 101

Palestinian Authority, 42, 71, 97;
  anti-Semitic graffiti on walls of, 23;
  cooperation with Israel Security
  Agency, 17; reports of Al-Qaeda
  cells in, 8
Palestinian Islamic Jihad, 26, 138, 165;
  claim of responsibility for attack,
  100; women in, 9, 114–15
Palestinian–Israeli conflict, compared
  with children's squabble, 129
Palestinian Preventive Security, 26
Palestinian Women's Society, 137, 138,
  140
Paradise: ability to have children in,
  159–60, 161–62; alcohol in, 162,
  164, 166, 170; direct passage to, 9,
  174; getting Christians and Jews
  into, 165; male/female

expectations, 159–60, 161–64, 165; marriage in, 154, 162; as motivating factor, 9, 124, 127, 129, 132, 142, 152; as physical *vs.* spiritual, 169–70; Qur'an on, 86, 159, 160, 165, 170; sexual relations in, 162–63; virgins in, 109, 159, 160, 161–62, 165, 166

Parents: agreement with child committing suicide, 107; opposition to child committing suicide, 7, 8, 10, 88, 97, 114, 119–20; potential role in ending bombings, 175. *See also* Father; Mother

Partition plan, Unite Nations, 3

Paternal deprivation, 25–26, 26, 37

Patriarchy, 10, 15, 116–17, 139, 140

Peace initiative, 8, 17, 91, 101

Pentagon, terrorist attack on, 9, 42, 173

Peres, Shimon, 39

Permissible association between sexes, 4

Petah Tikva, 20

Photographing/videoing: suicide bomber before bombing, 11, 154; women in prison, 92–93, 94

Physical abuse, by father, 150–51

Polygamy, 141

Popular Front for the Liberation of Palestine, 59, 114

Popular music, indoctrination by, 171

Premarital sex, 60, 74

Propaganda: anti-Israeli, 34, 134–35; glorification of *shaheed*, 11, 147; hate, 171

Psychological factors: automaton/robot-like behavior, 46; characteristic, 7, 158; depression, 118, 143, 158; fantasies of becoming *shaheed*, 9–10; guilt, 172; jealousy/inferiority/ deprivation, 42–43; moral judgment, 172; sense of omnipotence, 131, 172

Qardawi, Yussuf, 168

Qatar, 139

Qur'an: on Israelites, 65, 111; on paradise, 86, 159, 160, 165, 170; on revenge/restraint, 56; on suicide, 53; on women, 63; on women and jihad, 112

Qur'an, Abdallah (child bomber), 55, 147 (His name is spelled incorrectly in the book.)

Rabin, Yitzhak, 32, 41, 42

Racism, in Israel, 18

Radical fundamentalism, 156

Radio, Israeli, 40

Ramadan, 72, 154, 159

Ramallah checkpoint, 139

Ramat Gan bus attack, 38

Al-Rantisi, 'Abd al-Aziz, 91, 125, 131, 155

Rape, 141, 148

Recruitment: of children, 2–3, 147–48, 152–54; dispatcher relatives and, 27, 41, 110, 130, 132, 145, 174; double-standard based on gender, 116–17; by family and friends, 4–5, 7, 114, 118, 152–53; psychological factors, 11–12; victimization of women, 2–7, 103, 127

Refugee camp, 20, 26; Balata, 36, 38, 123–24, 147; communal life in, 3, 22–23; Sabra–Shatilla massacre, 82–83

Regrets/remorse, lack of, 31, 34, 39, 88, 127, 129, 133

Religious institution, indoctrination by, 43, 171

Religiousness: of suicide bomber, 20; of suicide bomber dispatcher, 30, 36–37, 39–40

Remarriage, 146, 153; children of, 121; of mother of female prisoner, 77, 78; of wife of prisoner, 21–22

Revenge, 33, 56, 83, 87, 102–3, 103, 109, 115–16, 116, 127, 128, 133, 152, 154, 156

al-Riyashi, Reem, 1–2, 105, 139, 167, 168

Romantic relationship, 131, 132–33,
  151–52; Internet and, 163;
  thwarted, 102–3, 115
Russia, female suicide bombers in,
  113–14

Sabra–Shatilla massacre, 82–83
Salem, Ali, 175
Samiria, 92
Saudi Arabia: slaughter of Khaybar
  Jews in, 23; television in,
  141
Savings account, confiscation of female
  bomber, 4
Sbarro restaurant bombing, 70
Scholarships, 143–44
Schools: attacks on, 113–14, 126, 128.
  See also Education
Second intifada, xv, 8, 9, 17, 41, 84,
  100, 116, 128, 142, 143, 152
Second Lebanon War, 8
Self-sacrifice, 2, 5, 10, 43, 105–6, 115,
  152, 156, 175
Sentences: for female prisoner, 72, 80,
  81, 85; for suicide bomber
  dispatcher, 17, 18–19, 29, 36, 37,
  40
Sephardic Jews, 15, 18, 40
Settlements, 2–3, 73, 92, 95, 128–29,
  134
Sexual identity, of suicide bomber,
  47–48
Sexuality, hair as symbol of, 47
Shaheed (Muslim man who died as
  martyr for sake of Allah): adoption
  by terrorist organization, 100; bad
  acts canceled, 2; characteristics of,
  158; financial reward for family of,
  9, 23, 115; first, 59; as hero, 9–10,
  171; magic of, 145; reward after
  death for family of, 105, 164;
  secular, 9; sense of power and
  omnipotence of, 172; status of
  family of, 4, 10, 23–24, 31;
  "tortures of the grave" and, 163,
  164; as victim of Palestinian
  society, 155; visit to family of, by

potential suicide bomber, 120. See
  also Suicide bomber, male
Shaheeda (Muslim woman who died as
  martyr for sake of Allah): bad acts
  cancelled, 2;
constant thinking about becoming,
  112; as not hero, 171; reputation
  of, 103; "volunteered", 4–5. See
  also Suicide bomber, female
Shamir, Yitzhak, 41
Shari'a, on unveiled woman, 62
Sharif, Muhi a-Din, 38–39
Sharon, Ariel, 91–92
Sheikh Yussuf, 164–65
Shi'ite Muslim, 167
Shopping mall suicide bombing: in
  Afula, 9, 115–16; in Netanya, 172
Shuhadaa Al-Aqsa (Al-Aqsa Martyrs), 4
Shuhadah (dying for sake of Allah),
  105, 156–57
Simultaneous terrorist attacks:
  buses/underground trains in
  London, 11; psychological effects
  of, 11–12; on Twin Towers and
  Pentagon in United States, 11
Six Day War, exposure of Palestinians
  to Israeli society during, 15–16
Skyjacking, xv, 9, 42, 171, 173
Sports, opposition to women in, 138
Sri Lanka, female suicide bombers in,
  113
State of Israel, Palestinian unwillingness
  to accept, 111, 126, 129
Suicide: Christianity and, 173; Judaism
  and, 172–73; for personal reasons,
  115, 175; social forces in Arab
  society and, 12–13, 156; social
  forces in Western society and,
  12
Suicide attack: at Afula shopping mall,
  9, 115–16; at Café Apropo, 34–35;
  double attacks, 14; in Gaza Strip,
  2, 105–6, 115, 139, 167; in Haifa,
  9, 83–84, 100, 166–67; increase in,
  xv; Jaffa Road bombing, 114;
  Jerusalem bus bombing, xiv; in
  London, 11, 119–20, 175;

Maccabim checkpoint bombing, 115; at Moscow movie theater, 113–14, 166; at Netanya shopping mall, 172; psychological effects of, 11–12; at Sbarro restaurant, 70; at schools, 113–14, 126, 128; at supermarket in Jerusalem, 1, 120; at Tel Aviv fast-food restaurant, 171; on United States, 9, 42, 171, 173

Suicide bomber: assumption of free/voluntarily choice, 1–2; child, 2–3, 55; compared with smart bomb, 45; emotional disturbance among, general lack of, 9–10; group activity of, 11–12; psychological preparation of, 11; physical preparation of, 11; recruitment of (*See* Recruitment); typical profile, 1993–1996, 8; "volunteered", 2. *See also Shaheed; Shaheeda*; Suicide bomber, female; Suicide bomber, male

Suicide bomber, female: action of as "legitimate adventure", 112; clothing of, 112; confiscation of savings account of, 4; first, 139, 146; forced into becoming, 3–6; gives own money to recruiter, 117–18; increase in numbers of, 113–14; in Kuridsh PKK, 113, 123; male escort for, 112, 113; motivating factors for attacks (*See* Motivating factor, female suicide bomber); recruitment and training of, 2–7; respect and, 4; sexual exploitation of, 4, 117. *See also Shaheeda*; Women, in prison

Suicide bomber, male: motivating factors for attacks (*See* Motivating factor, male suicide bomber); recruitment of (*See* Recruitment; Training); rewards for martyrdom (*See* Paradise); stipends for family of, 9; videos of, 11. *See also Shaheed*

Sunni Muslims, 166, 167

Sunni Palestinians, collaboration with Hezbollah Shi'ites, 167

Supermarket suicide bombing in Jerusalem, 1, 120

Syria, support of Hamas by, 8

Tamil Tigers (LTTE), 113

Tanzim, 95, 103, 127

Technology: cellular phones, 141; influence on Arab society, 16, 140–41, 163, 168; Internet (*See* Internet)

Television: indoctrination by, 148–49; influence on Arab society, 16, 89, 140–41, 163, 168

"Tortures of the grave", 163, 164

Training, suicide bomber, 3, 5, 117

Turkey, female suicide bombers in, 113, 123

Twin Towers, terrorist attacks on, 9, 171

Victims: child, 34–35, 38–39, 57, 83–84, 88, 116, 172; child suicide bomber view on, 154; dehumanization of, 10–11, 42, 43, 173, 174; female soldier, 26–27; humanization of, 43, 131; lack of distinguishing among choice of, xv

Virgins, in paradise, 159, 160, 161–62, 165, 166

Visitors, prison, 20, 38, 72, 92–93

War of Independence (Israel), 3

Washington, DC, terrorist attack on, 9, 42, 173

Watch metaphor, 52

Weapon: explosive belt, 3, 5, 10, 11, 103, 132, 148, 149, 152, 154, 168; explosive device, 46; explosive undergarments, 106; explosive vest, 11; hand grenades, 2, 7, 154; remote control device, 147–48

West Bank, 2–3, 21, 58–59, 129

Western clothing, female, 3, 70, 72, 90, 93, 112, 137, 167, 168

White supremacist, 42

Widows, 78, 121; "black widows", 113

Women: ability to visit mosque, 159; dowry and, 25, 103; hair covering for, 46, 47, 50–51, 62, 67; military action forbidden to, 157, 165–66; oppression in Arab society, 7–8; sports and, 138; value of, 122 (*See also* Mother). *See also* Clothing, female; Marriage; *Shaheeda*; Suicide bomber, female; Women, in prison

Women, in prison: children of, 90–91, 94, 95, 96–97, 98–99, 167; cigarette smoking by, 76, 82, 95, 101, 102; clothing of, 72, 90, 93, 100, 101, 107, 119; eating arrangements, 91; emotional problems of, 107; exercise/sports, 76; femininity and, 3, 85, 93, 94, 101; food, 76, 91; guards, relationship with, 76, 81, 134; hygiene products, 125; indoctrination of, 104, 134; medical care for, 73; photographer visit to, 92–93, 94; physical attack by other prisoner, 72, 73, 105, 135; relations among, 69–72, 75–76; religiosity of, 70, 72; Russian, 76; security prisoners, 69–79; status among, 120; trauma of imprisonment, 104, 105; visitors to, 72, 92–93. *See also* Clothing, female; Gender factors; Motivating factor, female suicide bomber; *Shaheeda*; individual woman

Work, for Palestinian: in Gaza with Arabs, 32, 33; in Gaza with Jews, 30, 32, 33; in Israel, 20, 29–30, 47

World Trade Center, 42, 173

Ya'alon, Moshe, xiv

Yassin, Ahmad (Sheikh), 1, 47, 50–68, 92, 155; on absolution/repentance, 60–61; on age of understanding, 54–55; on collaborators, 1, 59–60; on death, 54; death of, 67, 125; on drugs and Islam, 61–62; on economic status of *shaheed*, 58–59; on freedom of religion, 52; on gap between achievements in East *vs.* West, 62–63; on honor, 174; on infidels, 65; influence of, 67–68; on Islamic Movement and peace process, 67; on Israelites and land, 64–67; on jihad, 52, 53, 57–58; on justice, 51–52, 129; on mothers, 123, 138; on motivating factors, 56, 58–59; on *mujahad*, 54, 57; on nature of man, 61; on peace, 51, 53; on peace treaties, 53; on polytheists, 52–53; on prophets, 65–66; on repentance, 60–61; on restraint, 56–57; on revenge, 56; on *shaheed*, 53–56, 57–58; on suicide, 53; transcription of interview with, 51–67; on true believers, 61; on victims of bombing, 57; on Western culture, 62–63; on Western technology, 62–63; on women, 62–64, 167–68; on women, covering of hair, 47, 62, 67

Yavneh, 33

Yehuda, Machaneh, 45

Yussuf (Sheikh), 164–65

al-Zahar, Muhammad, 172

Zanoubia (Queen), legend of, 46, 47

al-Zarqawi, Abu Musab, 100

About the Author

ANAT BERKO, who holds a Ph.D. in criminology and served as a Lieutenant Colonel in the Israeli Defense Forces, is a research fellow at the Institute for Counter-Terrorism and lecturer at the Interdisciplinary Center in Herzliya. An expert on suicide terrorism, she also conducted research for the National Security Council. Her family fled from Iraq to Israel when the State was founded.